WRITING
TELEVISION
SITCOMS

WRITING
TELEVISION
SITCOMS

Evan S. Smith

A Perigee Book

A Perigee Book
Published by The Berkley Publishing Group
A division of Penguin Putnam Inc.
375 Hudson Street
New York, New York 10014

First edition: September 1999

Published simultaneously in Canada.

The Penguin Putnam Inc. World Wide Web site address is
http://www.penguinputnam.com

Library of Congress Cataloging-in-Publication Data

Smith, Evan S. (Evan Scott), 1956–
    Writing television sitcoms / Evan S. Smith. — 1st ed.
       p.   cm.
    Includes bibliographical references and index.
    ISBN 0-399-52533-5
    1. Television authorship.   2. Television
    comedies.   3. Televison plays—Technique.   I. Title.
    PN1992.7.S64   1999
    808.2'25—dc21   99-23459
                                                          CIP

Printed in the United States of America

10   9   8

For Christine, Connor, and Ryan
Alison and Dan

Acknowledgments

A number of terrific people helped to make this book happen. First, I would like to thank the writer-producers listed below. These generous folks took time out of very busy, very successful careers to give their input, and several reviewed the manuscript. With combined credits that read like a *Top 20* list of TV's best comedies, they are:

Sandy Frank (whose credits include *Late Night with David Letterman, In Living Color, Working Girl, Fresh Prince of Bel Air, Martin, Jamie Foxx*);

Ian Gurvitz (*A Fine Romance, Wonder Years, Delta, Get an Life, Fra*ⁱ *Wings, Becker,* creator of *The Tony Danza Show*);

Irma Kalish (*Family Affair, My Three Sons, Gidget, Please Don't Eat the Daisies, F Troop, Bob Newhart, Good Times, Too Close for Comfort, The Facts of Life, 227, Maude, All in the Family*);

Lawrence Konner (*Little House on the Prairie, Family, Working Girls, Almost Grown,* and feature films *Jewel of the Nile, For Love or Money, The Beverly Hillbillies, Mercury Rising, Mighty Joe Young*);

Maxine Lapiduss (*Normal Life, The Tracy Ullman Show, The Crew, Dear John, Charles in Charge, Baby Talk, Roseanne, The Jeff Foxworthy Show, Home Improvement, Ellen*); and

Matt Williams (creator or co-creator of *Roseanne, A Different World, Home Improvement, Carol & Company, Soul Man,* and co-producer of the original *Cosby Show*).

In addition to contributing advice, Matt Williams also gave us permission to include a story outline from the hit series *Home Improvement* in this book.

I would also like to thank . . .

My editor, Sheila Curry. Insightful and supportive, she has been an invaluable partner in this project.

Andrea Mattei, the capable editorial staffer who brought me to Sheila.

My colleagues at the Newhouse School, Syracuse University's renowned college of communications. It is a pleasure to work with people who are as interested in creating and exploring as they are in analyzing and preserving.

Shauna Moore, my tireless research assistant, whose position was entirely funded by the Newhouse School.

The staff of the venerable American Film Institute in Los Angeles. They were the first to recognize the potential of premise-driven comedy.

Lastly, I thank the many writers, performers, teachers, friends, and family members who have made me laugh, and who have taught me a thing or two about comedy writing.

CONTENTS

Introduction   1

PART ONE:
WRITING PREMISE-DRIVEN COMEDY

1: The Game Plan   7
   Career Paths   8
   Getting Started   10

2: First, Some Theory   12
   The Mechanics of Laughter   12
   Characteristics of Comedy   14
   The Importance of Tension   18

3: Putting Theory into Practice   19
   Seamless Humor   19
   Consistency   20
   Comedy Output   20
   The Traditional Approach to Sitcom Writing   21
   A Different Approach—Premise-Driven Comedy   23

4: Level One—Comedy in the Story Premise   25
   Predicaments   27
   Character Mix   32

Style of Comedy   37
Casting   40

5: Level Two—Comedy in Sequences and Scenes   42

Compound Story Predicaments   43
Stir Up the Character Mix   43
Mix and Match   44
Three Things to Remember   44

6: Level Three—Comedy in Dialogue and Actions   46

Building Jokes   47
Setups   47
Punch Lines   54
Funny Actions   64
Miscellaneous Comedy Tips   67
About All of These Labels   69
Developing Your Comedic Voice   70

PART TWO:
WRITING A PROFESSIONAL SCRIPT

7: Doing Your Homework   75

Why Write Spec Scripts?   75
Which Series to Pick   76
Researching the Series   78
Studying the Premise   80

8: Developing an Episode Premise   83

Advice from Our Producers   83
Dreaming Up Stories   84
Turning Ideas into Springboards   86

9 Developing the Story   90

The Importance of the Story   90
Creating a Beat Sheet   91

Story Structure—Linear vs. Thread 92
Story Threads vs. Subplots vs. Ensemble Stories 94
Stories Without Endings and Serialized Stories 95
Character Arcs 96
Story Tips 96
Comedy's Impact on the Story 98
Dramatic Structure vs. Broadcast Format 99
Creating Funny Characters 101
Remember the Mix 102
Character Types 103
Visiting Characters 106
How the Production Process Affects Your Script 108
Nail the Story, the Rest Is Easy 110

10: Writing an Outline 111
Writing to Sell, Not Educate 112
Building an Outline 113
How It Should Look on Paper 115
Stylistic Tips 118
Rewriting an Outline 121
Advice from Our Producers 122
A Sample Outline from *Home Improvement* 123

11: Writing the First Draft 140
Just Do It 140
Writing Scenes 141
Harvesting Comedy Built into the Premise and Scene Levels 144
Professional Script Format 144
Writing Scene Descriptions 145
Writing Dialogue 147
Miscellaneous Tips 150
Planting Exposition 151
Advice from Our Producers 153
When That First Draft Is Finished 156
Rewriting the Script 157

When Rewriting by Yourself   162
Advice from Our Producers   163
Once the Script Is Finished   165

PART THREE:
A BATTLE PLAN FOR LAUNCHING YOUR CAREER

12: Step One—Developing a Strategy   169
The Job Market—It's Not 1995 Anymore   169
How the Writer Fits In   172
A Writer's Work Week   173
Writing Is a Business   175
Ageism   176
Putting Food on the Table   176
Must You Live in Los Angeles?   179

13: Step Two—Landing an Agent   181
Do You Have to Have an Agent?   181
Developing an Agent Hit List   183
Before Picking Up the Phone   187
Making the Call   189
Submitting Your Material   190
Testing the Waters If You Don't Live in L.A.   192
Following Up   193
If You Fail to Land an Agent   194
You Get an Offer!   196
Signing the Contract   197
Once You Have the Agent   198

14: Step Three—Getting Your Work Out There   199
Scouting the Market   199
Hiring Windows   201
Working with Your Agent   202

Which Scripts to Send 203
Being Picky About Jobs 203
Cold-Calling Producers 204
Keep Writing 205
Writing in Teams 206
Rejection 207
Dealing with Writer's Block 207
Protecting Your Work 208
Who Keeps the Copyright? 211
Joining the Writers Guild of America 212

15: Step Four—Pitching for Assignments 215
The Call Comes In! 216
Preparing for the Pitch 216
The Pitch 218
Advice from Our Producers 219
What Might Happen 222
The Contract 223
The Money 225

16: Step Five—Landing a Staff Job 227
Landing a Staff Writing Job 227
Office Politics 229
Roundtable Writing 230
Advice from Our Producers 231
Contracts and Compensation 234

17: Step Six—Climbing the Ladder 237
Moving Up 237
The Care and Feeding of Agents 238
Taking a Development Deal 240
How Do You Sell a New Series? 241

In Closing 243

Appendix A: Script Format Guidelines   245
Appendix B: Additional Resources   265
Endnotes   271
Index   275

WRITING
TELEVISION
SITCOMS

Introduction

If you picked up this book either you are related to me (put the book down, Ma) or you are interested in becoming a sitcom writer. Or you are already a sitcom writer, but things are slow, your agent isn't returning your calls, and suddenly you're thinking that med school isn't such a bad idea.

Well, whether you are looking for a creative muse or career advice, you are in luck. You hold in your hands the official if-I-could-only-buy-one insider's guide to the craft of sitcom writing.

Why is this *the* book to read? Several reasons . . .

I. IT IS NOT 1995 ANYMORE

The sitcom business has changed radically in just the last few years. Creative control has shifted from writers to suits. New technologies have redefined content boundaries and generated more jobs. Would-be writers are landing staff positions fresh out of college instead of learning their craft via freelance assignments. While comedy basics, the things that make us laugh, will always remain constant, out-of-date professional advice can cost you a job, many jobs, your whole career.

2. A NEW WRITING METHOD

This book presents the first published description of *premise-driven comedy*, a writing method that focuses on developing a story's humor from the ground up. I have taught this approach in a variety of well-received classes and seminars, including presentations at the famed American Film Institute.

3. Depth of Material

This book focuses exclusively on comedy writing, and is designed to help both beginning and established writers. It is divided into three comprehensive sections:

- Part 1 of the book focuses on comedy writing theory. This section draws fresh insights from existing schools of thought and then describes my method for creating premise-driven comedy.

- Part 2 of the book explains how to write a professional script by putting comedy theory into practice. This section follows the same steps that a professional writer takes as he generates ideas, creates an outline, and lays down dialogue. Along the way, it describes the real-world dynamics that would come into play if you were working on an actual script assignment, facing impossible deadlines and frantic producers.

- Part 3 offers up a no-nonsense battle plan for getting work. Since most writers would rather spend their time writing than groveling for a job, this book presents an aggressive, step-by-step strategy designed to get you employed and back at the keyboard as quickly as possible. This plan ranges from broad goals to subtle strategies, and provides numerous insider tips.

While this book is written expressly for sitcom writers, the subjects that it covers—from comedy writing theory to story structure, to pitching techniques, to job-hunting strategies—should prove useful to all comedy writers.

4. Author's Credentials

There aren't a lot of people who have worked on three different sides of the (sitcom writing) desk. During my twenty years in the business, I have served as a sitcom writer (for studios such as Paramount, MTM, and Twentieth Century Fox), and as a vice president of programming (developing both comedy and drama projects for network television), and as a lecturer on comedy writing theory and screenwriting techniques.

Been there, done that ... and that ... and that. Which gives me three perspectives on this highly competitive field, which doesn't hurt.

5. ADVICE FROM SUCCESSFUL PRODUCERS

To supplement my own knowledge, I have solicited input from a number of leading sitcom writer-producers. These people, as noted in my acknowledgments, boast credits that include most of the top shows produced in recent years. Six are directly quoted in different sections of the book and several reviewed the original manuscript.

6. EASE OF USE

For quick and easy reference, this book is divided into the three distinct sections mentioned above and each chapter includes numerous subheadings. Important definitions, names, book titles, addresses, and phone numbers are presented *within* the text, where they will be of most use, rather than in lists buried at the back of the book. To supplement these references, additional resources are presented in appendix B.

Naturally, anyone who is serious about writing sitcoms needs to do her homework. You should read television scripts, film scripts, plays, critical reviews, attend classes and workshops, watch television, go to the movies and the theater, and read novels that won't even come close to getting optioned by Hollywood.

But first, to get started, if you are looking for that official if-I-could-only-buy-one insider's guide to writing sitcoms—you should probably read this book.

Part One

Writing Premise-Driven Comedy

One

The Game Plan

You want to write? You feel a need to write? You'd love to see your work produced, your name up on the screen? Maybe make a little money? Okay, lots of money. Tons. And you want a Porsche and a beach house, in Malibu, right next to Brad Pitt's. Yeah, yeah, sounds good.

Well, sorry, no guarantees on the money or that house thing. Try selling computers, become a lawyer. (Sell Brad a computer, become his lawyer.)

But if you enjoy writing for writing's sake, and if you tend to express yourself with humor, then I have good news: You can actually earn a living by writing sitcoms. Sometimes a very good living.

Check a TV schedule—over fourteen hundred original sitcom episodes were produced last year.[1] (That includes shows produced for broadcast, pay cable, basic cable, syndication, and satellite networks.) Someone is writing these shows, and making as much as eighteen thousand dollars, in up-front fees, per episode. Plus residual fees. Plus money if they work on a show's staff, money from development deals . . . But let's talk about that later.

Sure, some writers are paid huge fees to write feature films, but look at the numbers. About four hundred fifty mainstream films were produced in the U.S. last year, but only a quarter to a third were comedies and many of those were written "on spec." (Meaning, you starve for the three months to ten years it takes to write the thing, and just pray that you—or your ex, after the divorce—can sell it after it is finished.)

In television, most of your compensation is paid up front as you write the script. And the odds of your work actually being produced are much greater, which can greatly increase your income. And you have a better shot at protecting the integrity of your work, because television is dominated by writers while film is a director's medium.

So if you want to work as a writer and keep eating too, sitcoms are not a bad way to go. Sure, it's a competitive field, extremely so. And it's hard, hard work. But so is a job at McDonald's, IBM, or a doctor's office, if that is not where you really want to be. Right?

The question is, how does one become a sitcom writer?

CAREER PATHS

We will get into the nitty-gritty details of the sitcom business—the politics, the players, the jobs—later in the book. But before you invest energy in this career path, it might help to have a general sense of what lies ahead.

Think sunny Los Angeles. Picture a manicured estate off Sunset Boulevard. There's a pool, a pool boy, lunch by the chaise lounge . . . No, you don't live here, some producer does. But you might, someday—how do you think that producer got there? For right now, you're new in town. Maybe you're unemployed, without an agent or a promise of work. But you have a little talent and the sense to realize that life is short. If you don't take your shot, you will always regret it. Always.

So, you get a job to pay the rent and you start networking. And you write. And write. You write sample scripts, called *spec scripts*, for existing television series. These spec scripts are the calling cards that you will use to, hopefully, land an agent. (Sorry, but the odds are a thousand-to-one against anyone actually buying your wonderful spec scripts, as I will explain later; their sole purpose is to get you work writing new material.)

To land that agent, you submit your samples to every industry person you can reach, trying to get someone who knows someone who knows someone to read your scripts. Eventually, if the work is good, an agent will take you on. Then, you and he, or she, will circulate your samples to sitcom producers and executives until someone deems them good enough to hire you.

Getting hired can happen in one of two ways. First, you might be invited in to pitch for a freelance assignment.

A freelance assignment is an assignment, given by a show's producers to an outside writer, to write one episode of an existing series. You pitch ideas; the producers pick one or assign you an idea of their own; you write an outline, and then maybe the first and second drafts of a script. In and out, you're done in three to five weeks. And you pocket enough change to cover twelve months of rent or maybe a dinner at L'Orangerie.

Then, you keep writing spec scripts, you keep circulating your material, as you try to scare up your next job. (The episode credit that you have already earned adds greatly to your marketability.) If you are good, and tenacious, you might eventually land a job *on staff*. Meaning, you are given a contract for a set amount of time—weeks, maybe months—that pays you a huge amount of money to work full-time on a series. Typically, you work in an office at the studio lot where the series is produced. You put in sixty, seventy, or more hours a week, writing alone and in groups, attending production meetings, watching rehearsals, and eating lots of take-out food. Working on staff is crazy, exhausting, fun, challenging—and it pays very, very well.

If you are good, if you are well liked, and if the show and your producers survive long enough, your contract gets renewed. You work your way up through the ranks, trying to become a producer. You move on to different shows, get promotions, and earn more money. And maybe, someday, you will even get a chance to produce a series that you have created, or run a production company that produces several different sitcoms. Or maybe you will parlay your success into directing assignments or jobs in feature films. Or, like Conan O'Brien, your writing skills might propel you into a career in front of the camera.

If you are talented, tenacious, and a little bit lucky, working your way from freelancer to producer can happen very quickly. A surprising number of sitcoms are run by thirty- and thirty-five-year-old producers.

Of course, circumstances are different for everyone. I said earlier that your first writing job can happen in one of two ways. The traditional path described above, starting out with a freelance assignment, has recently become less common. Nowadays, more and more new writers start their careers by landing a staff gig *as their very first job*. They're given a short but renewable contract and a couple of months to prove themselves. Whether they survive or not, they've got a great first credit and can move on from there.

Where do sitcom writers come from? Everywhere. Some are recent college grads who hopped a plane to Hollywood the day after commencement. Some writers start out as an executive's assistant or a producer's secretary. They write samples and schmooze their boss until he or she tosses them a freelance assignment, and they're on their way.

Other writers come from completely different professional careers, having already established themselves as successful lawyers, artists, doctors, or executives. Bored with their jobs, they finally find the courage to try their luck at writing. These people tend to have a little money in the bank, which helps them to weather the financial ups and downs that sometimes face a new writer. (Of course, money in the bank does not guarantee a successful writing career.)

Still other people back into the business through pure coincidence, utter dumb luck. They are in the right place at the right time, and suddenly someone hands them a writing job. Maybe they are related to someone, they are someone's drinking buddy, they impress a producer at a party . . . whatever. They land the first job and off they go.

> **NOTE:** *Whatever your background, it is important to look before leaping. Before you move from Wisconsin or resign from that cushy corporate job, please consider the advice presented in chapter 13 of this book regarding ways to prepare for your assault on Hollywood. After all, it is a lot easier to crank out winning sample scripts or reel in an agent if you don't have the added pressure of a landlord screaming about overdue rent.*

GETTING STARTED

The first step to launching your career is to write a couple of dynamite spec scripts—the samples that will, hopefully, get you that agent and your first job. (No, do not start out by hounding producers and executives for work; how can anyone hire you if you don't have any writing samples to show them?) These spec scripts have to be fantastic, better than the produced episode you watched last night on TV. Otherwise, why should anyone be impressed? ("Gee, this *Drew Carey* spec is worse than the episodes I see every week—let's hire this guy!")

To get started, I suggest the following game plan: First, before you write anything, continue reading part 1 of this book, "Writing Premise-Driven Comedy." It will give you a better understanding of comedy writing theory, and it will arm you with a powerful method for weaving seamless, premise-driven comedy into your script. (Why not just dive in and start writing something? Because it is too easy to become married to scenes and jokes that, in the long run, might hurt your script.)

Then, begin writing your script as you read part 2, "Writing a Professional Script." The steps described in that section mirror the steps followed by professional sitcom writers.

Finally, once you have written at least one polished spec script, a sample good enough to show to professional contacts, you can use the strategy presented in part 3, "A Battle Plan for Launching Your Career," to attack the job market.

Of course, you have the option of skipping directly to part 2 of the book if you want to start writing a script right away. Or, if you have at least one script that represents your best writing, you can begin the job search outlined in part 3. However, I advise that you not rush into things. After all, you usually get only one shot at impressing a contact. If you submit anything less than your best writing, that producer or exec will probably inform her assistant that she does not need to see any more of your work in the future.

Ouch—there goes one potential employer. Forever.

So, instead, why not start at the beginning—with comedy writing theory.

Two

First, Some Theory

For over two thousand years, scholars have argued about what causes laughter and about how comedy works. The thing is, most of these theorists—dramatists, philosophers, physiologists, psychoanalysts, evolutionists—seem to have drawn very similar conclusions, but are too busy sniping at each other to notice the fact.

Why should you care?

Well, several of the widely shared yet universally contested concepts espoused in their theories have evolved into important tools of the professional comedy writer. So while we wait for scholars of the field to develop and embrace a single unified theory of comedy, let's look at a few of these ideas.

THE MECHANICS OF LAUGHTER

First, we should consider the basic mechanics of humor-related laughter (as opposed to laughter triggered by mental illness, physical disorders, or other less-than-humorous causes). Sigmund Freud declared, in his book *Jokes and Their Relation to the Unconscious*, that laughter is a "discharge of psychical energy."[2] Meaning, we invest energy in suppressing our feelings about a subject, but laughter can serve to release (or discharge) those inhibitions, giving us pleasurable relief. A number of other theorists before and after Freud have offered similar emotion-based, laughter-as-release theories; note Dana Sutton's declaration, in his more recent book *The Catharsis of Comedy*, that laughter is a "purgative" that relieves an audience of bad feelings.[3]

Of course, physiologists who hear such blatantly intuitive theories (based solely on observations of human behavior) get a little upset. They object because Freud and other "philosophical types" usually fail to address the tangible roles that chemical, nervous, and muscular functions play in making laughter happen. Physiologists like to describe laughter in terms of contracting muscles, the expulsion of air, and an interruption of one's respiratory cycle. But, as for what causes these actions? That's harder to explain. Famed theorist Herbert Spencer tried, in an article titled "The Physiology of Laughter," by suggesting that "nervous excitation always tends to beget muscular motion."[4] Funny, but "nervous excitation" sounds a lot like "psychical energy," and "muscular motion" might well describe a "discharge" via laughter.

If physiologists appear perturbed by the emotion-based models that Freud and his friends preach, evolutionists seem downright offended. In Robert Storey's article "Comedy, Its Theorists, and the Evolutionary Perspective," he declares that such "philosophers of comedy" must be given a wide berth. After all, he states, smiles and laughter are clearly "evolved responses" that developed because they strengthened the human gene pool, thereby promoting man's survival.[5]

To explain laughter's function, evolutionists refer to formal studies of primate behavior and the actions of human infants (who have yet to be influenced by social conventions). Their findings suggest that the human smile evolved from our early ancestors' bared-teeth display, which, in certain circumstances, was used to express hierarchical submission or reassurance within the troop; today, modern man uses his smile to indicate submission, reassurance, friendliness, and low-key amusement. Similarly, evolutionists theorize that laughter originated (in our ancestors) as a bared-teeth, loudly vocalized response to a hostile threat; today, man laughs in response to a humorous incongruity rather than a life-threatening predator.

On another front, physiologists and evolutionists jointly criticize the emotion-based, laughter-as-release theories by pointing out a simple fact of biology: Laughter does not directly cause physical relaxation, as claimed, but instead accelerates respiration, increases circulation, and raises blood pressure.

So, who is right? And, when sitting at the keyboard, puzzling over a punch line for *South Park*, do we really care? First—all are right, to some extent. And second—yes, we care.

As much as the above scholars disagree about emphasis, justification, and labels, all keep alluding to one vital element of laughter—*tension*. Call it "psychical energy" or "nervous excitation," proclaim it biological rather than emotional in nature, the bottom line is that some form of tension is necessary to laughter, and therefore to comedy.

Just as dramatic tension is released through the resolution of story conflict, comedic tension is paid off through a punch line. Extrapolating from the above theories, it seems reasonable to speculate that, many times, comedic tension is not supplied by a simple joke setup or mere wordplay alone. As we will explore in the coming chapters, other factors—the stress in our lives, universally shared gripes, even dramatic tension—can contribute to the comedic tension that makes a joke work.

Confused? No problem. Just remember the concept—tension, then a release. For a better understanding of how it applies to writing that joke for *South Park*, let's discuss some common characteristics of comedy.

CHARACTERISTICS OF COMEDY

Though theorists are still struggling to explain the mechanics of laughter, they have known for centuries that certain kinds of stimuli can cause us to laugh. Here is a brief list of traits that can be found in most jokes or funny situations.

I. INCONGRUITY

Wit lies in the likeness of things that are different, and in the difference of things that are like.

—MADAME DE STAËL (1766–1817)

When a thought or action is incongruous with the situation at hand, we often find that funny. Picture *Seinfeld*'s Kramer being hired as a Calvin Klein underwear model . . . or *The Drew Carey Show*'s Mimi giving makeup tips to the much prettier Kate . . . or psychiatrist *Frasier* trading schoolyard taunts with his brother Niles. Simply join two dissimilar notions together and the incongruity generates a—you guessed it—*tension* just begging for release.

Freud describes a related process as the "displacement" of an audience's train of thought; as in, the setup for a joke causes an audience to have certain expectations, but the punch line yanks the rug out by providing a very different, incongruous payoff. The result? Tension is discharged and the audience laughs.

Some modern evolutionists prefer to view humorous incongruity in terms of an audience's "mastery" of a joke. Meaning that, through the course of hearing the joke, from setup to payoff, the audience moves from confusion to understanding. The audience hears the punch line, instantaneously deciphers and masters the incongruity, and laughs in triumph at its accomplishment. (An amusing note: The "philosophers of comedy" so often belittled by modern evolutionists came up with their own "bewilderment and illumination" theory over a hundred years ago.[6])

Whatever the explanation, what matters to us—practicing comedy writers—is the concept of using an incongruous twist as a comedic payoff. We can accomplish this by exploiting similarities and differences to turn a simple situation into a funny predicament, or a boring character into a comic figure, or a normal response into a funny punch line. (Arnold Schwarzenegger was not just another supertough cop tracking the most brutal of killers—he was the *Kindergarten Cop*, forced to teach a class of five-year-olds while pursuing his manhunt.)

How do we come up with these incongruities? By using free association. By opening our minds to unique, unexpected connections. By looking at situations from different angles. By asking the question that all comedy (and drama) writers regularly chant, "What if? . . ."

2. SURPRISE

A no-brainer, right? Everyone knows that once you have heard the punch line of a joke, it just is not as funny the second time around. (Unless you are the one telling the joke, in which case the audience must be at fault.) The reason is that once we know the outcome, the incongruity is resolved, the tension dissipated. There is nothing left to "master," so the joke is no longer funny.

On another level, all humor incorporates some element of surprise within its structure. When we create a funny scene or joke, we try to reel the audience in with a realistic setup, then hit them with a surprise twist at the end. Why delay the punch line? Because otherwise, "Take my wife . . . please!" becomes "Please take my wife!" The surprise twist is lost and the joke falls flat. (We will discuss setups and punch lines in chapter 6 of this book.)

Use surprise to get laughs—save the punch lines and payoffs for last.

3. TRUTH

When a thing is funny, search it for a hidden truth.
— GEORGE BERNARD SHAW, *Back to Methuselah*

Tell a joke that carries a thread of truth, that strikes a chord with the audience, and that joke will seem doubly funny. You win extra laughs for being not only amusing but also clever and insightful.

Look at *Seinfeld*. Entire story lines were based on things like having a bad hair day or arguing with a Soup Nazi—the little things in life that we can all relate to. (We have been there, Seinfeld is us!) The subjects explored in these stories and jokes were small and seemingly unimportant, but they rang true. By capitalizing on the tensions in our everyday lives, a setup for one of these bits reeled us all the way in, producing a bigger laugh (release of tension) when we heard the punch line. (Hats off to Jerry Seinfeld and producer Larry David—they unearthed a comedy gold mine when they created a series that was, as several self-parodying episodes put it, "about nothing.")

Obviously, truth means different things to different people, particularly when one is dealing in insult humor. Bigots find truth in prejudice expressed as a punch line, while most people are greatly offended by the same joke. Writers should consider both their audience's point of view and their own standards of taste when developing material.

And, of course, not all jokes or funny bits incorporate a shared truth. Some jokes consist solely of a playful incongruity or wording, or some amusing physical comedy. The joke is the joke, that is all you get. An example from *Friends*:

> MONICA
> Joey, stop hitting on her. It's her wedding
> day.
>
> JOEY
> What? Like there's some rule or something?[7]

How can truth help our writing? Well, first, we should examine our audience's perspective and see what truths become apparent. (After all, the audience for an eight o'clock show is different from that for a nine o'clock show, the fans of *Moesha* are different from the fans of *Everybody Loves Raymond*.) And second, we should explore our own truths, the big and little experiences that we share with, oh, probably about a billion other people on the planet. Both efforts will turn up lots of funny material and keep us in tune with our audience.

4. AGGRESSION

There's no trick to being a humorist when you have the whole government working for you.

—WILL ROGERS (1879–1935)

Telling jokes is a great way to vent. Humor provides us with an outlet for our anger and frustrations by allowing us to disguise a verbal attack as entertainment. That way, we don't get punched by the attackee.

Whom are we attacking? The people and things that create stress in our lives—authority figures, oppressive institutions, personal antagonists. The boss, the post office, the brother Mom always loved best.

Freud says that such "tendentious" or "purposeful" humor not only provides an outlet for anger but also allows us to vent other repressed inhibitions.[8] He puts sex at the top of the list (big surprise, coming from Freud), noting that obscene humor provides a way of exposing that most delicate of subjects to an audience. The goal of an obscene joke can range from a flirtatious testing of the waters (when addressing a potential sex partner), to an act of malicious aggression (when forcing smut on an unwilling audience).

Whatever the intent, aggressive jokes can pack an extra punch for the same reasons that truthful jokes do—an empathetic audience laughs even harder because it identifies with the *content* of the joke, in addition to appreciating its comedic value. We enjoy the Will Rogers quote above for two reasons: because it provides a clever twist, and because we too are frequently annoyed by government blunders.

Of course, it is not always necessary (or, sometimes, even wise) to actually name the object of our joking aggression. More often than not, a writer alludes to the object by targeting a symptom or characteristic of the thing, or by going after someone who exhibits certain bothersome traits or represents a particular category of people. Consider this line from novelist P. G. Wodehouse (1881–1975): "It was one of those parties where you cough twice before you speak, and then decide not to say it after all."

While, on the surface, this observation seems to be directed at a type of party, the true target is that elitist class of society that revels in holding social functions solely to exclude and impress.

What role does aggression play in modern sitcom writing? It is everywhere! Aggressive humor is a standard component in sitcom stories, dialogue, and—most notably—in caustic characters like *Drew*'s Mimi, *Seinfeld*'s Elaine, and almost every character on *The Larry Sanders Show*. Why? Because aggression, like truth, promotes audience identification, which yields big laughs.

5. BREVITY

Every book, article, or thesis ever written about comedy includes that tired quote from Shakespeare's *Hamlet*, "Brevity is the soul of wit." Why? Brevity, mainly.

That line, better than any other, defines an immutable law of comedy. There is no mystery here, no theoretical construct to decipher. Centuries of practical experience have demonstrated that humor must be lean and mean, completely uncluttered. Otherwise, the incongruity gets lost, the surprise muddled, the truth diluted.

When in doubt, remember that less is more.

And in some cases, less might still be too much. A hundred years ago, Professor Theodore Lipps wrote that "A joke says what it has to say, not always in few words, but in *too* few words. . . . It may even actually say what it has to say by not saying it."[9] Remember "Take my wife . . . please!"? It says it all, without saying it. Enough said.

One last note about the characteristics of comedy. Scholars and writers identified these and other traits long ago, but have not always agreed on their relative importance. For additional modern perspectives, see Sol Saks's book, *The Craft of Comedy Writing*, and Melvin Helitzer's book, *Comedy Writing Secrets*. (Or buy lunch for a successful comedy writer.)

THE IMPORTANCE OF TENSION

By now, the reasoning behind my earlier speculation is probably clear. All theories of laughter, and all laughter stimuli, seem to depend on an underlying process of establishing, building, and then releasing tension. An *incongruity* creates comedic tension. A *surprise* twist releases tension. *Truth* and *aggression* increase tension. *Brevity* brings tension into high relief.

Often, much of the tension in a funny situation or an individual joke comes not from comedic structure but from shared stress in our lives. And the more tension in a joke, the bigger the release (or laugh).

It is helpful to keep these dynamics in mind when developing stories and sculpting jokes. Not that we should get hung up on labels and theories when trying to create—that's a surefire recipe for bland (but technically correct?) comedy. Instead, our goal is to explore these concepts so that they can float around in our subconscious, occasionally stepping forward to suggest or shape a bit of humor. And we can apply this knowledge in a more deliberate fashion during rewrites, when a couple of rules and tools can sometimes fix material that inspiration has left broken.

MOVING ON

It is one thing to analyze humor theory, another to apply it in one's writing. Let's take a closer look at how sitcom writers work.

Three

Putting Theory into Practice

Different writers have different strengths. Some are good with story structure, some with dialogue, some are related to the producer.

All comedy writers have good days, funny days, and bad, sad, can't-make-it-happen days. Sometimes a script will practically write itself, it just spills over with Grade-A humor. Other times, it just lies there, limp, dull, fodder for someone's eulogy. (Yours, once the producer sees it.)

Hey, comedy writing only looks easy. If there is one constant in the process, it's that all comedy writers share certain creative goals. These include:

SEAMLESS HUMOR

Good comedy writing is seamless rather than forced. Humorous situations should flow naturally from a story; they should not feel like a detour taken because the writer was desperate to cram in a few extra jokes. Likewise, funny dialogue should sound like something the characters would actually say; it should not sound like ill-fitting one-liners lifted from someone's standup routine.

A joke can be hilarious, the funniest thing that you will ever write, but if it does

Matt Williams: We have a phrase called "writer's hand." "That's funny, but it's writer's hand." It refers to self-conscious writing. It sounds like a sitcom writer. You can feel their hand writing the line and [hear them] chuckling, as opposed to the line coming organically out of the moment, out of that character's mouth.

not belong in your script it will break the audience's suspension of disbelief. It will distract viewers, leaving them with the impression that they have just been subjected to a joke.

Not good.

Even the broadest of comedies can boast of seamless humor, as long as its jokes remain true to its overall premise. Consider wacky classics like *I Love Lucy* and *Gilligan's Island*, or films like *Animal House* and *There's Something About Mary*. As outrageous as they were, the comedy that they offered seemed completely organic and natural. The payoff? Their viewers found it easy to relax and go along for the ride.

CONSISTENCY

Good writers, either deliberately or instinctively, struggle to maintain consistent levels of humor in their scripts. Meaning, they provide an amount and type of humor that is appropriate for the story they are writing, and they maintain those levels from beginning to end. Weak scripts, inconsistent scripts, tend to bounce back and forth. A funny sequence might be followed by a serious scene, followed by a stretch of dry humor, followed by loads of physical shtick. At the story's beginning, the audience is cued to enjoy a certain amount and type of comedy; but when these expectations are frustrated by inconsistency, the audience loses interest.

In sitcoms, the style of humor is dictated by the creators of the series premise. The challenge is to identify and consistently reflect that style in the episodes that you write.

COMEDY OUTPUT

I have never heard a producer say "Too much humor in this script—make it less funny."

Sitcom writers are always looking for ways to increase their comedy output. After all, the average half-hour script eats up two to three solid jokes *per page*. (Once in a meeting, I actually had an executive congratulate me with the pronouncement that he had counted ninety jokes in my script. Obviously, the guy needed a hobby.)

Of course, comedy writing is not just a numbers game. You are always trying to improve a script, always looking for that next joke that is just a bit better than the one already sitting on the page.

The challenge is to come up with enough terrific humor to satisfy your audience, and yourself, *without* forcing the jokes. Because, as much as your producers will always clamor for more comedy, the last thing that you want to hear anyone say is "This script is too 'jokey.' " (Meaning that your script is thick with obvious setups and predictable punch lines.) So much for seamless humor.

> **NOTE:** *Audience responses seem to come in three forms: a smile, a grunt or chuckle, and a full-fledged laugh. Broad, wacky, physical comedy—comedy that incorporates lots of outrageous situations and big surprises—usually generates a healthy number of laughs. Sophisticated, subtle, adult humor—comedy distinguished by wit and clever repartee—is more likely to garner quiet smiles. Picture Urkle doing a series of pratfalls for the first, and Frasier jousting with Roz for the second.*

THE TRADITIONAL APPROACH TO SITCOM WRITING

How do sitcom writers achieve these goals? How do they create seamless humor, consistent humor, more humor?

In the industry today, much of this work is left to the *rewriting* process. Consider how most writers and writing staffs operate. The average writer starts work on a spec script, his next writing sample, by developing an episode premise and quickly cranking out a first draft. Too often, he does not bother to write a story outline first, which is a bad idea, unless you are one of those obnoxious types who can completely map out a story in your head. Prior to circulating the script, the writer and his trusty readers (friends, wife, the mailman) examine the first draft to identify weak spots. The writer makes his revisions and sends the script off.

Many times this system works just fine. The writer correctly identifies script problems and turns out a dynamite spec. However, putting so much of the creative burden on the rewriting phase can have a downside. There is a tendency to address all script problems, some of which have nothing to do with a lack of humor, by trying to cram additional jokes into the dialogue. This can easily result in forced humor—the writer ends up with one very funny, but very bad, script. And no job.

Freelance writers working on an actual assignment and writers on the staff of a show operate in a similar fashion, except that they usually work from a written outline. (This outline has either been supplied by the show's producers or created under their supervision.) The standard approach is to have one writer or a writing team pump out a first draft of the script, which is then subjected to a seemingly endless cycle of rewriting. Much of this rewriting takes the form of "roundtable writing," a process in which five, ten, or more writers jointly go through a script, rewriting line after line, hunting for opportunities to wedge just one more joke into the material. Efforts to repair and improve the script usually last all the way through the shooting process, with revisions being tossed to actors even as the scenes are being filmed or videotaped. (As anyone in Hollywood will tell you, it seems that three-quarters of all writing done is rewriting—you rewriting you, you rewriting others, others rewriting you.)

Most of the time, roundtable writing is a great way to increase a script's joke count and remedy story problems—I guess that's why it became a tradition in the first place. And, no question, last-minute rewriting is an invaluable tool for fine-tuning a script. It allows the producers to adjust for a performer's timing, or account for unexpected staging problems, or capitalize on someone's brilliant last-minute inspiration.

However, as with the individual working alone on a spec script, placing so much of the creative burden on the rewriting process can have drawbacks. Again, the repeated attempts to bump up a script's joke count make it easy to fall back on a little forced humor here and there. (Particularly if you have fifteen to twenty different "voices" contributing to each draft.)

Also, continuous rewriting can lead to micromanaging a script's humor to death. Great jokes from an early draft are frequently dumped for weaker jokes in a later draft, simply because the newer jokes are still fresh enough to seem funny. (Some writers would scoff at this observation, arguing that "Your best work is what you will write tomorrow!" This is a good point, but so is "If it ain't broke, don't fix it.")

An even bigger problem is that continuous rewriting can inadvertently damage other parts of a script, from story structure to character development. Sure, that scene from *Dharma & Greg* is funnier now that you have added the one-eyed monkey. But how did that monkey get into Dharma's bathroom in the first place? (And what happened to his other eye?) Meaning, you must do yet another rewrite, or several, to fix a new story problem. And no doubt, some of those great jokes that everyone loved in earlier drafts will begin to seem stale in the additional rewrites, so . . . I guess you'll be replacing them too.

Not that I am lobbying against Hollywood's time-tested traditions of rewriting and roundtable writing. Those practices are extremely useful, even necessary. As the French poet Paul Valéry once declared, "An artist never really finishes his work; he merely abandons it." (Of course, I'm not sure that the guy ever wrote sitcoms.)

My point is that these vaunted traditions have their limitations. When managed by talented pros, vigorous rewriting can result in seamless, consistent, rich humor. (Witness *Roseanne*, *The Simpsons*, and the original *Cosby Show*, all of which were heavily rewritten.) But, when managed by less experienced types, of which there are now many in the business, the results can get ugly.

I believe that some folks in the sitcom industry have come to depend too heavily on the rewriting process. And economics is probably to blame. As production costs have soared, and a recent wave of federal deregulation has spurred television networks to become program producers, the financial stakes have gone way up. Executives have gotten more and more involved in the creative process in an effort to protect their company's investments. But this means more script notes from more sources—which is probably not the best way to hone fiction.

What would I suggest? A slight shift in effort. How about a writing approach that does not rely so heavily on "fixing it in post"? (Translation: When sloppy directors can't get something right during a shoot, they often opt to fix it in postproduction; sitcom writers are among those who enjoy using this phrase as a putdown—even though this is the very same approach used to write many of today's sitcoms.) Why not try an approach that gives you, especially if you are writing alone, a better shot at doing your best work?

A DIFFERENT APPROACH—PREMISE-DRIVEN COMEDY

Our favorite drama writers explore all opportunities to build conflict into their stories—be it "man against nature," "man against man," "man against self," what have you. These writers start with an interesting story premise, then compound dramatic tension when they create story sequences, and again when they create individual scenes. The result is a story that is both organic and rich.

Anonymous: It used to be that there was one star that maybe you'd have to deal with, and one network executive. Now it's fifty studio executives—that you have to pitch the idea to before you even get to the network—and then seventy-five network executives. And then the talent has their manager and agent clear everything. It's exhausting and it's the reason that there's so much pablum on TV. . . .

The executives think that if only they had paid more attention, that show would have been really good, when arguably it's the exact opposite. It was their attention that screwed it up. . . .

I'm of the mind that you can never receive too much input. But at the end of the day, the head writer on the show should be the one who makes the final decisions.

Similarly, the best sitcom writers instinctively integrate *comedic* tension into all levels of their work—from episode premise, to sequence, to scene. By the time they get down to writing dialogue, the comedy that they have planted at the first levels of the script automatically produces more laughs, bigger laughs, and more seamless laughs than are otherwise possible.

The key is to focus a little energy on laying comedic tension into your episode premise. Then, build on that tension and draw from that tension as you create sequences, scenes, and dialogue. It is a simple, intuitive approach, without any tricks. While it is certainly not intended to replace rewriting, this method can help you to draw as much comedy as possible from the stories that you create.

Creating premise-driven comedy means working from the ground up. . . .

Four

Level One—Comedy in the Story Premise

Just picture: There you are, sitting down to start work on that new script for *Just Shoot Me*. And you think to yourself, "Time to go for some of that premise-driven comedy. But how, dammit, how?"

Simple. You start by weaving funny elements into the premise of the episode. (Do not worry about scenes and dialogue yet; focus on the overall story.) The comedy that you plant at this first level of your script will automatically generate funny situations and jokes throughout the material. (Making your work easier!) Plus, the resulting humor will seem natural and seamless, because it grew out of the story rather than having been crammed into it.

To illustrate, imagine this story line: a housewife gets a chance to be on a game show. She answers the questions, wins a washing machine, goes home happy. End of episode. An interesting story? No. Funny? Don't think so. But if we play with the premise a bit . . .

The housewife gets her chance on the game show. She answers the questions just fine, until . . . she is tricked into admitting, on national TV, that her husband's boss is secretly bald! The boss is celebrity Alan Brady, her husband is Rob Petrie, and suddenly we have a great story line for a sitcom titled *The Dick Van Dyke Show*. Laura must confess to Rob, Laura tries to save Rob's job, Rob tries to save Rob's job. It is a classic episode, hilarious throughout, and all because of comedy that grows out of the story premise.

Consider another example, this one from a feature film: Two guys, buddies, witness a mass murder—eight or ten people are machine-gunned to death before their eyes. The two pals are spotted by the killers but they manage to escape. The pals run off to another city, trying to disappear, but run smack into the killers!

Interesting story? Sure. But funny? Maybe to psychos. Most people, hearing this description, would expect to see a tense thriller full of jeopardy, suspense, and violent death. But, tinker with that premise and you might get . . .

The two guys witness the massacre and they need to escape . . . so they don disguises—dresses! They pretend to be women, and join an all-female band that is leaving town for a gig. (Giving us men in drag, a classic comedy device.) To complicate matters, both guys fall for the same gorgeous woman, another band member. One of the guys—dressed as a woman, of course—inadvertently ends up sharing a bed with the goddess, and must struggle to maintain his disguise in the face of great temptation. The other takes on a second disguise, posing as a rich playboy, so that he can court the woman. But, at the same time, he is forced to play female best-friend-and-confidante when the woman needs to discuss her new beau (him!). Then the gangsters show up, there is mix-up after mix-up—

The movie? *Some Like It Hot*, a fabulous film that stars Jack Lemmon, Tony Curtis, and Marilyn Monroe. What might have been a tense thriller, a bloody gangster flick, is transformed into a hilarious G-rated family comedy—all because of funny elements woven into the film's premise.

How do you accomplish this in your writing? How do you lace comedy into a story premise? I will list four ways, and then we will explore each in detail:

PREDICAMENTS

Design an escalating series of predicaments into your story. The incongruity inherent in each situation will generate comedic tension, and that tension will be compounded by each subsequent, larger predicament.

CHARACTER MIX

Think character *relationships* rather than just . . . "Plumbers are funny, I'll make this guy a plumber." The Elaine character on *Seinfeld* was not that funny by herself; she was a neurotic, frustrated career woman who whined a lot. But when story lines had her bouncing off an exasperating kook like Kramer, an obnoxious underachiever like George, and a kindred spirit like Jerry, her role in the character mix spawned countless funny bits.

STYLE OF COMEDY

This has to do with genres, types of humor, amount of humor, and consistency of humor. The producers of a sitcom make these decisions when they create a series. The writer's job is to identify and exploit these decisions in the episodes that he or she writes.

CASTING

In most instances, writers have little say in casting decisions. But, consider the impact that these decisions can have on humor at the story level; imagine how differently you would tailor a role for Jim Carrey versus one that you would write for Drew Carey.

Very talented writers instinctively apply all of these tools when creating a story. Less talented writers do so occasionally. Unfortunately, occasionally doesn't get you work.

PREDICAMENTS

Webster's defines a predicament as "an unpleasantly difficult, perplexing, or dangerous situation." Gee, sounds like a laugh riot.

Yet predicaments can generate humor. How? By creating tension. As long as the viewer perceives that characters facing a predicament will not come to any real harm, that tension can be used to produce comedy. (It can be shaped into a humorous incongruity that calls out for a funny payoff.) Of course, we must first cue the audience that our story is meant to be funny, or jokes based on a character's unfortunate predicament might seem offensive and fall flat.

A funny predicament confined to one scene will pump up the humor for those few pages. But a sustained predicament built into the story premise can generate humor in scene after scene, from "Fade In:" to "End of Episode." (Think of Jack Lemmon and Tony Curtis in those dresses.) Create a funny predicament at the first level of your script and it can become a joke-producing machine for the duration of your story, or at least until said predicament is resolved.

NOTE: *Permanent predicaments are often built into the overall premise of a sitcom. Remember those seven people stranded on* Gilligan's Island? *When trying to think of funny story lines for an individual episode, a writer might start by exploring any permanent predicaments that already exist* *within the series premise. "No phone, no lights, no motorcar" might suggest the perfect story predicament for your episode.*

There is another benefit to creating escalating predicaments. A continuing, unresolved predicament in your story leaves your viewer hanging. It creates a sustained expectation, an underlying suspense, as he or she waits for the final payoff. The great thing about this? Situations and jokes that are *not even related* to the predicament seem funnier because the viewer is operating with a heightened sense of anticipation. (Cool.)

Want some examples? Here are some classic predicaments that have been featured in sitcom episodes. They should look familiar—they have been used time after time, in show after show. Some of them have even been listed in screenwriting books as examples of stories to write. Am I suggesting that you should rehash old story lines? No. These models are presented here for only one reason: They provide great examples of how you might build funny predicaments into an *original* story premise.

THE BIG LIE

A lead character tells a lie during a weak moment; either he wants to impress someone, or he gets caught in a compromising situation, or he wants something that he cannot have. The lie leads to another and another, each bigger than the last. (Tension, tension, tension.) The situation gets out of hand, eventually backfires, and laughter ensues.

Example? *Drew Carey* names his pet as an insurance dependent in order to get its vet bills paid. When questioned about this mysterious male dependent, Drew panics and claims that said dependent is Drew's gay lover (Drew is straight). When proof is demanded, Drew is forced to bring his friend Oswald, posing as the lover, to a corporate meeting to prove that Drew is gay. Naturally, the scheme falls apart and Drew is humiliated—a typical sitcom ending.

Technically speaking, the funny incongruity created by the first lie grows larger and larger with each new lie, but is finally resolved when the truth is revealed at story's end. In episodes featuring a "big lie," the guilty character sometimes gets carried away by the good fortune generated by his lies. (For example, Bart Simpson claims that he has performed some heroic deed, then starts to believe his own press.) Sometimes the character finds himself faced with a moral dilemma, in which he must choose between his interests and those of a more deserving character. Usually, the big lie is eventually exposed and order is restored. However, some episodes end with a clever twist that allows the character to escape with his dignity and "the prize" intact.

THE BIG SECRET

In these stories, a lead character discovers a secret about another character, but is somehow prohibited from sharing that information. (He usually blabs the secret to assorted friends, and has several close calls in which he almost blabs to the person involved.) Often, things start off simply enough, then turn into a huge, dying-to-tell burden. Rachel's *Friends* are delighted when she declares that she will finally tell Ross that she loves him—but then he climbs off an airplane with a new girlfriend on his arm, and everyone must hold their collective tongue. Ross finally discovers the truth, but only after a number of scenes have milked humor from this predicament.

Sometimes these stories feature a loose-lipped lead who proclaims that, for once, he will maintain absolute secrecy—then doesn't. Sometimes a secret is passed on but misinterpreted, leading to funny complications. At other times, those who know the secret finally become so incensed that they take desperate action; they confront the two-timing husband or expose the corporate scam, only to discover that they have misinterpreted the situation and caused a humiliating scene.

THE MISUNDERSTANDING

One character misinterprets something that he is told or that he overhears, and then gets into trouble when he acts on the misinformation. Comedic tension is created the second that we, the viewers, realize that the character has misunderstood. It builds each time the character does something that makes the predicament worse.

Example: *Larry Sanders* tries to send a crude, insulting fax to a media critic he hates, but accidentally directs it to his sidekick, Hank, instead. Hank, gravely offended, tells his producer that he intends to quit, and badmouths Larry to an actress whom Larry is pursuing. It seems that all will end well when Larry makes friends with the critic and Hank learns that the fax was not intended for him. But a final twist in the story reveals that Hank, in an attempt to do Larry a favor, has just forwarded the scathing fax to the critic.

A ROCK AND A HARD PLACE

A lead character of the series must choose between two very good things or two very bad things. Should *Frasier*'s Niles stand up to the bully and win Daphne's affection, or should he crawl away and keep possession of his teeth? Should *Home Improvement*'s Tim take Jill out for that long-promised anniversary dinner, or should he join his buds at the Truckosaurus Tournament of Champions?

These predicaments often involve growing levels of deceit and they often take the form of a moral dilemma. In the old days (say, the pre-*Married . . . with Children* era), the lead character could be counted on to eventually choose the high ground, sacrificing her interests for another character's. Now, just as often, the lead will shamelessly pursue the more selfish goal, but end up losing everything by the story's conclusion. (Or not; the days of selfish deeds always being punished are long gone.)

THE SUREFIRE SCHEME

The second a lead character says the words "Trust me, what could go wrong?" we all know what lies ahead. Be it *Taxi*'s Louie DePalma or *Spin City*'s Michael Flaherty, that character is about to unleash a surefire plan to get rich or get laid, or both. Of course, he and his cohorts immediately encounter an escalating series of unexpected problems, bad decisions, and foolish risks, all of which land them in hot water. Usually, by story's end, their surefire scheme completely backfires. The characters are worse off than before, and we enjoy a pleasing release of tension as order is restored.

SOMETHING THAT ROCKS THE BOAT

In these stories, all is normal in sitcomland until some event rocks the boat. Sometimes this event takes the form of a past acquaintance or a relative coming to visit. For example, an old girlfriend pops up to threaten *Dharma & Greg*'s relationship, or to introduce the son that Greg didn't know he had. Or *Drew*'s folks get kicked out of their condo, so guess where they plan to live. Or a hunky new neighbor drives *Friends*'s Monica and Phoebe apart as they fight over the guy.

These stories create tension by threatening the status quo. They often build up to some sort of showdown, an emotional confrontation during which misunderstandings are revealed. Then they usually end with the boat-rocker returning to wherever it is that he came from.

TIME BOMB

These stories feature a race against time. The characters get themselves into a predicament in which they must accomplish an impossible goal by a fast-approaching deadline. Of course, the harder they try, the worse matters get. How often have we seen the story in which a teenager throws a big party while the folks are out of town? The place gets trashed, a treasured vase is broken, then—uh-oh!—the folks call to say they will be home early!

Right, too often. Other variations include rival characters competing on a dare, a character boasting himself into an impossible deadline at work, or characters hurrying to exploit a big opportunity before others discover that it exists.

TRAPPED IN A SPACE

You pick—a bank vault (*Married . . . with Children*), a locked broom closet (*Friends*), or a stopped elevator (every series ever produced). The lead characters get themselves trapped in a small space, usually accompanied by a pregnant woman or a closet claustrophobic, and must keep from killing each other as they wait to be rescued. Inevitably, one or more characters are overdue at some important event—a speech, a wedding, maybe *their* wedding. And, sometimes, their lives are actually in danger, with a clock ticking.

Why does this worn premise work? It's a pressure cooker. The small space forces opposing characters to remain in close proximity, which gets sparks flying. Plus, the concept of being trapped creates tension in all of us at some primal level, since being trapped usually leads to getting beaten, eaten, or sent to jail. Plus, missed appointments add even more tension, and they open up lots of story possibilities.

SEX

These predicaments often involve an aggressive pursuit, featuring a lead character as either the pursuer or pursu-ee. An example: Dick, of *3rd Rock from the Sun*, shows kindness to an antisocial librarian. She, misinterpreting his gesture, jumps him in a fit of passion—just as his girlfriend, Mary, appears. Dick is confused, tries to placate and plead, but every action he takes just makes things worse.

Other times, there is temptation on both sides. A lead character suddenly finds himself in a compromising situation with a willing, desirable acquaintance. Should he or shouldn't he? There are usually some small complications—like a wife and twelve kids waiting at home. Or maybe both parties work at the same place. Or a boss or best friend is already involved with the acquaintance. Or the characters must confront issues involving promiscuity, pregnancy, disease, or sexual harassment.

THE DEAD BODY

Talk about tension—stick one of your characters with a dead body and the possibilities are endless. Does she have to hide the corpse? Will she be blamed for the death, even accused of murder? Must she assume the stiff's identity to avoid a disaster, or close a big deal?

There are also plenty of dead body predicaments that do not involve man-handling a corpse. *Murphy Brown* gets trapped into giving a eulogy for a person she loathed. *The Simpsons* screw up some delicate funeral arrangements. The Bundys (of *Married . . . with Children*) join in a feeding frenzy over an inheritance. Or a reluctant character has to break the news to the new widow. Or someone gets stuck with the stiff's nasty little dog.

Again, I am not suggesting that you should rehash old plot lines such as these. (We will discuss techniques for creating *original* stories in chapter 8.) I have listed the above "classics" only because they are great examples of how to build funny predicaments into an episode premise.

If you want to study more examples of classic sitcom plots, check out Milt Josefsberg's book, *Comedy Writing*. Or, better yet, sit down and draw up a list of recycled stories that you have seen; you could probably cough up another twenty examples, and the exercise would be time well spent. (*Esquire* magazine even published a parody of recycled sitcom stories in March of 1993, in an article titled "The Ten Basic Sitcom Plots.")

Lastly—don't smirk too much. If you become a working sitcom writer, you will someday take a second glance at a wonderful story that you have just thought up, only to realize that . . . Yikes! You have just recycled that old Big Lie model. Well, do not despair. Those old predicaments keep popping up for two reasons—they reflect human behavior, and they are funny. As long as you apply them in a fresh manner, true to your characters, you can still use (reuse) them.

CHARACTER MIX

Place *Seinfeld*'s Kramer in any situation—in an elevator, at the post office, in a corporate meeting—and funny bits just pour out onto the page. But put his friend Elaine in the same situations and what happens? Do jokes automatically materialize?

Put *Frasier*'s dad, Martin, in an elevator or *Drew*'s friend, Kate, in a post office, and we get the same result. Some characters are just inherently funny, anywhere, anytime, because of their design. (And because of the actors who play them.) Other characters—more normal characters?—are less funny out of context. They get most of their laughs through involvement in story predicaments and interactions with other characters. Elaine is funniest when reacting to Kramer, sparring with Jerry, or haranguing George. Most of Martin's humor comes from his role as both parent to, and dependent of, Frasier. Kate is a blue-collar babe who provides a sexy foil to her pals, and whose one-of-the-guys status entitles her to join in what would normally be males-only banter.

NOTE: *Interestingly, when the* Seinfeld *series first began, Elaine was George's opposite—a competent, socially adept careerist. However, later in the series, she evolved into George's twin—an insecure, neurotic loser. It appears that the useful contrast she originally offered in this character mix was gradually sacrificed for the sake of easy laughs. Which was unfortunate, because Elaine's original character—a rare portrayal of a strong, capable woman—sparked many of the more sophisticated story lines that the series featured in its early years.*

My point? When creating characters for a sitcom (a subject that we will discuss in part 2 of this book), pay attention to the character mix. To maximize opportunities for generating humor, the characters should complement rather than duplicate each other. Each should actively contribute something fresh to the mix. Perhaps he or she provides a conflicting point of view, as the original Elaine did; characters who have different opinions usually end up in conflict, which creates tension, which can be turned into comedy.

Or perhaps the character might have a tendency to get himself and others into trouble, as *Home Improvement*'s Tim Taylor does. The result? Conflict, and comedy.

Or the character might behave in a strange manner or live a bizarre life-style, as Kramer did. The reactions from other characters, and contrasts with other characters, can be funny. And the strange character's behavior often results in other characters being roped into unusual predicaments.

Whether you are creating a cast of series regulars for a new series or a one-shot visiting character for a single episode, the concept remains the same. Here are a few more of those classic sitcom models; these are based on character relationships rather than story predicaments.

ROLE REVERSAL

This dynamic occurs when a character is forced to assume a role that is contrary to his nature. He is then confronted with numerous obligations, expectations, and obstacles that he is ill equipped to meet. Picture a young dad who suddenly finds himself a single parent to three toddlers. How many times have we seen that concept? Of course, sometimes there are two dads, or six kids, or even three men and a baby.

There are the episodes in which one character assumes another's job responsibilities (role) on a dare, with disastrous but funny results. And episodes in which one character gets roped into pretending that he is another character's lover or spouse, even though both characters actually hate each other. Tension? Comedy? You bet.

One of the most interesting examples of role reversal, at the series premise level, occurred in the late eighties. America was gaga over cheerful family sitcoms like the original *Cosby* show. But then came the FOX network and two shows titled *Married . . . with Children* and *The Simpsons*. Role reversal? Instead of featuring the nice, friendly families that audiences were used to seeing, these two series featured *antifamilies*. Irresponsible mother Peggy, slut sister Kelly, childlike parent Homer, sassy son Bart . . . In both shows, a classic premise was turned upside down, roles were reversed, and the result was fresh comedy. Audiences tuned in and the new network took off.

FISH OUT OF WATER

Write a character into a world where they don't belong, and you will end up with a mix of individuals who have dissimilar social skills, cultural traditions, educational backgrounds, religious points of view, intelligence levels, even eating habits. These differences will spawn conflict and humor. Remember the *Beverly Hillbillies*? Think of all the funny episodes that were based entirely on some small, simple contrast between the Clampetts and their neighbors. As in, Dr. Granny treats Mrs. Drysdale to a hit of her 100-proof tonic. Or Jethro decides to become a sophisticated Beverly Hills playboy. Or the family mutt impregnates the neighbor's thoroughbred poodle.

Another example of how a fish out of water can spice up a show's character mix is the hour-long series *Northern Exposure* (a show that was more a "dramedy" than a sitcom). Snooty Manhattan-bred Dr. Fleischman found himself stranded in the remote village of Cicely, Alaska. The contrast between his aggressive, demanding nature and the calm, soothing ways of the community generated many a story line and much humor—all because of decisions made at the series premise level.

ODD COUPLING

Create a character mix that forces two complete opposites to exist in the same space, and funny things will happen. The best example of a series (and a play, and a film) that featured a pairing such as this? *The Odd Couple*, of course. In that series, Felix and Oscar differed in countless respects—clean freak vs. slob, cultural snob vs. blue-collar guy, sensitive man vs. crass lug. The two men argued about everything from personal hygiene to politics, and this resulted in a wealth of funny stories, funny scenes, and funny lines.

Other examples of odd coupling in a show's character mix include Tim and Al in *Home Improvement*, Fran and Mr. Sheffield in *The Nanny*, and even the diverse character mix featured in *Gilligan's Island*. At the episode level, one might create a temporary odd-couple situation by importing a visiting relative, romantic interest, business associate, etc., whose contrasting personality completely disrupts the life of a lead character.

SEX

Yes, we already named sex as a means of generating story predicaments, but it can also be useful when creating a character mix. (And can one really discuss sex too much?)

In terms of relationships between characters, it is sometimes useful to create or exploit an ongoing sexual tension between two leads. Meaning, you might create two characters who urgently need to consummate their relationship and become full-fledged lovers, but are somehow prevented from doing so. Consider the Niles-Daphne bond on *Frasier*; how many story lines have grown out of the simple fact that needy Niles is hopelessly in love with Daphne, but too afraid to make his move? On the show *Friends*, how much mileage has been gotten out of the on-again, off-again, on-again relationship between Ross and Rachel? And let's not forget the ever-smoldering passion shared by *3rd Rock from the Sun*'s Sally and Officer Don.

Occasionally, if producers start running short of original story ideas in a show's fourth or fifth season, they weaken and allow characters to consummate a sexual tension. Sometimes the decision works and other times it damages the character mix. Consider the effect on *Cheers* when Sam and Diane finally got together; the producers realized their mistake, broke the pair apart again, and even duplicated the original sexual tension when designing Diane's replacement, Rebecca.

Another type of character mix might exploit sex by featuring two lovers, or spouses, who enjoy a healthy, in-your-face sex life. Examples include the couples in *Step by Step*, *Mad About You*, and *Dharma & Greg*. Comedy in these shows frequently comes out of disruptions to the physical relationship—such as kids interfering with planned "date nights," a passing criticism blown out of proportion, or a fear that the healthy relationship is growing stale.

In recent years, producers have grown increasingly bold about incorporating homosexuality into a show's character mix. On *The Larry Sanders Show*, Hank's gay assistant, Brian, provided a wonderful foil to his oafish boss; Hank's moronic, self-obsessed personality was made all the more obvious by its contrast to his assistant's sensitive, intelligent nature.

When series lead *Ellen* came out of the closet, her admission created all sorts of comedic tension; it completely reinvigorated the show's character mix. Her friends reacted in amusing ways, funny conflicts arose at work, and her tentative forays into the gay community generated lots of laughs. Unfortunately, the series came to dwell so heavily on gay dating issues that it failed to find (or keep) an audience, and the series was soon canceled.

PRETENSE

When a comedic character pretends to be something that he is not, he is usually doomed to exposure and humiliation. As Freud describes it, the character has "seized dignity and authority by a deception," and needs to be taken down.[10]

Consider the character mix on *Frasier*. Frasier and his brother Niles both reek of self-importance. As lovable as they are, their superior attitudes and affluent lifestyles make them ripe targets for those feelings of aggression that we discussed earlier (in the section titled "Characteristics of Comedy"). The brothers' pretense is particularly obvious every time one of them behaves in a foolish or childish manner, which occurs frequently. Fortunately, the creators of the series provided the perfect means of drawing comedy from this pretense; they balanced the character mix with Martin, Daphne, and Roz, three down-to-earth individuals who are well suited to knocking Frasier and Niles off their high horses whenever needed.

Other examples of how pretense has been incorporated into a series premise include *NewsRadio*'s pompous Bill McNeal (played by the late Phil Hartman), *The Nanny*'s snooty C.C. Babcock (Lauren Lane), and *Home Improvement*'s klutzy Tim Taylor (Tim Allen). Each of these characters regularly puts on airs or feigns knowledge of some topic, making him- or herself a prime target for a comeuppance.

At the episode level, a writer can either exploit pretense that has been built into a show's character mix (if any), or lure a normally unpretentious character into putting up a pretense. Either way, the bluff will usually backfire by story's end. Bart Simpson cheats on a test to gain special treatment—then finds himself overwhelmed by life in the gifted-student lane. *Seinfeld*'s George Costanza pretends to be a timid tourist in order to attract an ebullient New Yorker—but she eventually dumps him because he seems incapable of surviving in the Big Apple.

Lastly, any discussion of character pretense has to include that old standby, the tired story line that screams "this show's producers are burnt out"—the class reunion episode. As in, a lead character is anxious to impress her former lovers and rivals at her high school reunion, so she pretends to be rich, thin, happily engaged, and/or married. Usually, the charade is uncovered in the final act. And these stories often end with a double twist, in which an obnoxious rival turns out to be an even bigger fake than the series lead. Tension is relieved, order is restored, and all ends happily.

NOTE: *If you want a real treat, find a copy of the* Taxi *episode in which Bobby substitutes for Louie at his high school reunion. The story seems mar-*

*velously fresh and funny even today, because the writers found a new take
on an old premise.*

The above archetypes are presented to illustrate how character relationships, not just funny characters, can be used to generate comedy. You could come up with more classic examples if you tried—which might be a worthwhile exercise, since these pairings are used again and again in all forms of comedy.

STYLE OF COMEDY

While the last two sections ("Predicaments" and "Character Mix") dealt with comedic elements that might be woven into a story premise, this section will deal with overall stylistic approach. A writer needs to know, to sense, what type and what amount of humor are appropriate for his story. And his style of humor must be consistent throughout the script.

In a completely original script, such as a pilot script for a new series, there are many decisions to make—you are creating the series from scratch. However, if you are writing for an existing series, the producers have already done this job. Your task is to study their series in depth so that you can identify and match the show's style of comedy. This is important—if your script does not look, sound, and feel exactly like the episodes that are produced every week, you don't get the job. No matter how funny your material is, no matter how exciting the story.

In chapter 7 we will discuss specific steps that you can take to analyze a series. For now, let's focus on how different styles of comedy can affect humor in a story.

GENRES, SORT OF

First, let's talk genres. And, just to illustrate a point, let's talk feature films rather than sitcoms, because a sitcom can, conceivably, present a different genre every week. (*The Simpsons*'s Homer might be featured in a romantic story one week, and a sci-fi tale the next.)

In films, most stories fall into a particular genre or incorporate several different genres. What's a genre? It's a class of stories that share certain attributes. For instance, love stories usually feature two people who start out as strangers or even enemies, but who are inevitably drawn together. Typically, the seemingly mismatched couple encounters a series of romantic obstacles but is forced together just long enough for sparks to fly.

In a detective genre, we expect to see murder victims and an investigation.

The hero is usually a surly outsider, a man with a past, whose search for clues leads him into great personal danger and, possibly, a romantic entanglement.

Other genres include horror, suspense, action, sci-fi, buddy-cop, coming of age, personal redemption, etc.—each of which is distinguished by its own set of attributes. While some films feature only one genre, most combine several. Look at the first *Robocop* movie—part sci-fi, part horror, part action, part buddy-cop, part comedy. Whether you like this type of film or not, it did an excellent job of blending a diverse mix of genres.

Why are genres important? Because audiences expect to see certain story elements when they watch a particular genre. Writers can either play to those expectations or, better yet, cut against them (to surprise viewers by reversing the norm).

Okay, but what do film genres have to do with writing sitcoms? Well, while sitcoms do fall into broad categories—domestic, odd couple, out of the closet with a vengeance, etc.—these categories are not synonymous with genres. By themselves, sitcom categories do not clue us in to the set of attributes that help to define a given series. Technically, *Married . . . with Children* and the original *Cosby* series were both domestic sitcoms of the eighties, each featuring a family unit in a home environment. But, clearly, that's where the similarities ended. Same category, different story attributes.

To complicate matters further, as noted above, a television series might feature a different genre every week, since each episode features a new story.

My point is that, when writing for sitcoms, it might be useful to think of each series as being its own genre. The premise of each series dictates a unique set of attributes that writers should include, and that the audience expects to see, in individual episodes. On a broad level, this might include elements such as a tendency to provide moral lessons in the final sequence, or the use (or avoidance) of controversial story themes. In terms of comedy, a show's attributes might range from *Seinfeld*'s Kramer having body spasms whenever he hears surprising news, to *Home Improvement*'s rule that the audience may never see Wilson's face.

In short, each series features a distinct style of comedy, and those attributes must be reflected in your script. If you are having difficulty getting a feel for a show, it might help to just start asking specific questions, such as these:

Where Does the Humor Come From?

Does most of the show's humor come from funny predicaments? Specific characters or relationships? The characters' environment?

Does the show deal in small, human stories or in outlandish, bigger-than-life predicaments? Or in small stories made outlandish?

Is the show's comedy generated by internal events or initiated by visiting characters?

How Broad or Subtle Is the Humor?

Does the show go for big belly laughs (usually the province of broad, wacky sitcoms) or just smiles and nods (typical of more adult, more sophisticated shows)?

Does it indulge in incredible fantasies such as alien encounters and Halloween spooks, or are all of its stories realistic and plausible?

Is most of the humor in the series visual or does it come out of dialogue?

How Does the Humor Affect the Story?

Does humor merely leaven or does it dictate the story?

Does humor overpower credibility, sacrificing story logic for the sake of laughs?

Do episodes climax with an explosive comedy run in the final act or maintain an even level of humor throughout?

Are the stories influenced by classic comedy genres, such as farce (mistaken identities and misunderstood actions), parody (campy sendups), or forties romancers (witty repartee)?

Of course, the best way to get a feel for an existing show's style of comedy is to watch episodes and read produced scripts. Then the trick is to write a script that uses that show's conventions in a fresh, exciting manner.

Even better, write that rare episode that expands a show's premise; create a visiting character worthy of becoming a series regular, open up a new story direction, or reveal a facet of a relationship that warrants further exploration.

BE CONSISTENT

One last, very important thought. Once you have studied a show and gotten a feel for its style of comedy, be consistent in your writing. New writers, bad writers, new bad writers, frequently make the following mistakes:

Too Funny to Pass Up

You come up with a fantastic joke or predicament, so funny that even your dad laughs, but it just doesn't quite fit the character or story. ("There's Kramer, a horse, two dwarves . . . and in this scene, Kramer's a lesbian!")

Sorry. But if that marvelous gem is not consistent with the show's style of comedy, you must dump it. Otherwise it will damage your story, distract the reader, cost you the job, and ruin your career.

Suddenly, it doesn't seem so funny, does it?

The Genre Shuffle

New writers frequently shift comedic genres midstory, ruining a script. Typically, they start out by writing in a style of comedy that is appropriate for a show, but then lose focus. ("After the beer-belching contest, *Drew* visits a kid in the hospital; the boy's on a respirator, dying, his mom just got killed . . .") Suddenly, the tone of jokes, the number of jokes, and the pacing of jokes change, disrupting the feel of the material. The result? See above, under "cost you the job, ruin your career."

In short, be consistent. If your writing is true to a show's style of comedy, your jokes will flow naturally.

CASTING

Why is casting listed here? Casting is not a part of sitcom writing, and unless a writer is also a producer—or is sleeping with a producer—he or she has little influence in this area.

But casting can have a big effect on comedy in a story, so we should take a quick look.

To illustrate, imagine that your agent just called—you've won a shot at pitching for Jim Carrey's new sitcom! You dive right in, developing a long list of story lines that feature broad, physical comedy: Jim gets stuck in a gorilla cage, Jim studies ballet, Jim accidentally gets shock therapy.

You show up at the pitch meeting, raring to go, but discover that . . . oops, your agent made a tiny mistake. The star isn't Jim Carrey, it's Drew Carey. And Drew doesn't do pratfalls. Drew doesn't have a rubber face. Drew doesn't get shock therapy.

Suddenly, casting's impact on comedy in a story premise is painfully clear. You politely excuse yourself from the pitch meeting, and rush over to your agent's office to share this revelation with him.

How can we make this lesson work for us? Part of studying a series (a subject that we will discuss later) involves looking at the actors' comedic strengths. Play to those, exploit those, and your comedy will flow naturally from the characters that they portray. Bob Newhart gives marvelous understated reactions, so use this by subjecting him to outrageous events and pairing him with outlandish characters. Ellen DeGeneres can play the same types of physical gags that made Lucy famous, so give her a chocolate factory or some vita-meata-vegamins to work with. Kelsey Grammer is able to portray pompous while still remaining likeable, so lure him into being pretentious, and then knock him down. Bill Cosby has perfected the role of the put-upon parent, so let those kids loose.

At the same time, there are instances when casting against type can bolster an episode's comedy, especially when filling guest roles. (Casting "against type" means casting an actor who is known for traits that are the opposite of those that define the character she will portray.) Shortly after *Ellen* came out of the closet, an episode of her series featured Emma Thompson and Sean Penn playing themselves, but with one small twist—both actors pretended that they were actually closet homosexuals, anxious to proclaim their "true" sexual preference to the world. The acts of casting known heterosexuals against type, and then poking fun at their supposed sexual insecurities, added tons of comedic tension to the story line. (Role reversal, but through casting.)

While we have discussed the idea that some folks in the sitcom world rely too heavily on the rewriting process, comedic timing is one area in which that emphasis is absolutely necessary. No matter how good the final script is, it is still important to fine-tune the material during run-throughs. Sometimes the producers and the director can only spot a weak bit when it surfaces during a rehearsal. Other times, run-throughs will kick up a bright new idea or two that didn't show up on paper.

In short, casting affects the writing process from beginning to end—something to keep in mind when you attain producer status, or start sleeping with that producer, and can finally influence those decisions.

MOVING ON

We have explored several ways to weave comedic tension into a story premise. Our next goal is to build on that tension, and draw from that tension, as we create sequences and scenes.

Five

Level Two—Comedy in Sequences and Scenes

After brainstorming until your ears explode, you finally come up with the perfect episode premise for a script. And it's funny. You have explored all of its comedy potential and it's got prime-time Emmy written all over it.

Now it is time to get serious, time to beat out the story (a process that we will discuss in chapter 9). As in all fiction, a sitcom script must have a dramatic structure, a beginning-middle-end, that is both logical and compelling. The difference is, yours also has to get laughs.

So you sit down to map out individual sequences and scenes. (A *sequence* can be defined as a series of consecutive scenes that feature one continuing action, such as a chase sequence. A *scene* is a segment of story that occurs in one location over one period of time; change either the location or the time and you have started a new scene.) While developing the story's dramatic structure, you should also explore the next level of comedy in your script. How? Well, you already planted some humorous sequences and scenes in the premise when you created it; they are the hooks that made the story seem funny in the first place. If you conjured up a "Joey goes to the sperm bank" premise for *Friends*, perhaps you envisioned a sequence that features Joey being embarrassed when he makes his first deposit. Or scenes that feature his friends' surprised reactions when they discover what Joey is doing.

But don't stop there. Don't leave the rest of the humor burden to dialogue alone. As you shape your story, you should harvest a few more of the comedic elements that you planted in the premise. Here are some ways to do so:

COMPOUND STORY PREDICAMENTS

Joey wants to be a sperm donor? And his friends seem surprised? Crank up the comedy by complicating Joey's situation—add more layers of funny predicaments. When Joey goes to make his first donation, maybe there's a slight misunderstanding—he thinks that he actually gets to sleep with the prospective mother. Or maybe he misunderstood the donor application, and somehow gave the impression that he is a famous heart surgeon (when, in fact, he only plays one on TV). And perhaps his friends discover the mistake, and argue over whether they should intercede. But they arrive too late. Or they hurt Joey's feelings. Or, or, or . . . There are a ton of funny options, *all driven by the original premise.*

Compound a predicament at the story level and the comedic tension doesn't just double, it increases geometrically. And it prolongs the duration of the funny predicament over a larger section of story, creating more laughs and bigger laughs. It isn't just *Drew* dreading having to attend some uptight company function—he gets stuck with Mimi as his date.

What is the difference between predicaments used at this level, in sequences and scenes, and the type used in the overall premise? Not much. You can compound a story predicament by adding additional layers of the same type of predicaments. A Big Lie can lead to Bigger and Bigger Lies, until everything backfires in a funny way.

Or, you can mix and match. Maybe a Big Lie puts a character between a Rock and a Hard Place. With a Dead Body. Trapped in a Space. (Again, these crusty examples are presented only to make a point; your goal should be to come up with fresh predicaments, drawn from your original premise, that compound your script's humor.)

The primary difference between predicaments at the first and second levels of your script is that those used in sequences and scenes are usually more finite events, that tend to occur in real time. The predicament pops up, plays itself out, and then gets resolved, all in one continuous segment of story.

STIR UP THE CHARACTER MIX

Hollywood screenwriting guru John Truby counsels that drama is about "people acting against people, not things." I am sure that he would say the same thing about comedy.

A great way to draw comedy from a sitcom story is to stir up the character mix. The show's producers wove humor into the overall series premise when they created the original mix, an ensemble of amusing characters who are supposed to interact in funny ways. Now, as you map out sequences and scenes, you can extract even more comedy from that mix by *temporarily* shifting character roles or relationships. (This applies whether or not your episode premise already plays off the show's character mix, via role reversal, fish out of water, or some other comedic device.)

For example, the character mix of *Seinfeld* included a neighbor whom Jerry hated—the infamous Newman. In a typical episode, Jerry and Newman found themselves arguing, competing, even feuding, with each other. But some episodes generated a lot of laughs by temporarily changing the character mix. They featured a sequence in which either Jerry or Newman had to approach the other for assistance or advice; the two characters reversed roles and formed an unnatural alliance that ran contrary to the original series premise. Comedic tension doubled because we were waiting for not only the resolution of the episode's story predicament but also the inevitable collapse of the temporary alliance. The payoff was extra sweet when that collapse occurred, the boys resumed their feud, and order (the character mix) was restored.

MIX AND MATCH

Obviously, you can also generate humor at the sequence and scene level by mixing story predicaments and character shifts together. If your episode premise involves *Friends*'s Rachel trying to keep her love for Ross a secret from him, you can complicate things by having Ross ask her to befriend his new girlfriend, the woman whom Rachel wants to kill. Then the girlfriend makes things even worse by asking her new chum Rachel for advice on how to seduce Ross. Rachel's original predicament is *compounded by a second predicament*, the request from Ross, and then made unbearable by the requirement that she *shift character roles* to play confidante to her unknowing rival. Tension builds throughout the sequence, generating comedy that flows naturally from the story.

THREE THINGS TO REMEMBER

As you explore comedy at this, the second level of the script, here are three things to remember:

ESCALATION

Just as a dramatic plot line should become more involving and compelling as it progresses, so should the comedy in a script. Otherwise its development seems too linear, or flat, or even anticlimactic. Yes, the jokes have to be funny from page one. But usually the predicaments, and the comedic tension that they cause, should escalate to a sort of comedy climax in the script's final scenes. (In fact, some series always feature a raucous *comedy block*—a big grouping of very funny jokes—at the end of each episode.)

LOOK TO THE SERIES PREMISE

It often seems that the best stories are drawn from a character's foibles, his or her human weaknesses. While many a sitcom episode has been based on importing some funny situation from the outside world, you can't go wrong by looking back at the original series premise to find ideas. At the least, the material that you come up with will flow naturally from the characters and seem true to the show.

BE CONSISTENT

When mapping out your sequences and scenes, remember the importance of maintaining a consistent style of comedy. Find the right mix—the right tone of humor, the right amount of humor—and make sure that it is reflected in all sections of your script. Otherwise, if some sequences seem hilarious while others read like a funeral announcement, you just might have a problem. Take time to review and reshape your scenes before writing any dialogue—it's better to do it at this stage than when your judgment is clouded by funny jokes.

MOVING ON

If you plant humor in a story premise, it is easier to create funny, natural sequences and scenes. Now that we have developed a story chock full of comedy, let's discuss the art of writing funny dialogue.

Six

Level Three—Comedy in Dialogue and Actions

Now comes what many consider to be the most enjoyable part of screenwriting—dialogue. If you have done your job right, you have constructed a story that is not only fresh and exciting, it is also a comedy-generating machine. It is brimming with humorous situations and characters that automatically suggest a number of funny lines. And since those lines are *drawn from* the story rather than *forced on* it, they should sound completely natural. (If you haven't done your job right, if you haven't explored the comedy potential of your premise, then you must now generate most of your humor through jokes and wordplay alone, which is not always an easy task.)

How do you take advantage of all of your groundwork? How do you make that premise-driven comedy pay off? Well, the raw materials are in place, so now it comes down to turning your funny ideas into funny jokes—setups and punch lines. Only we're not talking those obvious one-liners that pepper a comedian's monologue. Humor in dialogue should be absolutely seamless. Every funny line should sound just like something a character would say (under the given circumstances of a scene).

How do you create these seamless, just-like-a-character, non-monologue-like jokes? It helps to know a little about basic joke mechanics because the do's and don'ts of building jokes apply whether you are writing gags for Carrot Top or a clever retort for *Frasier*. Along the way, we'll look at excerpts of produced sitcom scripts to illustrate how clunky joke elements can be magically transformed into smooth, funny dialogue.

NOTE: *As much as I believe that writers can benefit by studying comedy theory and the creative process, I don't recommend getting too hung up on joke mechanics. The funniest lines that you create will probably just pour out onto the paper while you are writing away, born of instinct rather than conscious thought. So, yes, arm yourself with technical knowledge, but be aware that its greatest value lies in editing and repairing, not creating.*

BUILDING JOKES

You know the basic model—setup, then punch line. More precisely, a setup, or straight line, introduces the subject of the joke and hints at some complication or incongruity, producing tension. The punch line supplies a twist that resolves the joke in an unexpected fashion, releasing that tension. Laughter and gainful employment follow.

While punch lines always get the big headlines, setups are the true unsung heroes of joke warfare. Here are a few pointers to remember when beginning a joke:

SETUPS

THE SETUP SHOULD BE REASONABLE

The goal of a joke is to reel the audience in with a reasonable setup, then club it over the head with an unexpected punch line. The key to reeling the audience in is to present a situation that seems completely feasible, logical, even unremarkable. Otherwise, if the setup seems improbable or odd, the audience will know that something is up. The surprise of the punch line will be lost and the audience will get away.

Consider the setup in the following joke from an episode of *Just Shoot Me*; Maya has gone to the hospital because her father, Jack, and his young (second) wife have just had a new baby:

NOTE: *The script excerpts that follow are* not *printed in correct script format.*

```
(MAYA ENTERS AND STOPS AT THE NURSERY WINDOW. SHE
SCANS THE BASSINETS FOR THE NAME GALLO AND FINALLY
SPOTS HER LITTLE HALF SISTER. . . . )
```

> MAYA
> She's just beautiful. (BEAT)
> How's Allie?
>
> JACK
> Amazing. She was only in labor for two
> hours—and no drugs.
>
> MAYA
> How about you?
>
> JACK
> Just a Valium during the pushing.[11]

Anything remarkable about this setup? No. "In labor," "no drugs," and "How about you?" seem like perfectly normal bits of conversation. So an audience will swim right up, unsuspecting, ripe for that clubbing.

Sometimes a setup can seem completely reasonable but *still* be too obvious. In his book, *The Craft of Comedy Writing*, Sol Saks points out that there are times when it helps to intentionally misdirect an audience before "opening the trapdoor." A writer might "even go so far as to leave false clues [in the setup] to lead the audience astray."[12]

MANY SHAPES AND FORMS

A setup can consist of one line, several lines, or the same line repeated. Whatever shape it comes in, a setup usually contains at least two parts: the basic premise of the joke (to orient the audience), and a beat or two of development via complications or an incongruity (to create tension). Without the second part, development of the setup, there is not enough tension to make the joke pay off. Consider these lines from an episode of *The Parent 'Hood*:

> (T.K.'S WATCHING TV AS ROBERT ENTERS.)
>
> T.K.
> Mr. Peterson, can I order *Ultimate Fighting*
> on pay-per-view? It's only twenty-nine
> ninety-five.
>
> ROBERT
> Well, did you do your homework?

> T.K.
> Yeah.
>
> ROBERT
> Did you clean your room?
>
> T.K.
> Yeah.
>
> ROBERT
> Do you have twenty-nine ninety-five?
>
> T.K.
> No.
>
> ROBERT
> So close. But keep up the good work. [13]

If the writer hadn't bothered to include those beats of development in the setup to the joke, he would have ended up with . . .

> T.K.
> Mr. Peterson, can I order *Ultimate Fighting*
> on pay-per-view? It's only twenty-nine
> ninety-five.
>
> ROBERT
> Do you have twenty-nine ninety-five?
>
> T.K.
> No.
>
> ROBERT
> So close. But keep up the good work.

. . . which isn't that funny.

NOTE: *Comedy writers sometimes refer to this fundamental joke structure—setup, setup, punch line—as a* triple.

SPREADING OUT THE SETUP

In good dialogue, the jokes are invisible. The script doesn't read like a bad comedian's standup routine, rife with blatant setups and predictable punch lines. Instead, different parts of a setup might be spaced out within a scene, making them less obvious. Or elements of a setup might occur long before the punch line, even several scenes before it, comfortably laced into earlier dialogue. When the unsuspecting viewer finally does trip over the punch line, the joke not only scores on its own merit, it gets extra points for artful design.

Here's an example from *Friends*; Monica is upset because someone stole her credit card and went on a wild shopping spree:

> (MONICA IS SHOWING A VERY LONG CREDIT CARD STATE-
> MENT TO JOEY. . . .)
>
> MONICA
> . . . But look at how much they spent!
>
> RACHEL
> Monica, calm down. The credit card people
> said you only have to pay for the stuff you
> bought.
>
> MONICA
> Still, it's such . . . reckless spending!
>
> ROSS
> Uh, I think when somebody steals your credit
> card, they've kind of *already* thrown cau-
> tion to the wind.
>
> CHANDLER
> (LOOKING AT STATEMENT) What a geek. They
> spent $69.95 for a Wonder Mop.
>
> MONICA
> Uh, that was me.
>
> CHANDLER
> By "geek," I meant—Oh, the hell with it. You
> bought a seventy-dollar mop. You're a
> geek.[14]

By establishing that Monica is thrifty and geeklike, the above lines add to the joke setup that takes place in the next scene.

> (MONICA IS STILL ON THE COUCH, LOOKING AT THE CREDIT CARD STATEMENT. . . .)
>
> RACHEL
> Are you still going over that thing?
>
> MONICA
> (STARING AT STATEMENT) This woman's living my life.
>
> RACHEL
> What?
>
> MONICA
> (INDIGNANT) She's living my life. And she's doing it *better* than me! Look at this. She bought tickets to plays I want to see. She buys clothes at stores where I'm intimidated by the salespeople. She spent three hundred dollars on art supplies.
>
> RACHEL
> You're not an artist.
>
> MONICA
> Well, I might be if I had the supplies.[15]

If the previous scene hadn't helped to "set up" Monica's insecurities, creating an initial level of comedic tension, the last joke would have seemed far less potent.

NO HINTS

A setup should not hint at its punch line or it will ruin its surprise, and the joke. As always, less is more. Consider these lines from an episode of *The Simpsons*; Homer is hosting a barbecue and Barney shows up carrying a large beer keg:

> BARNEY
> Hey, Homer. Thanks for inviting me to your
> barbecue.
>
> HOMER
> Wow, Barney! You brought a whole beer keg.
>
> BARNEY
> Yeah. Where can I fill it up?[16]

If the setup had hinted at the punch line, the joke would have been ruined. As in:

> BARNEY
> Hey, Homer. Thanks for inviting me to your
> barbecue.
>
> HOMER
> Wow, Barney! You brought a whole beer keg.
> Is that thing full?
>
> BARNEY
> No. Where can I fill it up?

LIFE IS A SETUP

Many times, as discussed earlier in the book, universally shared miseries can serve as half of your setup. Go after someone or something that causes tension in people's lives, and that tension will feed right into your joke. Consider how much the following excerpt from a *Seinfeld* episode depends upon our ability to relate to a joke's premise; Jerry and Elaine are trying to rent a car, but the obnoxious rental agent, Lydia, is refusing to honor Jerry's reservation:

> JERRY
> Well, what was the point to the reservation?
> Why did I make a reservation?
>
> LYDIA
> I didn't take your reservation. Let me speak
> to my supervisor.

(LYDIA CROSSES TO HER SUPERVISOR.)

JERRY
(TO ELAINE) She's going to talk to her supervisor. You know what she's saying over
there? "Hey Marge, these people think I'm
talking to you so just pretend you're talking to me. Okay, now you start talking."

ELAINE
(PLAYING ALONG) "Oh, you mean like this? So
it looks like I'm saying something back to
you even though I'm not saying anything at
all."

JERRY
"Good. Now I'll say something else and they
won't yell at me because they think I'm
checking with you."

ELAINE
"Great. I guess that's enough. I'll see you
later."

JERRY
"Okay. Thanks. I'll go back and talk to them
and tell them I spoke to you."

LYDIA
(RETURNS) I'm sorry, my supervisor says
there's nothing we can do.[17]

Of course, life's contribution to joke setups isn't just limited to comedic-tension-building *shared miseries*. Sometimes quick references to *shared cultural experiences* can contribute to a setup. When the audience catches the connection, the joke wins points for being both clever and economical. Consider how few words were required to make the following jokes from *The Drew Carey Show* work:

(DREW IS AT HIS KITCHEN TABLE. . . . OSWALD,
KATE, AND LEWIS ENTER.)

```
        LEWIS
        Hey, Drew.

        OSWALD
        Hey, Drew.

        DREW
        Hey, Gome. Hey, Andy. (NOTICING KATE)
        Thelma Lou.

        KATE
        We haven't seen you at the Warsaw in over a
        week. Something wrong . . . Otis?[18]
```

TENSION ADDED BY STORY

A joke within a story has an advantage over a stand-alone joke—the comedic tension of its setup is often boosted by dramatic tension in the story. Meaning, if a predicament that has been woven into the story already has us on the edge of our seats, that overall tension contributes to the weight of the jokes in that story sequence.

Similarly, if tension exists in certain character relationships (e.g., the sexual tension between Niles and Daphne of *Frasier*), that character baggage might also contribute to the weight of a joke. This synergistic advantage, over individual jokes presented out of context, is subtle, but every little bit helps when writing comedy. (Which is why many of our favorite comedians give their monologues a structure, a beginning-middle-end, that develops and exploits dramatic tension.)

PUNCH LINES

Every writer uses different terms to describe a punch line—*switch, reversal, surprise, twist, a surprise twist,* etc. I think of a punch line as a sudden twist that makes both sense and nonsense; it resolves the setup, but from a totally different direction than the audience was led to expect. In doing so, it utilizes the characteristics of comedy that we discussed earlier—incongruity, surprise, truth, aggression, and brevity.

Here are a few things that you might want to remember when writing punch lines:

LAST THINGS LAST

In most cases, the punch line comes at the very end of a joke. Otherwise the surprise is lost, right? There is no incongruity left to conquer, no tension to release, no amusing payoff. The simple rule is put the punch line last.

DON'T "GO PAST THE JOKE."

In dialogue, the punch line doesn't just come at the end of the joke—usually, it also comes at the end of a character's speech. Otherwise, if the character keeps talking after successfully delivering a joke, he might trample the humor. Which is worse than never having joked at all.

If multiple jokes are included in the same speech, they are sometimes separated by scripted pauses (written as *dialogue cues*, which we will discuss later). As with the above, if the character plows ahead to the next joke before the audience has time to digest the last one, the punch lines might get trampled. (A talented actor will automatically sense that a brief pause is needed, but less . . . intuitive? . . . actors sometimes benefit from written cues.)

So, don't "go past the joke." Put the punch line where it belongs, and try to leave a space, some breathing room, after each joke.

> *NOTE: Can these rules be broken? Absolutely. On some occasions, the rhythms of a character's speech patterns are such that she will deliver the punch line and then add a related phrase or two. Maybe the character is naturally verbose, or rambling because of some story element, or adding humorous embellishment. If you feel that the additional words supply a necessary rhythm to her speech and are true to her character, then go ahead, add the extra beats of dialogue.*

TOPPING A JOKE

Sometimes a joke lends itself to a series of punch lines, one after the other, each funnier than the last. Writers love these jokes because they are so wonderfully economical. You make a joke and get the laugh, then add a second punch line, and maybe a third—all based on one setup!

Here are three examples in a row from an episode of *The Drew Carey Show*; Oswald tops Lewis's first joke, and then Lewis tops two of his own jokes:

```
(OSWALD IS AT THE KITCHEN TABLE . . . LEWIS EN-
TERS. HIS CLOTHES ARE TORN UP AND HIS HAIR IS
MUSSED.)
```

OSWALD
Geez! You okay? Who did this to you?

LEWIS
The lab monkeys at DrugCo got out and . . .
tried to make me their girlfriend.

OSWALD
I take it it wasn't that handsome monkey
you're always going on about.

LEWIS
(SITTING DOWN) They're testing this new
drug to help senior citizens regain their
sex drive. Next thing I know, Bobo was trying to bend me over a lab table. (BITTERLY)
After all we did for them at the Scopes
trial.

OSWALD
He didn't actually . . .

LEWIS
No. I was able to make myself look unattrac-
tive. But I'll never forget their hoots and
catcalls as I gathered up my things.[19]

And here's a more subtle example from *Friends*; in yet another sex-crazed monkey story, the characters are upset that Ross's pet has developed a nasty new habit—humping the furniture; first, Monica tops Chandler's punch line, and then—after Ross adds to the original setup—Phoebe delivers a third punch line:

MONICA
You've really got to do something about him.

ROSS
What? It's just a phase.

CHANDLER
That's what we said about Joey.

MONICA
Ross, how many things does he have to hump
before you realize it's a *life choice*?

ROSS
You know, you'd think you guys would be a
little more understanding.

PHOEBE
I know, but we're not.[20]

Not only does *topping a joke* bump up your joke count, it also increases the chances of getting big laughs. Why? Because the first joke establishes a momentum and gets the audience smiling. Then you hit them again and again—quickly, before they can recover. The audience is caught off balance, is surprised not once but several times, and loves you for it.

There are two things to watch when piling punch line upon punch line. First, you probably don't want to top a joke more than two times, max. Any more, and you might call too much attention to the joke. The audience will suddenly feel as if it is viewing actors-telling-jokes instead of an involving sitcom story.

Second, take care not to dilute a healthy joke by plowing over it with additional punch lines. Some jokes are best left alone. Perhaps they deliver an important dramatic moment, or they are critical to a scene's pacing, or they just feel like they say all that needs to be said on a subject. Rather than ruin a good thing, think twice before piling on punch lines.

RUNNING GAGS

Running gags are another great way to earn comedy bonus points. Tell a complete joke in one scene, then come back to it two or three times later in the story. (If you refer back to the original joke only once, the second joke is called a *callback joke*.) You create a *running gag* by having the same character restate the original punch line under different circumstances, resulting in a fresh laugh. Or a succession of different characters might restate the same punch line under different circumstances. Or one or more different characters might voice variations of the same joke, all playing off the original setup.

Sometimes, each time a repeating punch line pops up, it takes on a second meaning, making it both funny and clever. And, sometimes, the final installment of a running gag is presented with a twist or reversal, ending the joke series with a big laugh.

Consider this example, a simple callback joke, taken from a *Seinfeld* spec script; in the initial joke, George becomes convinced that a Rolex he sold to Kramer has the power to attract women, and is desperate to get the watch back:

>   JERRY
>   You're not buying into this . . .
>
>   GEORGE
>   Alice, Betty, Cindy—he's dating the whole
>   alphabet and I got nothing! I need this
>   watch.
>
>   KRAMER
>   Sorry.
>
>   GEORGE
>   But it's mine!
>
>   KRAMER
>   I bought it.
>
>   GEORGE
>   Do I have to grovel? Do you want me to
>   grovel?
>
>   KRAMER
>   I don't want you to grovel.
>
>   JERRY
>   Hold on—I'd enjoy a good grovel.[21]

The next installment of the gag occurs several scenes later, when Jerry and George are arguing in front of Elaine:

>   GEORGE
>   Honest? Honest again? Like you were honest
>   with Elaine about her big head?
>
>   (OOPS! ALL THREE REACT.)
>
>   ELAINE
>   What? You lied about my head?

>   JERRY
>   It wasn't a lie really—
>
>   ELAINE
>   And then you let me grovel like that?
>
>   GEORGE
>   Oh, he loves a good grovel.[22]

Here's another example, a running gag from *The Simpsons*. This series of jokes relies on visual humor; young Bart has inadvertently punched the school bully, Nelson, and now fears for his life:

>   (Nelson and the two excited weasels are dragging
>   Bart by the leg across the playground to a row of
>   garbage cans. Bart's head is BANGING over small
>   rocks, improperly put away softball equipment,
>   and a lost shoe.)
>
>   BART
>   (WOOZILY) I'm glad *that's* over. Boy, you
>   sure taught me a lesson. But it's all over
>   now, thank heavens. Now we're friends
>   again, right? Shake.
>
>   (CLOSEUP ON BART'S DAZED FACE. He looks like he's
>   trying to figure out where he's at. PULL BACK to re-
>   veal that Bart is now inside a garbage can.)
>
>   NELSON
>   (MENACING) You die again tomorrow, man.
>
>   (Nelson gives the garbage can a shove toward the
>   CAMERA. Bart's eyes open wider as the can tips.
>   LONG SHOT of garbage can bouncing, rolling, and
>   crashing down a hill. BART'S POV, INSIDE GARBAGE
>   CAN—garbage is being tossed around as we see the
>   world spin round and round outside the lips of gar-
>   gabe can. LONG SHOT OF HILL as garbage can bounces,
>   crashes, and rolls out of sight.)

```
BART (voice-over)
Man, I hate that guy.
```

(**FADE OUT. COMMERCIAL BREAK. FADE IN** at Simpson
Home. We hear clattering of rolling garbage can,
shortly before the garbage can rolls into view and
rolls to a stop. Bart climbs to his feet, takes a
few confident steps, then falls over. . . .)[23]

The second installment of this running gag comes a couple of scenes later;
Bart's mother, Marge, has convinced Bart that the bully just needs a little
understanding:

(Bart is toe to toe with Nelson, but instead of
looking afraid or combative, Bart has a sympa-
thetic look on his face. Bart is wearing a baseball
cap.)

```
BART
(GENTLY) Listen, I understand, man.

NELSON
What?

BART
(GENTLY) I understand. You're overweight
and not too good in school and you're not
very good-looking. That's why you lash out
at me.
```

(BART'S POINT OF VIEW: Nelson's fist coming
straight toward him. SOUND EFFECT: a sickening
thud. DISSOLVE TO SIMPSON HOME. Homer and Marge
are sitting on the couch. Marge is knitting. Homer
is reading the paper. Lisa is looking out of the
window.)

```
LISA
Here he comes!
```

(We hear the distant clatter of a rolling garbage can approaching. A moment later the front door opens and Bart crawls in.)

> BART
> (TIRED; A LITTLE MUFFLED) Hi, Mom. Hi, Dad.
> (COUGHS UP BASEBALL CAP)

(. . .)

> MARGE
> Good heavens! What happened, Bart?

> BART
> Nelson didn't like being understood.[24]

The third installment of this running gag comes two scenes later; Homer has advised his son that nobody ever went wrong by fighting dirty:

(Nelson starts to move slowly toward Bart, clenching and unclenching his hands. Suddenly an image of Homer's head appears in the sky.)

> HOMER'S IMAGE
> (SLIGHT ECHO EFFECT) Remember the family jewels, son.

(Bart remembers now. He rushes Nelson and WHACKS him below the belt. Nelson doesn't react right away. Then he snorts and begins to advance on Bart. . . . Bart looks up at Homer's image for further advice. Homer's image thinks for a moment, then shrugs.

CLOSEUP OF BART, with Homer's image looking down. Bart starts to run, but before he can take one full step, Nelson's hand reaches INTO FRAME, grabs Bart by the neck and yanks him OUT OF FRAME. Homer's image looks off screen, wincing and covering its eyes as Bart gets thrashed. SOUND EFFECTS: TERRIBLE THRASHING, DOZENS OF THUNDERING PUNCHES.)

```
BART (voice-over)
(GROANS) Whoa! Ouch! Ow! Ooh! Oh no, boys,
not the can, please.
```

```
(DISSOLVE TO FRONT YARD OF SIMPSON HOME. Lisa is
in the front yard when Bart comes rolling down the
street and comes to a stop in front of the house.
Bart crawls up to Lisa. . . . He is a mess, as
usual. Bits of his clothes are disintegrating and
falling off as he walks.²⁵
```

Note that in the second and third installments of this gag, we don't need to repeat all of the setup (i.e., Bart being stuffed into the garbage can); we go straight to the punch line of the garbage can rolling to a stop in front of the Simpsons' house.

Why do running gags earn extra laughs? Perhaps the audience is impressed by how clever you are for retooling one joke so that it can be used several times, often under very different circumstances. (And, no doubt, the audience is pleased with its own cleverness at having caught the subtle joke connection.)

Occasionally, a running gag will become a standard element of a show's premise, recurring in many episodes, or even every episode, of the series. For instance, *Seinfeld* got a laugh every time Jerry encountered his hated neighbor, Newman; each man greeted the other by pronouncing his name with obvious distaste, setting a humorous tone for the exchange that followed.

On a more gruesome level, *South Park* helped to make a name for itself by featuring a running gag in which a primary character, Kenny, gets killed *in every episode*. Each week the poor kid is subjected to a violent death, only to reappear—without explanation—at the top of the following week's episode. The gag generates lots of comedic suspense, because viewers are just waiting to see how Kenny will be killed in each story.

Finally, running gags are sometimes referred to as *runners*; however, many people also use this term to refer to a very minor subplot of a story, which might or might not be funny.

NOTE: *Sitcoms eat up a lot of jokes, at least two or three per page. So being able to play several punch lines off the same setup, by topping a joke or using running gags, can come in pretty handy. Both devices are economical and they encourage big laughs, which is important when trying to write joke-rich material.*

WHEN YOU CAN'T FIND THE RIGHT PUNCH LINE

Here's a tip: When you can't find the right punch line, go back and check the setup. Once I agonized over a joke through several drafts of a script, spending hours trying to replace a single weak punch line. A producer who was passing by my office tossed off a casual suggestion—"Change the setup?"

Hmm. I went back, tweaked the joke's premise, and suddenly—half a dozen great punch lines popped into my head. Problem solved.

The moral of this tale? Sometimes even producers have a good idea. And if a punch line isn't working, *check the setup*. See if you need to establish a different incongruity or a bigger contrast in the first half of your joke.

GO FOR LITERAL

When stuck for a funny punch line, see if you can exploit the literal meaning of the joke's setup. As Melvin Helitzer states in his book, *Comedy Writing Secrets*, by playing off "the literal meaning of a key word, we surprise the audience, who's automatically interpreted the expression with its traditional reference. It makes logic illogical. . . . 'Call me a taxi' [leads to] 'Okay, you're a taxi.' "[26]

Here's another example, from the late comedian Sam Levenson: "Somewhere on this globe, every ten seconds, there is a woman giving birth to a child. She must be found and stopped."

And, here's an example of a literal punch line delivered in dialogue, from an episode of *The Drew Carey Show*; Drew and his friends have gathered at their favorite bar to honor the spirit of Saint Patrick's Day:

> OSWALD
> Kate, you're Irish. What's Saint Patrick's
> Day all about?
>
> KATE
> In my family, it's about three hours of con-
> sciousness.[27]

The best part of these jokes? Responding with a literal punch line can earn you more of those comedy bonus points; you win for being both funny and clever, having surprised the audience by choosing an unexpectedly direct route to a payoff.

FUNNY ACTIONS

Okay, we have discussed how setups and punch lines can be smoothly woven into dialogue. Now let's get to the ". . . and Actions" part of this chapter. Meaning that sitcom writing isn't just about verbal humor, it also features funny actions and sounds. Here are some examples:

MANNERISMS

Recognizable actors and the characters that they portray are usually known for certain physical traits. They exhibit funny mannerisms that we have come to expect and adore. Kramer (Michael Richards) didn't just enter a room; he flung the door open and zipped inside. Drew Carey reacts to even the most astonishing news by not moving a muscle, and pausing a beat before giving a response. Kirstie Alley gets instantly weepy and flustered in any crisis, reverting to little-girl mode until she suddenly dreams up a new course of action; then, just as quickly, she's cheerful again and forging ahead. Some mannerisms are developed by actors (or are part of an actor's real-life personality), but many are originated by writers when they create new characters.

STAGE BUSINESS

Funny actions can take the form of an actor doing *stage business* while performing in a scene. Meaning, an actor might fiddle with something or perform an amusing physical action, both to get a laugh and to help define his character. Picture *Ellen* donning a hidden police wire to help trap a crook; true to her klutzy character, the wire slips down into her slacks, so she must do outrageous contortions to keep the elusive microphone close to the crook's mouth.

Sometimes stage business is designed to contrast with ongoing dialogue, to beef up comedic tension. Example: *Mad About You*'s Paul Buchman proclaims his undying love for wife, Jamie—while staring zombielike at a televised beauty contest.

Sometimes stage business can build up to its own punch line. As in, *Damon* finally stops fiddling with the fragile knickknack and puts it back on the shelf— then the shelf crashes down!

Sometimes a bit of minor business, unrelated to anything else in the story, might be used merely to increase the humorous tone of a scene.

A TAKE

A character is surprised, he reacts with a funny expression, and we laugh. Called a *take*, a *look*, or a *reaction*, the character's simple physical response is frequently the only punch line that is needed to complete a joke. While an actor might give a *double take* in extreme circumstances, a script should only designate *when* a take should occur—let the actor and the director decide what degree of reaction is appropriate.

SLAPSTICK

Falling, dropping, whacking, breaking things. Since Og and Mog first tripped into a tar pit, we've gotten laughs out of cartoonish violence and physical mishaps. Tension, surprise, aggression—these gags have it all. And they often utilize the same structure as a dialogue joke, moving from setup to punch line.

An example of a slapstick setup? One character gives his friend a loving pat; the friend pats back, a little too hard; the first character, irritated, gives a little shove back; soon the two friends are wrestling like maniacs on the carpet. The incongruity of the setup comes from friends making friendly gestures that suddenly turn hostile. It's surprising and it rings true, because we have all experienced similar (if less violent) misunderstandings.

Physical actions can also serve as the setup or punch line for a dialogue joke, as illustrated in this bit from an episode of *Seinfeld*: Kramer decides to test the strength of his latest invention, an oil-filled balloon, by dropping it out of a high window. Tension builds when Kramer trespasses in an office building to perform the test, and uses the help of a student intern even though the kid's college has canceled his internship (with Kramer). Just as Kramer counts down to the balloon drop, Jerry's new girlfriend appears in the parking lot below, pausing right at ground zero (launching the setup). Jerry yells to her but she misinterprets the warning. The oil-filled balloon drops and . . . Even though we don't actually see the aftermath, we get a huge laugh out of the (physical) payoff.

Slapstick humor is considered very broad, even unrefined, but it can be a great way to get big laughs—if broad humor is appropriate for your show.

FUNNY VISUALS

Some funny visuals don't involve physical injury. Perhaps a character starting a new job is required to wear a humiliating "House of Wieners" uniform. Or a couple of would-be lovers, dining in a restaurant, are so hungry for each other that they eat in a sexually suggestive manner. Or *Seinfeld*'s George Costanza, stripped down to his boxers, strikes sexy poses for Kramer's camera, only to have the embarrassing photos fall into Newman's hands. (Or was that *Drew Carey* in his boxers, ending up on public billboards as a poster boy for a new diet product?)

Sometimes these sight gags involve someone hiding something, such as an old girlfriend whom the wife doesn't know about, or a thousand pieces of a newly busted vase. As the guilty character lies to cover his tracks, the contrast between what he says and what we see (and know to be true) creates an amusing incongruity. It provides chuckles along the way and builds to a big, satisfying payoff when the truth is finally revealed.

Funny visuals are frequently used to get a laugh out of a character entering a scene. As in, "But who could possibly be so stupid?" followed immediately by Stupid's entrance. The joke has been done to death, but will probably continue to be used since it provides a convenient way to get Stupid into the story.

As with slapstick humor, a funny visual can serve as a setup or a punch line. However, not all sight gags are part of a fully structured joke. Some bits are just funny to see, or maybe they contribute to the dramatic tension of a scene.

Funny Sounds

Sometimes sound can supply a punch line or boost the humor of a joke. Any time that *Home Improvement*'s Tim Allen starts poking around a piece of machinery, you know that the thing is doomed; but the sparks, smoke, and explosion still make the moment funny. When *Ellen* finally chose to declare her sexual preference, she shared the private revelation with a close friend; the fact that two hundred strangers also heard her broadcast the secret over a public address system was what got the laugh.

Alliteration

On a far more subtle level, writers get a lot of mileage out of a simple phonetic tool—*alliteration*. By starting several words in the same phrase with the same sound, one creates a pleasing aural rhythm. Consider the effect it has on these lines from an episode of *King of the Hill*; Hank has rushed to the doctor after suddenly becoming ill:

```
HANK
How bad is it?
```

DOCTOR
Your heart's in good shape—considering you
seem like a man who butters his bacon.[28]

How does alliteration help this joke? Change the doctor's line to "...
butters his steak," and see if you notice a difference.

Freud suggested that our favorable response to aural rhythms evolved from
early childhood learning-play, when we first discovered the pleasurable effects
"which arise from a repetition of what is similar, a rediscovery of what is
familiar, similarity of sound, etc."[29] Maybe. Whatever the explanation, there
are some moments when a dose of alliteration adds just the right leavening to
an otherwise unfunny speech. By itself, it does not get a big laugh or even an
amused grunt; but sometimes it earns a smile or, at the least, keeps the material
from losing all comedic momentum during a more serious passage.

FOREIGN ACCENTS

Another (less subtle) source of funny sounds is the foreign accent. The
late Andy Kaufman injected new life into this worn comedic device when he
performed the character of Latka Gravas on the classic sitcom *Taxi*. Kaufman
created an original language of sorts for his character, and he (and the show's
writers) focused on more than just silly pronunciations and funny phrasings.
They got their biggest laughs by exploring the huge differences between
Latka's (fictional) native culture and life in the Big Apple. They went beyond
the obvious, superficial humor of mangled English to draw humor from the
character and his bizarre origins. (Not unlike the concept of drawing humor
from the premise of a story, rather than from wordplay alone.) The result was
a rich, hilarious, lasting characterization.

In today's politically correct environment, foreign accents tend to receive
rather delicate handling. Sitcoms still feature characters like Antonio of *Wings*
and Daphne of *Frasier*, but most seem reluctant to portray these characters in
anything other than a positive light. (Antonio might have been a simple man,
but he was not a fool, crook, or sleaze.)

MISCELLANEOUS COMEDY TIPS

Now that we have explored some of the basics of joke mechanics, here
are a few general tips about creating comedy:

LESS IS MORE . . . USUALLY

Always remember that less is more, whether you are trimming excess words out of a punch line or dumping an entire scene from a script. As Sol Saks notes in his book, *The Craft of Comedy Writing* . . .

> *Clarity* and *simplicity* are, again, desirable in all writing, but necessary in comedy. They are crucial ingredients because in comedy you *must* have your audience's undivided attention. If they puzzle over a word or thought ever so slightly, if they are distracted by an unnecessary word or phrase, you lose their concentration and the temperamental comedy disappears in a huff.

Saks adds that "the best comedy has *precision*, which, put simply, is the exact word in its proper place."[30]

A word or two can make a difference. Every syllable affects the rhythm of a joke. Every surplus word hurts your chances of keeping the audience focused until you can surprise them with the punch line. A good rule of thumb is that any time you ask yourself if something should stay in or not, you should probably go with "not."

There are some exceptions to the less-is-more rule. You might create a moment or a character for which *more* is more. Ellen DeGeneres sometimes uses this technique when portraying a character who is caught in an awkward situation; she babbles and babbles, then babbles about her babbling, making a bad situation worse by dragging it out. A person's natural inclination would be to say as little as possible and beat a hasty retreat, but Ellen's character gets laughs by going for more rather than less. To sum up, keep it lean and clean. Clutter and imbalance can kill a joke, unless they *are* the joke.

BIGGER REALLY IS BETTER

Comedy writers seem to agree that bigger is better. Exaggerate parts of a joke and you are more likely to get a big laugh. Laura Petrie didn't reveal Alan Brady's baldness to her friend Millie—she broadcast it to the entire nation. It wasn't just a couple of strangers who overheard *Ellen* proclaim that she was gay—it was an airport full of people. Little Kenny of *South Park* doesn't just take a ribbing every week—the kid gets killed. The lesson? Unless it runs contrary to a character's nature or the show's premise, think big when going for big laughs.

SMALL TRUTHS, BIG LAUGHS

A reminder: The truth can be funny! As any comedy writer will tell you, if you strike a universal chord with the audience, you will score big points. If you can't remember why, flip back to our discussion of the "Characteristics of Comedy" for a quick review.

ONE LAST RULE: THERE ARE NO RULES

Humorist James Thurber (1894–1961) once said that "The only rules comedy can tolerate are those of taste, and the only limitations those of libel."

Censorship is death to comedy. Yet, as mentioned above, we exist in an era of political correctness. Is modern humor suffering? Not really. In fact, savvy comedians like Chris Rock, Sinbad, and Ellen DeGeneres have boosted their careers by turning insult humor on its head. Lifting a page from the Woody Allens and Rodney Dangerfields of yesteryear, they have taken very non-PC jokes and directed them at themselves. Instead of maligning their own physical shortcomings, the new breed have targeted political hot buttons such as (their own) race and gender. They dish out seemingly insensitive putdowns, but it's hard to get angry when they themselves are the ones being insulted. Their approach lessens the pressure to be PC, which enables them to target even the most sensitive of subjects.

Yes, there will always be rules about what is or isn't acceptable comedy. But a writer's job is to tackle delicate issues, to be fresh and daring. So heed your own tastes—and those of your producers—and just go and be funny in the best way that you know how.

ABOUT ALL OF THESE LABELS

The problem with discussing joke mechanics is that you start tossing out a lot of labels and rules. It just seems so . . . mechanical. But I believe that, just as music composers study harmony and orchestration, comedy writers should learn the tools of their craft. Some writers disagree, arguing that one cannot learn comedy by studying joke structure and such. Yet when asked why a particular joke doesn't work, they describe the problem in the same terms presented above. (I guess they learned the stuff back in the womb or something.)

Not everyone is capable of writing comedy; but those who are naturally funny can certainly hone their writing skills by studying the creative process and learning the craft. So, watch shows, examine scripts, take classes, read books, and keep writing. And, if possible, find a professional mentor or two, as famed comedy writer Larry Gelbart (the *M*A*S*H* series, *Tootsie, Oh, God!, A Funny Thing Happened on the Way to the Forum*) managed to do early in his career.

> When I worked under Bill Manhoff's tutelage on *Duffy's Tavern*, I had just turned seventeen. Other than having the knack of being funny on demand—on being able to provide jokes that fit a specified situation—I was not familiar with the vocabulary of the trade, the articulation to describe what kind of punch lines those situations might require. If that sounds vague, perhaps it still is to me after all these years. I guess what I learned most from Bill was just punching away until what seemed the right line finally dawned on me or anyone else in the room.[31]

Learn the craft, develop your skills. How you do it doesn't matter.

DEVELOPING YOUR COMEDIC VOICE

Different writers have different strengths and each has her own take on what makes something funny. A benefit of developing a script's humor from the ground (or premise) up is that, whatever your strengths are—story structure, funny dialogue, physical comedy—this approach prompts you to explore all types of humor at all levels of the script. It encourages you to develop all aspects of your comedic voice rather than merely settle for, say, cramming funny jokes into unfunny scenes, because funny jokes are what you do best.

Conversely, this from-the-ground-up approach can also help you to identify and compensate for weaknesses in your writing. Are your characters dull? Are your stories too serious? Do your scripts start funny, then fade? It's hard to overlook these problems when your first priority is to draw comedy from the overall premise. When problems do surface, this approach gives you a better shot at identifying where you might be weak, so that you can train yourself to apply more energy in those areas.

MOVING ON

So ends our discussion of premise-driven comedy. It's a simple, intuitive approach composed of three steps:

• Weave funny elements into your story premise.

- Exploit and compound those elements at the sequence and scene level.

- Draw from your story's built-in humor to create natural, seamless dialogue and actions.

It's all about *building*, rather than *repairing*. Do your job right and you will get Laura Petrie winning a dishwasher—by humiliating her husband's boss. Or Jack Lemmon and Tony Curtis running from mobsters—disguised as female musicians. Or Frasier, Damon, Ellen, and Drew welcoming a new houseguest—the person who drove them into therapy at age twelve.

Now let's look at how comedy writing theory can translate into a professional sitcom script.

Part Two

Writing a Professional Script

Seven

Doing Your Homework

WHY WRITE SPEC SCRIPTS?

How do you get work as a television sitcom writer? By flashing a fancy Harvard degree? By submitting that play you wrote for Mom's church group? By showing off those clever articles about breast feeding?

You get sitcom work by showing that you can do sitcom work, by submitting spec sitcom scripts. (A *spec* is a sample script that consists of an episode of an existing television series, written without pay or the producers' authorization.) Before hitting the job trail, a would-be writer should have *at least* one dynamite sitcom spec under his arm. This section of our book will show you how to create that work sample by following the same steps used by working professionals.

Sure, some producers and executives boast that they like to judge writers by reading completely original work—stage plays, movie scripts, television pilot scripts, etc. But only a bold few actually hire new writers based solely on original material. Too frequently, the response is "Fantastic, great stuff. And do you have any sitcom specs I can see? Just to show the others, of course."

And, yes, the business has actually gone through a cycle, starting back in the late '80s, when a Harvard degree greatly increased the odds of a person getting work. Some top writer-producers had come from Harvard and that launched a hiring trend. (I was actually confronted with the Harvard thing during a pitch meeting once; I responded with "Sorry, I went to Brown. Guess that makes me, what, only 80 percent as funny?" Oddly enough, I didn't get that job.)

And, of course, there are other ways to break in. Exposure as a successful standup comedian might do it. Or, if your Uncle Morty runs a studio, that could definitely do it. But those clever breast-feeding articles? Don't think so. And even if you are blessed with an Uncle Morty, when he goes to twist some poor producer's arm, he'll still need a writing sample to stick in the guy's other hand.

My point is that many people in Hollywood like to sound encouraging and open-minded; it's flattering to them and it keeps them out of negative, confrontational conversations. But talk is cheap, especially for them. The truth is that the odds of getting work in a particular creative form are best if you can prove that you can write *in that form*. Analogy: You might be a great dermatologist, but how often are you going to be hired to perform heart surgery? (Other than at an HMO?)

In fact, the distinction goes even further than that. When hiring writers, producers differentiate between writing samples based on types of sitcoms. You submitted a *King of the Hill* spec? "Sorry, we don't do a cartoon show." A *Drew Carey* spec? "Loved it, but our show is more urban." A *Drew Carey* spec to a different show? "Sorry, too urban."

I know—a great script should be enough, shouldn't it? But trust me, producers are extremely discriminating.

If you are serious about writing for television sitcoms, *you should focus all of your creative energy on writing spec scripts* for the type of shows that you like to watch. *Do not* waste time writing a movie script. *Do not* write a one-hour dramatic spec, a play, or even an original series pilot. While you are letting yourself be distracted by some creative whim, more focused writers are cranking out a *Spin City*, then a *King of the Hill*, and then another sitcom spec. They are submitting sample after sample after sample to producers, and they are getting work. Your work.

Your new mission in life is to write a killer spec sitcom script. And write another, and another, until someone is paying you to write. To help you get started, this chapter will describe some homework that you should do before developing a story.

WHICH SERIES TO PICK

Decision number one: Which series should you pick for your next, or first, spec script? Jurgen Wolff, in his book *Successful Sitcom Writing*, offers some practical advice: Write for a "show you really like," a "quality show," "a show that has been on the air for at least one season" and is "likely to remain on the air for at least another season."[32] His thinking behind three of these points is obvious, but why is picking a "quality show"—a highly esteemed, critically acclaimed show—helpful?

Two reasons, I believe. First, most producers are television literate and therefore more likely to enjoy scripts written for better shows—the shows that they themselves would be inclined to watch. And second, some producers turn out cheesy shows but are convinced that their turkeys are on par with *Frasier* and *Seinfeld*; send them a script for an equally cheesy show and they will look down their noses at it. So, within the style of writing that you want to do (physical comedies, family-themed shows, young urban series, whatever), select the most esteemed of the bunch for your spec. Choose *Friends* instead of *Buds on the Make*.

Here are some other factors to consider, just to confuse you:

PICK A SHOW WITH HIGH RATINGS

Even if it's goofy, it will carry extra cachet. Plus, it is likely to be around for a few seasons, giving your spec a longer shelf life. (Television ratings are posted each week in trade magazines such as *The Hollywood Reporter* and *Variety*; track the numbers to see which shows seem healthy and to develop a sense of what the country is watching.)

AVOID OLD SHOWS

People are tired of watching them. Agents and producers are real tired of reading them. And they tend to get canceled just about the time you're typing "End of Episode" on that new spec.

ASK AROUND

Check with agents, writer friends, and contacts at shows and the networks to see what scripts are coming in every day. If everyone is writing samples for the same show, it will make it more difficult for your script to stand out. Conversely, you might discover that a new dark horse series is the hip show to spec and decide to jump on that bandwagon.

At this point, you might be asking "Gee, if my life's dream is to work on *Just Shoot Me*, shouldn't I only be writing *Just Shoot Me* spec scripts?"

Naw, too logical. The script submission process works like this: You write a sample script for *Show X* and submit it to every *other* show being produced in the hope of being hired to write a *new* script. Yes, you can submit your *Show X* sample to the producers of *Show X*, but the odds of them being impressed are slim; writing staffs are notorious for being overly harsh when judging specs written for their own show.

"But surely if they saw a great script—my script—they would want to buy and produce it? To save the hassle of developing a different one from scratch?" Sorry. That never, well, hardly ever, happens. Why? Probably some wasn't-created-here, Mama-never-loved-me thing. Whatever the reason, just know that if you want to write for one show, you are usually better off submitting a spec for a different, but similar, show.

Any exceptions? (Aren't there always?) If you have a strong connection to someone important on a show's staff, it sometimes does pay to submit a spec based on that person's show. Your contact will still be as critical when evaluating your script, but that might be outweighed by the flattery factor; jazzed that you like his show enough to crank out an episode, he might extend himself more in an effort to help (hire?) you.

Obviously, in a perfect universe, you could simply pick whatever brand-new show is going to be the hit of the next five seasons and write a spec for that. Of course, if you had that type of crystal ball, you'd be a billionaire by now.

RESEARCHING THE SERIES

In 1990, I invited writer-producer Stephen J. Cannell to appear as one of the guest speakers in a Producers Forum Series that I presented for the American Film Institute. When the discussion turned to writers' pitching strategies, he recounted a unique meeting that he had had years before. A noted film writer deigned to approach Cannell about doing an episode of a detective series that he (Cannell) was producing. The writer came in, they exchanged pleasantries, and Cannell invited him to unleash. The entire pitch? "Clowns." (PAUSE.) "Clowns?" "Clowns. Intriguing, you know? That whole clown thing. It just works."

And that was it. All he had. He had no idea what Cannell's series was about and he certainly hadn't prepared for the pitch. This was a bad move. It's an insult to the people who work on the show. You don't get the assignment and you don't get invited back.

What should you do instead? Writing is a business, your business, so take it seriously—do your homework. Before starting a spec script or going in for a pitch, study the show in question. If you haven't been watching it religiously, tape three or four episodes and analyze them. No time? You're going in to pitch this Thursday? Ask your friends or another writer; one of them might have stockpiled tapes of the shows you need. Or ask your agent or other industry contacts if they have or can get episodes. (However, you should try to avoid using up favors from these folks—it's better to have them helping you by tracking down job leads.)

If you have actually been invited to pitch a show, the production staff is usually happy to lend you episodes and scripts before you come in. Ask for tapes of "their favorite episodes," so it does not seem that you are unfamiliar with the show. You should also ask if they have a series bible and story breakdowns that you could look at. (A *series bible* usually contains character backstories and a detailed description of the show's overall premise. *Story breakdowns* provide synopses of episodes that have already aired and stories that are currently in development, and sometimes include descriptions of ongoing or planned long-term story arcs.) These additional materials can save you from pitching an idea that has already been done on that show and they often give valuable clues to underlying subtext in the series.

If you have not been invited to pitch a show, you might still get tapes and/ or scripts by calling and asking an assistant who works in the production office—on very rare occasions, one will take pity on you.

While studying taped episodes is important, it is even more instructive to read produced scripts from the show. (Especially those penned by the producers who give out the writing assignments.) Things look different on paper than they do on the screen, and your work will be on paper. So get several recent scripts and start reading. You can probably get produced scripts from the same sources named above. If not, you can find a number of published scripts from successful TV shows on the shelves of your local bookstore. Or a local college's communications department might have recent scripts in its library, especially if the school is in or near Los Angeles or New York City. Or, if it is geographically feasible, you can visit the libraries of industry organizations such as the Writers Guild of America or the Academy of Television Arts and Sciences.

Still stuck? Well, you didn't hear it from me, but rumor has it that a lot of television scripts have been posted at unofficial Web sites on the Internet. Type the name of a show into a search engine and you are likely to find yourself at some private home page that features written transcripts of recent episodes. Copyright laws probably dictate that you should not download or print the unauthorized scripts, but nobody can stop you from reading the things on-line.

NOTE: *Do not rely on on-line scripts to show you how an episode should look on paper; few Web postings are laid out in the correct script format.*

ANOTHER NOTE: *Got a VCR? Build a tape library. Record two or three episodes of every new series that hits the air. (If possible, include the show's pilot—it usually contains a lot of useful back story.) Then, when your agent calls to schedule a last-minute pitch for a show you've never seen, you'll be covered.*

STUDYING THE PREMISE

Sounds a bit technical, huh? Researching shows, studying them. The truth is, some very talented, very successful writers scoff at the idea of analyzing a creative work in such a deliberate fashion. At the same time, one of the most frequent complaints that producers have about spec scripts is "Sorry, but our characters would never behave like this." Your script might be funny, dramatic, and touching, but too bad, you just blew it—because you didn't know the show. So, as much as you might want to dive right into writing an episode, I suggest that you pause first to study the show's premise. Each television series has its own creative format. That format might change and evolve over the years, but the producers are the ones who will make those refinements. Your job is to follow the show's current format to a tee.

Scripts first, tapes first, it doesn't matter. Get some paper and start looking for patterns that define the show. If, along the way, you trip over a great story for an episode or a funny bit that you might use, scribble it on a separate page and *put it aside*; do not get distracted from your current objective of learning the show.

It is easier to study prerecorded tapes than to watch shows as they are broadcast. A VCR allows you to zip back and forth, and you can use its clock display to note the duration of scenes and the points in a story when events occur. If unfamiliar with a series, you might want to view the show once to get a feel for it, then go back to work through the material at your own pace.

Different writers look for different things when they block an episode out on paper. I usually list the following, from left to right: the number of the script page (or number of minutes into the taped episode) that the scene starts on; a descriptive phrase to identify the scene; and, vertical columns labeled "A", "B", "C", etc., in which I note the story beats that occur for each plot or subplot. Finally, I indicate each commercial break by underlining the scene that precedes it.

Then I ask a few questions, usually starting with *story*. These might include:

- What types of stories are used? (Small and personal? Wacky? Controversial stories? Stories about nothing?)

- Who is the audience for this show? What do they want to see?

- Is this an eight o'clock show (featuring softer stories designed for kids and teens) or a nine o'clock show (featuring harder-edged, more sophisticated material)?

- How many story lines does each episode feature? (Just an A story? Or one main A story with a B subplot? Or three to five story threads that are all equally important?)

- Do some story lines continue across several episodes?

- Do certain elements seem to be present in almost every episode? (Do A stories always feature Frasier while Roz only rates an occasional B story? Does each episode express a theme or end with a lesson being learned? Does each have a happy ending?)

- In terms of pacing, how long are most of the scenes? Is each episode composed of short, snappy scenes, or long, talky scenes, or some other identifiable mix?

- What are the standard sets? What other types of locations are sometimes used?

And, of course, I look at *characters*:

- Does the show feature an ensemble cast, a shared lead, or a single lead?

- Which characters usually drive the stories?

- Do characters experience growth in a story (even if it only lasts until next week's episode)? If so, what kind?

- What dramatic functions do the regular characters serve (e.g., rival, confidant, busybody, commentator, etc.)?

- How is each character distinguished by his dialogue and behavior?

- Is there some ongoing subtext that influences the characters' actions (e.g., romantic tension, emotional baggage, etc.)?

- How are visiting characters used?

Along the way, I make note of the show's *broadcast format*, the schedule of commercial breaks that interrupt its half-hour time slot:

- How many pages does this show's scripts average? What script format is used? (see appendix A for details)

- Does the show open with a title sequence and then go to its first scene, or does it start right off with a "cold open" (to hook the audience) and then go to titles?

- How many commercial breaks interrupt the body of the show, one or two?

- Are the story segments between commercial breaks of roughly the same duration, or is one usually longer than another? (For instance, *The Simpsons* used to feature a long first act, a shorter second act, and an even shorter third.)

- Does the show include a brief *tag* scene at the end, placed after the last commercial interruption but before (or during) closing credits?

And, of course, I look at the show's *style of comedy*. I might ask questions such as those listed under the earlier section dubbed, aptly, "Style of Comedy" (see chapter 4). In short, who and what make this show funny?

Lastly, as I make my way through the tapes and scripts, I automatically make mental notes of what I did or didn't like. What worked? What failed? What lessons can I apply to my own script?

Do I literally ask all of the above questions when studying a show? Of course not. Most of the answers are readily apparent and writing is not a fill-in-the-blank process. The above lists are offered merely as a guide, cues to trigger whatever questions will best peg a show's format for you. If you take the time to study a show, subtle elements in its premise will become apparent. If you weave those elements into your script, it will read more like an actual episode of the series—a huge plus in any producer's eyes. As a bonus, your exploration of the show's premise will probably turn up some great story ideas and comedy bits that would not have occurred to you otherwise.

So do your homework, unless you are one of those "very talented, very successful writers" who doesn't need to. Once you have picked a series and dissected the beast, good news—you are ready to begin work on your own script.

Eight

Developing an Episode
Premise

First, you need an idea for a story. It can be just two or three sentences that describe the basic premise of your episode. Of course, finding the right idea is easier said than done. Your job is to dream up a long list of possibilities, then pick the one gem that can be developed into a fantastic spec script.

Or, if you are generating stories because you have been invited to pitch an existing show (a process that we will discuss later), your mission is to develop ten to fifteen terrific ideas. If all goes well, the producers will pick one and pay you to write a script.

Or, if you already work on the staff of a sitcom, part of your job is to pitch new story ideas to your producers or maybe to the entire writing staff. Eventually, you will be instructed to develop a script based on a particular concept, though it might not be an idea that you yourself created.

What types of story ideas are you looking for?

ADVICE FROM OUR PRODUCERS

Here are what some of the producers interviewed for this book look for in a story premise. (The credits for each producer quoted in this book are listed in the acknowledgments.)

Matt Williams: I think the biggest thing is, what are you going to explore or expose about your lead character's personality? If you would say, "You know what, I want to expose one of Tim's insecurities," then you can build a story around that. I'm intrigued by that, because you're showing me something different about the character. . . .

Be true to the show's "world." Don't [write] that Tim Taylor (of *Home Improvement*) is going to have a wild affair behind his wife's back. That may surprise people, but it's not true. In the world that we've established, Tim would never cheat on this woman.

Lawrence Konner: Like drama, the essence of comedy is conflict. You have to be very clear on what each character wants from the other in every scene. I think jokes will fall flat, comedy will not work, if there isn't a sense of somebody wanting something from the other person. David Mamet talks about that as the central idea of all drama writing. It applies to comedy, as well, and I think that's where the laughs come from. . . .

I don't think an overly complicated story is going to impress anyone. I think a fresh story certainly will, but that's hard to come up with. So [at least try to come up with] a fresh spin on an old story, you know, a little bit of spin that we don't expect.

Ian Gurvitz: One thing that truly annoys me is whenever I see spec scripts based on worn-out clichés, like "the grandmother from hell," "the mother-in-law from hell." Whenever I see scripts like those, it's like a red flag indicating that the writer is not really capable of much original thought.

Sandy Frank: The story should really make sense in two ways: It should make sense action-wise, [meaning that the story should develop logically]. And it should also make sense on an emotional level; you should know exactly what the characters are thinking and feeling and wanting at each moment. Because viewers really do identify with characters emotionally, and also because that's what the executives are going to be bugging you about from day one.

Okay, but how do you come up with ideas for an episode?

DREAMING UP STORIES

Get a piece of paper and write down every story idea that comes to mind. Just scribble a few words for each, no more than a phrase or two—details will only bog you down. (Several ideas probably occurred to you when you were studying your chosen series, so begin by listing them.)

Then look at the show's overall premise to see what its built-in humor might suggest. Review our discussion of premise-driven comedy and start thinking escalating predicaments, character mix, cast strengths—ways to create an episode full of comedic tension. George Costanza is virtually unemployable—what if he got the world's neatest job? Drew and Mimi abhor each other—what if they had to room together? Niles secretly lusts after Daphne—what if she needed a fake husband to fend off a suitor?

Next you might ask questions such as these:

- Has your life been affected by an event or discovery that could launch a good story?

- What universal truths strike you as being funny and episode-worthy?

- What controversial subjects would you like to explore?

- What recent news item might be turned into an episode?

- What unique (as in, scary/alluring/needy/vengeful/insane/disaster-prone) visiting character might spark a story?

- How about a parody of some big movie? Or another TV show? Or an overblown celebrity?

- What if your characters got involved in a mystery?

- Is there a unique (and affordable) location that suggests a story?

- What ghost from the past might pay a visit?

- Who or what deserves a really good comeuppance?

- What if a main character's lifelong dream came true? Or her worst nightmare?

And, of course, there's always the infamous dream-sequence episode. (Just kidding; those stories are usually too gimmicky to make for good spec scripts.) Or you can dream up a new batch of trigger questions and see what stories they suggest.

Still nothing? No ideas? Then take this book back and see about a refund. Med school is still an option.

More likely, you now have fifty or a hundred one-liners in front of you. Some are wrong for this show, some aired on TV last week, and some are just lame. But a few should seem doable. The next step?

TURNING IDEAS INTO SPRINGBOARDS

Once you have developed a long list of story ideas, the next step is to winnow it down. Skim through the list, crossing out the obvious losers. Seen it before? Have no idea where the story might go? Just not funny? Dump it.

When you hit a promising idea, if you think of additional elements that might enhance or develop it, scribble them down in the margin so that you don't forget those options. Then go through the list again. Compare each idea to the others. Which stories seem most interesting? The easiest to make funny? Which stories would you most like to see on TV? In addition, consider the following:

LAG TIME

If you write about current events or a new fad, is your story going to seem dated before you even finish the script? How will it hold up four months from now? Eight months from now?

DON'T NAME CELEBRITY GUEST STARS

If you pitch a *Just Shoot Me* story that features Denzel Washington as a guest star, and you, personally, can guarantee that Denzel will take the role, then congratulations—you just sold a script. However, if you can't guarantee a celebrity's participation, it is best to avoid naming that person in your story.

USE INSIDER INFORMATION

If you have been invited to pitch a show and you discover that the producers are anxious to explore a certain type of story, try to meet that need. A few years ago, an executive at a network gave me a tip that the producers of a show were looking for a chance to bring a previous guest star back for another episode. When I went in to pitch, I tossed out a story featuring exactly that type of guest star. I then (bending the "celebrity" rule just mentioned) casually suggested that the perfect person to play the guest role might be, oh, the very guy that they wanted to have back. By the end of our meeting, not only had I been hired to write that script but the producer was claiming credit for the casting idea.

REMEMBER WHOSE SHOW IT IS

Most stars get real unhappy when supporting or visiting characters get the main story lines. Producers are sensitive to this, so you should be too. The exception? You receive inside information that the producers feel that a particular supporting character is being underutilized. Pitch some great stories that feature that character and you might get hired.

AVOID HOLIDAY EPISODES

They seem less appealing out of season and sometimes feel as if their merit is partially due to holiday spin. (An unjustified emotional perception that can, nevertheless, diminish your spec script.)

DON'T RELY ON PHYSICAL COMEDY ALONE

Some shows derive a large portion of their laughs from physical comedy. Unfortunately, that plays better on a screen than it reads in a spec script. And some executives and producers are just not very good at visualizing scripted physical gags. (Myth has it that some executives even boast that they don't bother to read stage directions, just dialogue—meaning that they skip over much of a script's humor.) My point? If a show is very physical, then write it physical. But make sure that your dialogue is chock full of verbal humor too, because some of your readers will judge your script primarily on that basis.

As you go through your re-revised list of story ideas, a few more ideas will fall away and others will start to shine. The next step is to develop the more promising concepts into springboards, to see which can be turned into full-fledged stories and which are merely funny ideas.

A *springboard* is a three-to-five sentence description of a story. The first line or two set up the basic premise of the episode, and the next couple of lines hint at funny, intriguing complications that will occur. Springboards present the beginning and middle of the story to hook the listener, but do not always include a resolution. They are a sitcom writer's primary selling tool, the pitch that you throw at producers in the hope of getting a script assignment. Some writers refer to them as *log lines*, a reference to the brief episode descriptions provided in weekly TV logs.

An example of a springboard?

Drew is in heaven, he finally met the woman of his dreams. There's just one little problem—turns out she's also dating Drew's boss. And what's worse? She's Mimi's sister.

This simple pitch presents a setup and two complications, but no resolution. Why did I omit the ending? Because some springboards work better if you leave the producer hanging, hungry for more. If he wants to hear the ending, he can always ask. Better yet, he can pay you to write it.

NOTE: A high concept idea is similar to a springboard, only more compressed and dynamic. In just a line or two, it presents an exciting, instantly recognizable story hook. As in, "Arnold Schwarzenegger is . . . The Nanny." (A writer friend of mine coughed up this idea but didn't follow through; two years later, someone else brought out a film titled Kindergarten Cop. *Oh, well . . .)*

Some writers like to incorporate titles of hit films or series into a high concept line, such as "It's Die Hard *meets* Babe—*terrorists take over a farm, but one little piggy's not going down easy!" These title-dropping concepts are now considered cheesy but, if they are the best way to get your idea across, who cares?*

To repeat, as you go through your list this time, try to envision how each premise might be developed into a story. Write the ideas out as rough springboards, limiting yourself to no more than a few lines for each. Why? Because if you can't articulate the essence of a story in a few lines, it might be too muddled a concept to successfully flesh out (or sell to a producer). So make the effort, write your thoughts down. And don't kid yourself into believing that a horribly confused story concept will magically straighten itself out later. It won't.

Obviously, as you develop your stories, you should discard any unwieldy ones. If you can't come up with an ending or the plot seems clichéd or contrived, toss it out and move on.

Here's a question: What if you are writing for a show that uses multiple story threads, three to five equally important plots, rather than a single main story? (A show like *Friends*, for example.) Should you create separate, fully developed springboards for each story thread? No, not at this exploratory stage. Two or three lines for each premise should suffice as you weigh different ideas. Later, when you select several to weave together, you can fill in the gaps.

NOTE: When it comes to writing, everyone works differently. When something important occurs to me but I don't want to interrupt the current focus of my work, I write the idea on a separate page (rather than risk forgetting it). Under the heading "Characters," I might list ideas for visiting characters, funny character bits, unique dialogue traits, etc. Under the heading "Story," I note story reminders, funny jokes or situations, alternative story directions. Under the heading "Notes/Questions," I list practical to-do's such as reminders to double-check a peripheral character's name or get a producer's fax number. Obviously, you should do whatever works for you; this is just one approach to keeping things on track.

Eventually, after much thought, you will end up with that one perfect idea, that well-shaped premise, that is guaranteed to launch an Emmy-winning script. But do you really have to write all of this stuff down, go through all of the steps listed above? Many writers do not. Some go through the steps but do it all in their heads, creating/winnowing/structuring without putting a single word on paper. Others base a script on the first idea that occurs to them, and are talented enough to create great material. Again, do what works for you. Do whatever you need to do to create a great premise.

Then it's time to start writing a story outline, right? Well, almost . . .

Nine

Developing the Story

THE IMPORTANCE OF THE STORY

You've got a great premise and you sort of know where the story goes, so why not unleash those creative juices and start writing the script?

Well, some writers can. A talented few can create a wonderful, enthralling story as they work their way through a first draft. But most of us need a road map. Without it, our stories tend to go astray and hit a series of dead ends. We take weird paths to solve story problems and end up with a script that seems disjointed, forced, patched together.

Is this such a big deal? You bet. In my twenty years as an executive, writer, and teacher, I have come to believe that story is the single biggest reason that a project will succeed or fail. (By my definition, characters are integral to story; they drive the story and their arc of development is realized through story.) In the sitcom business, what determines whether you get a script assignment? The stories that you pitch. What are writing staffs trying to fix when they keep working until 3:00 A.M.? Flawed stories. What are viewers really talking about when they discuss "boring," "ridiculous," "she'd never do that" episodes? Bad stories.

Recognizing the importance of story, sitcom producers require that an episode's plot be figured out, *on paper*, before a writer goes to script. Sell that brilliant premise of yours during a pitch, and your first task will be to write a formal outline. If you are hired as a freelance writer, you might write it yourself, and rewrite it, following notes given by the producers. Or the producers might sit with you and practically dictate the entire story, which you will then clean up and put into outline form.

If you are on the staff of a show, you might write the outline yourself, after creating the story with the producers or just getting notes from the producers. Or the producers might write the outline themselves and hand it to you. Or the entire writing staff might sit together and verbally pound out the story, after which someone (probably you) will write up the outline.

One way or another, the story ends up on paper. The good thing is that, if a producer asks you to write an outline, you get paid to do so. (More on this later.)

Should you bother doing all of that extra work—creating an outline—if you are writing a spec script by yourself? Definitely, you need that roadmap. In fact, though the standard hiring route is to go directly from premise to outline, I recommend that you do another step in between. I recommend that you create a beat sheet.

CREATING A BEAT SHEET

A *beat sheet* is a one-page blueprint of the story's structure.

A traditional half-hour sitcom episode features one main story line, which is usually composed of five to nine big plot points, or beats. If the show also features one or two subplots, which occupy less screen time, each of those usually rings in at only three to five beats.

Since the late eighties, a second breed of sitcom has become equally popular—sitcoms that feature multiple story threads instead of a single main story line (with or without subplots). Each story thread is a main story in its own right, featuring one of the show's lead characters. However, since all of these threads still have to be crammed together into a half hour of television, each one incorporates fewer story beats and occupies less screen time than a traditional main story. *Friends* is an example of a show that features thread structure: In a single episode, one story features Rachel, another Ross, another Joey, and a fourth Monica. All of these stories are main stories, of roughly the same dramatic weight, but time restrictions limit each thread to an average of three to six beats apiece.

So how do these story lines and beats translate into a beat sheet? First, let's clarify the meaning of *beats*. A beat is a moment, a discovery, or an incident that alters the main character(s)'s goals, and/or cranks up a story's dramatic tension. As Linda Seger notes in her book, *Making a Good Script Great*, story beats sometimes consist of two parts, an *action* that forces a *reaction*.[33] For example, *Home Improvement*'s Brad doesn't just lose his mother's one-of-a-kind watch; the second half of the beat is that he then decides to cover up by replacing the watch with a fake.

A beat sheet is simply a list of the beats that define your story. By providing a clean, at-a-glance look at how your episode develops, it enables you to quickly see whether each plot line works or doesn't work. To keep the full focus on story, each beat should be written in the briefest possible form; it should be just a phrase or two, not even a complete sentence, that provides the gist of what happens. For instance, the previous paragraph's example might be reduced to: "Brad loses mother's watch—decides to replace with fake."

Beat sheets are powerful tools because they enable a writer to identify fatal story flaws before it is too late; meaning, before the flaws have been completely obscured by clever scenes and funny dialogue. If you look at that sheet and the story doesn't build, is not logical, is not funny, does not surprise and seduce, then it's back to the drawing board. And consider yourself lucky for having caught those flaws now, when they are easiest to fix.

> **NOTE:** *There is another industry definition of* beat sheet *that refers to a type of story outline sometimes used by producers of dramatic series. Those multipage outlines are usually distinguished by numbered scenes, truncated grammar, and functional scene descriptions.*

One last thought regarding beat sheets: When an episode features multiple story lines, it is probably easiest to sort out the beats for each individual story first, and then figure out how to weave the different stories together later. Of course, if a great sequence of integrated beats suggests itself early on, run with it.

Given that stories are composed of beats, and that beat sheets are a great way to track a story's development, how does one create a compelling story line?

STORY STRUCTURE—LINEAR VS. THREAD

I once heard that "if movies are larger than life, sitcoms are smaller."

At a very basic level, many sitcom stories tend to follow a well-worn path. First, a lead character encounters a new problem or opportunity, and goes to outrageous lengths to solve that problem or pursue that opportunity. (If his actions were logical rather than outrageous, there would be no story.) Then, running into an escalating series of obstacles, he takes inappropriate actions to achieve his goal. (That goal often changes and becomes more imperative as events proceed.) By end of story, the character's misguided efforts backfire on him; exposed and embarrassed, he learns the error of his ways. Sort of.

This pattern of development is nothing new. It's the same linear structure model that was described by Aristotle over two thousand years ago. To paraphrase from *Aristotle's Politics & Poetics* (a book that you should probably have on your shelf), a story is composed of three sections: The *beginning* introduces a complication to a character's life, launching the story. The *middle* section presents developing action, a series of *revolutions* and *discoveries*, which drives the story forward. The *end* resolves the story conflict, often through a reversal of fortune for the main character.[34]

Notice the similarities between these two models? The same linear, or "three-act," structure that you see in a conventional sitcom story is also used in conventional movies, one-hour series, books, myths, fables, etc. (Notice that I use the qualifier *conventional*—not all story lines follow the Aristotelian model, as we will discuss below.)

Looking more closely at sitcoms, we see that the three acts of an individual story line usually unfold in the following manner:

- The first act, the beginning, is very brief because you don't need to introduce characters and settings; they are already in place if you are writing for an existing sitcom. Within a page or two, and in just one or two story beats, a complication occurs that sends the lead character off on some sort of mission.

- The second act is the longest. Taking up half to three-quarters of your story line, it is the journey, or quest, that your character pursues as he tries to achieve his goal. Dramatic tension should escalate as he goes— jeopardy mounts, stakes increase, the character's actions become more desperate, etc. As Hollywood screenwriting guru John Truby counsels, a writer tackling her second act should "think development, not repetition"; meaning, each scene should build on preceding story, not repeat material that was covered in earlier scenes. Second acts often end with some huge revelation or event that leaves your character facing a major dilemma.

- The third act usually takes up about a quarter of your story line. The pace picks up as the tale reaches its climax—characters confront each other, the truth is revealed, and the story is resolved. The main character loses as often as he wins, but somehow the episode usually manages to close with a happy ending.

Please note that I have described the above model as the structure of an *individual story line*, not an episode. As previously discussed, some sitcoms regularly feature four or five *story threads* instead of a single main story. However, each of these threads features the same three-act structure as described above. The primary structural difference is that, due to time constraints, story threads are shorter—they feature less dramatic development—than a traditional main story line. (The synergistic effect of multiple story threads being woven together gives them as much dramatic power as a traditional sitcom's single main story.)

How might each of the three acts break down into an average number of pages per script? It's impossible to say since every story is unique. For point of illustration only, here is one example: In a typical fifty-page sitcom script (written in "tape format," which is explained in appendix A), an episode that features a *single main story line* might break down as follows: five to ten pages for the first act, about thirty pages for the second act, and ten to fifteen pages for the third.

Again, this is just one example, based on a traditional, linear, one-main-story episode. If you are writing for a show that features thread structure, a typical episode might include four story threads, each taking up roughly a quarter of the fifty-page script. Where each act of each thread might appear page-wise is impossible to say, because the different threads could be woven together in any number of ways. (Remember *Seinfeld*?)

STORY THREADS VS. SUBPLOTS VS. ENSEMBLE STORIES

Story threads, as defined in the preceding section, are main stories that feature main characters. Time limitations require that these threads be shorter, less developed, than traditional main stories. Though several story threads are woven together to fill out an episode, and though they connect with each other at different points in an episode, each thread usually features a totally separate, unrelated story.

Subplots are short, secondary story lines that usually feature a show's supporting characters. Subplots sometimes present stories that are totally unrelated to an episode's main story, or that *seem* unrelated until they dovetail with the main story late in the episode. Other times, subplots might present stories that parallel the episode's main story; meaning, they explore a similar theme or dilemma, and occasionally provide the key to resolving the main story. Example: *Home Improvement*'s Tim Taylor has been acting like an insensitive chauvinist, but doesn't recognize his own (mis)behavior until he scolds son Mark for behaving in a similar fashion.

Ensemble shows differ from shows that utilize *thread structure* in several ways. Take sitcoms such as *Taxi* and *Frasier*, for example; though it might seem that an ensemble show features an interesting cast of equal characters, a second look usually reveals that one of the characters is more equal than the others (e.g., Alex Rieger, Frasier Crane). It might feel as if the less-equal ensemble characters get as much story time as the lead, but if you count up the number of episodes that feature each character (or the dollars that each actor rates during contract negotiations) it becomes clear that most ensemble shows are actually wrapped around a single lead character. What is more, though other members of an ensemble cast might "star" in different episodes of the series, they are starring in a single main story line rather than in one main thread woven in with other main threads. Lastly, the distinctions between thread structure and subplots in an ensemble series are sometimes difficult to see because supporting characters and subplots in ensemble shows get a lot more screen time than those in a traditional series.

STORIES WITHOUT ENDINGS AND SERIALIZED STORIES

Some sitcoms will introduce a story thread or a subplot and then just cut it off in midstride. We see a beginning and a middle, but no end. *Seinfeld*'s Kramer might spot an ad for a crazy product, order it, show it to Jerry . . . and that would be all. Nothing else would happen, there was no resolution.

Was this a sign of sophisticated writing, a bold decision to mimic the many unresolved threads that occur in real life? Sure. That, or the show was running long so they just chopped out the ending. Either way, occasional unresolved story lines such as these can add a fresh sense of reality to a show.

On another front, some sitcoms also utilize *serialized* story lines, or *story arcs*. These are stories that are spread out over a number of episodes. Example? Someone meets, dates, and dumps a new boyfriend over the course of five episodes. We still get a beginning, middle, and end, but they don't all occur in one half-hour sitting.

NOTE: *Prime-time television series are sometimes referred to as* episodic television, *to distinguish the form from TV movies and soaps. The primary difference between episodics and soaps is that installments of the former usually tell a complete story (or episode) in one sitting, while installments of the latter contain segments of serialized stories that are spread out over a number of shows.*

CHARACTER ARCS

What about character arcs and character development? Do sitcom characters grow to new levels of maturity and enlightenment as a result of their weekly adventures?

Yes and no. Structurally speaking, sitcom characters will frequently follow the same pattern that we expect to see in drama. They might start off an episode by behaving in a selfish or self-centered manner regarding some issue. During the second act, they take inappropriate actions as they try to achieve some goal. At story's climax, they realize the error of their ways and finally do the right thing. A lesson is learned, all is well, "The End." Until the next episode.

While long-term psychological growth is usually an important dramatic element in movies, books, and other forms of fiction, you don't see much of it in a series like *Men Behaving Badly*. The characters are who they are, and by next week they will have forgotten any lessons that they supposedly learned this week.

There are exceptions. For instance, sometimes the producers of a domestic sitcom will have their characters—most often the kids—learn from their mistakes as they mature. They will still make and remake mistakes over and over again, but the *types* of mistakes that they make will change as they and the series evolve. The issue is no longer "Will *Sabrina* cheat on that test?" but rather "Will *Sabrina* cheat on Brad?"

STORY TIPS

As long as we are talking about story structure, here are a couple of important things to remember:

YOUR LEAD CHARACTER SHOULD DRIVE THE STORY

Even if you use a visiting character to bring a story into an episode, that story should feature your lead character. The show is called *Frasier, Moesha, Dharma & Greg*—not *This Week's Visiting Character*. Your lead character should be the one pursuing the goal or evading the crisis. His decisions and actions should be what move the story forward. And your lead character should be the one who resolves the story at episode's end, even though his actions will often result in his being exposed and humiliated.

CONFLICT—IT'S A GOOD THING

Anyone who has graduated from third grade can tell you that conflict is an essential element of drama. Well, good news, conflict is also a great source of comedy. Unfortunately, a lot of inexperienced writers shy away from scenes that feature characters really going at it. They walk their leads right up to the brink of some juicy confrontation, but then pull back. They send the characters off in a different direction instead and we, the audience, are left feeling cheated.

Be brave. Throw your characters into hot water, because that's when things really get interesting. The funny thing is, once you do, sparks fly and stuff starts happening, and these scenes often end up being your favorites.

MILK A CHARACTER'S FLAWS

As in many dramatic stories, sitcom plots often grow out of a main character's weaknesses, or his tendencies to get himself into trouble. An example from *Seinfeld*: George Costanza meets a terrific woman, someone who actually finds him appealing—but fault-finding George dumps her because she has one minor flaw, a big nose. Kramer then helps the woman to get her nose fixed and starts dating her, much to George's dismay. The lesson? By exploiting a character's flaw, stories such as this can generate natural, seamless humor, because they grow right out of the show's premise.

ONE STORY LINE PER CHARACTER

While the lead characters of a series usually have some involvement in all of the story lines in an episode, each plot or subplot in an episode should feature a different person. Spread the stories around. One character gets the main story, another gets a subplot, another gets a second subplot, and so on. In a show that utilizes thread structure, each lead character gets only one thread—or, some weeks, no thread—and also serves as a supporting character in the other lead characters' threads.

STORIES SHOULD BUILD AS YOU GO

While stories need to be funny and interesting from the very first page, they should become more involving as you go. Typically, your biggest dramatic moment occurs in the third act, partly because it takes the first two acts to establish the importance of whatever issues are at stake. Fortunately for you, working to develop premise-driven comedy (which is all about building from the ground up) will help your story to develop in a compelling manner.

TIME FRAME OF THE STORY

Traditionally, a sitcom story line lasts for only a few days, a week, or maybe a couple of weeks. The argument given is that a longer time span would dilute the dramatic tension of the story. ("How urgent can a story be if it runs for six months or more?") Some episodes, such as a baby-delivery show or a trapped-in-an-elevator show, are even played out in real time; the story spans only a half-hour or several hours, unfolding at roughly the same pace for both characters and viewers.

> **Matt Williams:** Every sitcom episode has to build up to one key dramatic moment, what [the story's] really about. It can build to a key decision that your protagonist has to make. It can build to a key discovery that a character makes. It can build to a key moment of reconciliation. But everything in your story builds up to and away from that moment, which, ninety percent of the time, is in your block comedy scene.

More recently, however, adventurous sitcoms have enjoyed success by taking liberties with the time frame of a show. For example, *The Simpsons* will interrupt a normal scene to flash forward twenty years for a ten-second glimpse of the future, then cut back to present day without missing a beat. In its final year, *Seinfeld* featured an entire episode that ran in reverse; some critics took shots at what was an obvious gimmick, but viewers had no problem following the story line.

Does this mean that you are free to ignore time-frame traditions if writing a spec script? I reluctantly suggest that you do not. Some execs and producers tend to mistake innovative story elements for a lack of familiarity with their show. (Or worse, bad writing.) I recommend that you save those cool time-frame ideas for when you are already on the staff of a show. Then, they—and you—are more likely to be given serious consideration.

COMEDY'S IMPACT ON THE STORY

In sitcoms, how are story lines affected by comedy? Typically, we see the following:

CHARACTERS AND EVENTS ARE FREQUENTLY EXAGGERATED

It's not just *Drew* accidentally spilling coffee on some boring report—he wipes out the one document that is key to his getting that new promotion.

GOALS AND STRATEGIES ARE OFTEN SILLY OR OUTRAGEOUS

If the character's plan for reaching some goal was rational and logical, there wouldn't be a story to tell. The audience is happy to suspend disbelief and accept the idea that sitcom characters almost always ignore obvious solutions.

THE ISSUES AT STAKE ARE USUALLY SMALL

Sitcoms aren't about abortion debates or nuclear holocaust. Sitcoms are about parking tickets and forgotten anniversaries. They are issues that we can relate to, and that don't cost millions to portray on the small screen.

Of course, there are different ends of the scale. A sophisticated, adult, "nine o'clock" sitcom is likely to feature entirely credible situations and deal in human truths; its comedy usually comes from fresh characters and clever dialogue. On the other hand, very broad sitcoms live by one rule—anything for a laugh! Story logic takes a backseat to funny jokes. (Which is not to say that weak story development is okay; an outrageous episode must still build and resolve in a compelling manner.)

DRAMATIC STRUCTURE VS. BROADCAST FORMAT

So far, when we have discussed the three acts of a sitcom story, we have been referring to a script's *dramatic* structure. But the word *act* is also used as a purely technical term, coined by network scheduling types, to describe a segment of an episode that occurs between commercial breaks. This and other elements that interrupt a show define its *broadcast format*.

To clarify, that marvelous script that you are writing will probably be interrupted by an opening credit sequence, commercial breaks, and a closing credit sequence. Your job is to study the series that you wish to write for so that you can duplicate its broadcast format (i.e., its standard pattern of scheduled interruptions) when you write your outline and script.

Here is where things get a bit confusing. The timing of commercial breaks does not necessarily coincide with the transitions between the three *dramatic* acts in a typical episode. The commercial break that comes "right after the first act" (speaking broadcast-format-wise) might actually be located halfway through the second act (speaking dramatic-structure-wise) of your story. So the different uses of the term *act* can seem confusing.

Why do you care? Because, when you write your outline and your script, you are supposed to break your story up into segments that reflect the *broadcast format* pattern regularly used on your chosen show. As I will explain later, you will be typing "ACT ONE, ACT TWO, etc." at points that do not necessarily coincide with *dramatic* act breaks in your story.

Should you worry about this now? No. Now you should concentrate solely on building a good story. You can figure out where to insert commercial breaks later, when you write the outline.

How does a show's broadcast format normally play out? As previously mentioned, some series always start the half hour off with a brief *cold open*, or *teaser*. They show the first scene of the episode to get viewers hooked, then go to opening credits (the title sequence), then a commercial break, and then they come back for the first act (speaking broadcast-format-wise) of the episode. These openings are popular because that first nugget of story is more likely to grab a viewer's interest than is a credit sequence that he's already seen fifty times.

Other shows might start with the opening credit sequence, then go to the first commercial break, and then come back to the very first scene, which starts the first act.

The main body of an episode is interrupted by one or two more commercial breaks, dividing it into two or three acts. Often, just before each break, an act will end with some sort of cliffhanger, large or small, to lure viewers back after the commercials. When the next act starts, after the break, that new act usually begins by having one of the characters briefly recap what has happened in the story, to reorient viewers.

At story's end, some shows finish the last act, go to commercial, come back for closing credits, and that's it.

Other shows might finish the last act, go to commercial, and then come back with a brief tag scene. A *tag* is a very quick final scene tossed in just for laughs (and to hold viewer interest through the previous commercial break). While tags often play off one of the episode's story lines, that story line has usually already been resolved at the end of the last act. Closing credits often follow a tag scene but, since the early nineties, some shows (e.g., *Friends*) have chosen to run credits down one side of the screen *during* the tag scene, making those hard-earned credits practically unreadable.

Other creative twists on the traditional cold-open, no-open, tag-or-no-tag strategies have included: *Seinfeld*'s opening and closing monologues (which were eventually discontinued); variations in *The Simpsons*'s opening credits, that included Bart writing funny phrases on a school blackboard and an ever-changing family-on-the-couch scene; and *Ellen*'s use of tongue-in-cheek openers that had nothing to do with the episode's story lines.

CREATING FUNNY CHARACTERS

You are trying to achieve two goals when working on characters in your script. First, you must remain true to the voices and personalities of the show's continuing characters. Otherwise, your script might be funny and compelling, but . . . something's not right, Raymond just doesn't sound like Raymond. (People notice the difference. Especially producer-type people.)

Second, you should strive to make any visiting characters that you create both fresh and three-dimensional. They are a great way to convince producers that your writing skills go beyond an ability to mimic an existing show's format.

Where do you start when studying existing characters or creating new ones? You start with your gut. When you think of an existing character, what strikes you first? If you had to describe her personality in one sentence, what adjectives would you use? Why exactly does that character work or not work for you? (Be specific. Write it down if you have to.)

Creating a new character? What traits came to mind when you first conceived him? Did you picture him only in terms of how he could facilitate your story, or as a living, breathing personality? (Again, be specific.)

Then, look a little deeper. Lajos Egri, in his book *The Art of Dramatic Writing*, suggests that characters are best defined by their "physiology, sociology, and psychology." He lists different traits for each of these three dimensions in an effort to help writers get a feel for a character:

- For physiology, he tics off traits such as sex, age, height, weight, posture, appearance, and physical defects;

- for sociology, he lists items such as social class, occupation, education, familial history, religion, race, politics, and leisure-time activities;

- for psychology, he lists morals, ambitions, frustrations, temperament, attitude, complexes, and IQ.[35]

Must you take the time to explore all of the traits that Egri describes, for all of the characters that will appear in your script? No, of course not. The point (mine and, I speculate, Egri's) is that an examination of *specific attributes* can provide valuable clues to a character's personality. *You decide which traits are most telling*, for which characters, and develop those. (Personally, I usually focus on the character's emotional base—his dreams, flaws, and weaknesses, the things that make him most human.)

How do you develop traits that will make a character *funny*? Good question. The answer is different for every character in every story. Fortunately, most of the time, some amusing traits will automatically occur to you when you first dream up a character.

If you want to develop more of that character's humor, or if you can't see any humor in a character, try exploring traits that make a character seem *incongruous within his environment*. (Remember the important role that incongruity plays in humor?) Here are some examples: *Taxi*'s Louie De Palma was a little man who belittled big people—the show got lots of laughs by capitalizing on Louie's short height, a *physiological* trait. *The Beverly Hillbillies* were millionaires living in a community of millionaires—but their lack of education and social standing, *sociological* traits, made them incongruous, and funny. Within the Clampett clan, Jethro's complete lack of an IQ rendered him unique in his elitist environment—a *psychological* trait that generated loads of humor.

So explore incongruities between characters and their environment. The tension created by these dissimilarities can make your characters seem fresh and distinctive, and should suggest a lot of comedy.

REMEMBER THE MIX

In addition to deciphering an existing character's traits, or creating an interesting blend of traits for a new character, remember to assess his role *in the character mix*. While we come to know characters by observing their goals, fears, and actions, the manner in which they interact with others is just as enlightening.

Most sitcoms are star vehicles that feature a single lead character and a supporting ensemble, but some other series (e.g., *Friends*) feature multiple leads. In either case, the continuing characters in a show frequently act as a family unit. This unit might be led by a strong parental figure (e.g., *Family Matters'* Carl Winslow) or by the biggest baby of the bunch (e.g., *Home Improvement*'s Tim Taylor). And, the family ties might be more figurative than literal—witness the groupings in *Cheers*, *Murphy Brown*, and *NewsRadio*.

Whatever the mix, the show's continuing characters should be the ones who drive the stories forward. They should face the same types of problems that the show's viewers face, and they should be anything but perfect. (Perfect is boring, and most sitcom story lines grow out of characters getting themselves into trouble.)

How should the leads interact with each other and the rest of their sitcom family? Actively, dynamically, with sparks a-flyin'. As in life, a sitcom family is most interesting when everyone is going at it. Nobody cares if a lead character is debating global politics with an outsider, a character whom we don't know. But get two series regulars arguing over which way to hang toilet paper, and that we'll watch.

CHARACTER TYPES

Interestingly, one can often spot recurring character types in television sitcoms. In his critical essay, "Comedy, Its Theorists, and the Evolutionary Perspective," Robert Storey identifies four personality types that are commonly found in comedy: "the fool, the wit, the rogue, and the hero." While these types can be found in all forms of fiction, Storey suggests that the first three keep recurring in comedy because audiences are happy to laugh "*at* the fool, or *with* the wit, or (ambivalently) in complicity with the rogue's transgressions."[36]

Of course, the concept of recurring character types is nothing new in drama. Remember Joseph Campbell? Character archetypes in world mythology? Well, you can find a few in comedy too. See if some of these sound familiar:

THE SUPPORTIVE PARENT

As previously described, many sitcom families are led by a wise, insightful, supportive parent type. Because this character is usually more sensible than other "family" members, many of his stories grow out of problems that others have caused. And much of the comedy that comes from this character type is generated by his reactions to funny situations around him. Often, this is the character that provides the guidance that another character needs when making some important decision. Carl Winslow of *Family Matters* and Jill Taylor of *Home Improvement* are prime examples of a supportive parent.

THE IDIOT SAVANT

Often playing the child to a "supportive parent," the idiot savant is a character who makes up in insight what he lacks in IQ. This person is the trusting, innocent simpleton whom the others deem lovable but inferior—even though he is usually the one who blurts out a simple-but-brilliant solution when disaster looms ahead. Idiot savants come in all shapes and sizes. They generate a lot of their humor by giving literal responses (punch lines) to joke setups, and by stating truths that nobody else dares to mention. Woody Boyd of *Cheers*, and "Coach" Pantusso before him, are classic examples of an idiot savant.

The Idiot Idiot

Another childlike character, this type rarely provides an insight to compensate for his idiocy. He is just dumb, funny, and lovable, a constant source of trouble. (Trouble that, happily, spawns lots of funny predicaments.) Idiot idiots are usually featured in broader comedies and their antics often involve a lot of physical humor. (They are the "comic fools" noted above.) Think Barney Fife of *The Andy Griffith Show*, Luther Van Dam of *Coach*, and Joey Tribbiani of *Friends*.

The Clown

The clown is usually an intelligent, rational adult—who falls down a lot. She generates stories and comedy by being inept, clumsy, and awkward. Clowns often stumble into outrageous physical predicaments, which are made all the more funny by their frantic efforts to extricate themselves. The greater the potential for embarrassment, the more a clown is guaranteed to screw up. Classic sitcom clowns include Lucille Ball, Dick Van Dyke, and, more recently, Ellen DeGeneres.

The Operator

The operator is a close cousin to the "rogue" mentioned above and the "trickster" frequently featured in ancient myths. This character is always on the make, looking for some golden opportunity. Not only do his ill-conceived schemes create funny predicaments, but his seeming inability to quit when he is ahead keeps the stakes rising and the comedy coming. Think young Bart of *The Simpsons* and Michael Flaherty of *Spin City*.

The Mentor

The mentor, another mythic character type that appears in modern sitcoms, is a source of wisdom for other characters; however, those other characters often don't seek his advice until they have already screwed up a situation big-time. Mentors, unlike supportive parents, are frequently cast as peripheral characters in a sitcom family. Their distance from the main story action enables them to be more objective when assessing a dilemma. (Which is just as well, since, wise beings that they are, they are less likely to become ensnared in the type of snafus needed to drive a sitcom episode.) Eldin Bernecky of *Murphy Brown* and Wilson of *Home Improvement* are examples of a mentor.

THE CONFIDANT

The confidant is another source of advice, though his advice, unlike the mentor's, is often bad. Taking the role of a best friend, a trusted associate, an uglier sibling, confidants are usually just a bit of a loser compared to the show's lead; they get fewer dates, have worse jobs, and are a degree less intelligent. However, they are always eager to discuss the lead's schemes, suspicions, fears, or what he should wear to the ex-girlfriend's wedding. Think Lewis and Oswald of *Drew Carey*, and Robert of *Everybody Loves Raymond*.

THE IRRITANT

Some characters exist solely to make other characters miserable, which creates conflict, which leads to comedy. The irritant might range from merely being an obnoxious person to having a specific hostile agenda (directed against another character). On *Drew*, the self-centered boss, Mr. Wick, falls into the first category, while pit-bull Mimi falls into the second. On *Just Shoot Me*, the obnoxious-with-an-agenda character of Dennis falls somewhere in between.

THE ROMANTIC INTEREST

Per our earlier discussion of stories driven by sexual tension, the romantic interest is the character that makes another character "tense." Typically, a lead character desires the romantic interest, but that person is unobtainable because of a gap in social status, a career conflict, or some other obstacle. (The couple clearly belongs together but—this being sitcomland—only we, the audience, can see that.) In other cases, two leads both serve as romantic interests (to each other) in a healthy relationship; they frequently question and test their relationship, but always reaffirm the strength of their bond by story's end. In *3rd Rock from the Sun* Dick and Mary are an example of the first relationship, and *Dharma & Greg* are an example of the second.

THE CRITIC

Many sitcoms feature a character who is always criticizing the people around him. This critic—the "wit" named above—is usually very clever and blunt, and often dead on in his comments. He gets some of his laughs by dishing out snappy insult humor, and some by having his own wisecracks (born of pretense) backfire on him. In the latter case, either his target gives back better than the critic gave, or the critic discovers that his crack was unintentionally cruel ("That'd almost be funny—if her puppy wasn't *dead*."). Examples of this character type include Carla of *Cheers*, and both Frasier and Niles of *Frasier*.

So there are a few recurring character types that can be found in today's sitcoms. Do they appear in every show? No. When producers create a new show, do they just pick one character type from column A and two from column B, etc.? No. (We hope not.)

In fact, to describe these behavior patterns as "recurring character types" is probably too restrictive. While some characters do stick to a particular mold pretty closely, most share a blend of these and other traits. And that blend can shift from week to week, and even *scene to scene*. Frasier might play supportive parent to his dad in one episode, and childlike idiot to the man in the next. Mimi might play the supreme irritant for two-thirds of a story line, and then grudgingly serve as mentor to help Drew through a third-act crisis.

It is probably most useful to think of these "types" as just another way to get a handle on how a show's characters interact. Or as a way to describe a character's mode of behavior in a particular scene.

> **Matt Williams:** How the characters think is more important to me than what the characters say. For example, on the *Mary Tyler Moore Show*, there was an episode in which Mary was in the bathtub, and Ted came into the room by mistake. Ted accidentally dropped his keys into the tub, and he looked down like he was going to retrieve them. He did not say a word, but the audience just burst out laughing. Why? Because they knew how Ted thought. He just looked down, and then she just looked up, and I think the line was, "Don't even think about it."

VISITING CHARACTERS

Many sitcom stories feature one or more visiting characters, individuals who appear in only one episode or in a string of successive episodes. (Characters who pop up irregularly throughout a season, or over the life of a series, are usually referred to as "recurring characters.") While, as noted above, you should try to make visiting characters fresh and exciting, there are a few things to remember:

NOT TOO FRESH AND EXCITING

Visiting characters should not outshine the series regulars. If a newcomer gets too much screen time or seems too appealing, the show will feel off-balance. (And you can bet that the show's producers will get a nasty call from their star's agent, proclaiming that his client is suddenly feeling used, abused, and undervalued.) After all, America tuned in to see the series regulars, not some stranger. Does that mean that you should write low-key, boring visitors? No, just remember that while an outsider might bring a story into an episode, that story should become a regular character's concern. And keep a lid on how much dialogue you throw to your (fresh and exciting) visiting characters.

REGARDING OPPONENTS

Stories come from conflict between people, which makes a dramatic opponent—half of said people—a very important character. If you are going to tell a juicy, compelling story, and the opponent is a visiting character, that opponent should be as powerful as, or even more powerful than, the series regular who is featured in the story. Otherwise, there isn't much of a story to tell; the series regular would quickly trounce his opponent and the conflict would be over.

Should a series regular always beat his opponent? Hardly. Remember, in comedy, the third act of a story line often climaxes with the lead character losing a fight and being humiliated. Which is funny.

Who is the opponent in a romantic story line? While there are often a number of parties who present obstacles to true, if temporary, love, the biggest opponent is usually the romantic interest him- or herself. Whether a love relationship spans the life of a series or only a single episode, the two characters that belong together frequently start out as rivals or enemies. They are made for each other, but are too busy doing battle to realize that fact at first. The pleasure of the story comes from seeing them go through hoops until they finally succumb to their happy fate.

Lastly, as with all characters, the opponent in a story should have human dimensions—his own value system, goals, fears, point of view, etc. A "bad guy" who is simply bad for bad's sake seems poorly drawn and uninteresting. *Drew*'s Mimi might be a beastly opponent, but we sense that she has her own dreams and insecurities, that she suffers when others taunt her, and that she—on rare occasions—will reach out to another person.

SERVING YOUR STORY

On a practical level, here are some other things that you might consider when creating a visiting character:

- Who might be the best person to introduce the story?

- Who might help to relay important exposition? (*Exposition* means information that a viewer must have if she is to understand a story.)

- Who might help to keep the story moving?

- Who might serve as the best foil to the regular characters?

AVOID REPETITION. AGAIN

As with story structure, one should think development rather than repetition when creating characters. Avoid introducing visiting characters who are merely a carbon copy of a series regular, *unless* that similarity is part of the episode's comedy. For example: *Frasier* gets some competition in the pop-psych world—a new radio rival looks, sounds, and thinks just like Frasier, and is getting bigger ratings.

HOW THE PRODUCTION PROCESS AFFECTS YOUR SCRIPT

This chapter is about the art of turning a promising episode premise into a solid story. However, there are a few realities of television production that you should be aware of when writing a sitcom script. Meaning, your creative instincts must sometimes be tempered by budget and time constraints, such as the following:

LOCATIONS AND SETS

Ever notice how most sitcom episodes take place indoors? In just a few rooms? It's a money thing. Those rooms, called *standing sets*, are crammed together on the floor of some big Hollywood sound stage (or, on rare occasions, a New York sound stage). A sitcom usually features three to four standing sets, plus a couple of *swing sets* (seldom-used sets that can be swung out of storage when needed). And that's it. An office, a coffee shop, a living room, a bar where everyone knows your name are the spaces where all of a sitcom's stories take place.

All? Okay, sometimes, reluctantly, a show's producers will invest in new sets if they are critical to a strong script. Maybe a hospital room, a subway car, or a gate at the airport. But are those producers happy to spend that extra money? No. In fact, not only are they unhappy when they see spec scripts or freelance scripts that call for multiple new sets, the perception is that the writers of those scripts are uninformed. To avoid that label, be thrifty. Try to direct your story lines so that they can take place in the show's regular (standing and swing) sets. If you must venture elsewhere, fine, but limit yourself to one or two new sets, tops. (Of course, once again, when you are on the staff of a show, your ideas regarding new locales will probably get a better reception.)

What about all of the locations used on *Seinfeld*? And on *The Simpsons*? What about all of those family shows that travel to Hawaii or Europe for a couple of episodes? Well, when you are producing a series as successful as *Seinfeld*—a billion-dollar, moneymaking machine—yes, you can get extra money for additional sets and location shooting. And when you are writing for an animated show like *The Simpsons*, yes, you can call for whatever exotic sets you want—it's a cartoon! And those trips to Hawaii? Those are stunts dreamed up to attract viewers during network sweeps months. (*Sweeps* refers to a critical audience-rating period that influences how much a network can charge advertisers for commercial time.) Costly? Sure, but the producers see the trips as a way to attract new viewers, and land a free trip to Hawaii. (Who could blame them?) Are such travel stunts a good idea for a spec script? Never. Again, their use in a freelance writer's script would only serve to indicate that the writer is out of the loop.

SPECIAL EFFECTS

Special effects are expensive to produce and time-consuming to shoot. Sure, you can call for some basic *mechanical effects*, effects that can be produced by a prop person or effects technician right there on the set; these include things like smoke, breakable mirrors, and levitating objects. And there are a number of flashy *optical effects*, such as objects radiating light and images superimposed over other images, that can be easily created. But otherwise sitcoms are not the place for car crashes, exploding buildings, and morphing monsters. While an occasional sci-fi or fantasy series like *Sabrina, the Teenage Witch* might call for exotic effects on a regular basis, most shows never use the stuff. So, while that idea about the *Wayans Brothers* being shrunk to the size of peas might get big laughs from your Aunt Phyllis, it is best to follow a show's lead regarding its use of special effects.

STUNTS

As with special effects, stunts cost money and time. They require trained personnel, a coordinator, performance fees, etc. Unless a show has employed stunts in the past, you should probably avoid including any in your script.

NAIL THE STORY, THE REST IS EASY

Building a story is hard work. That is why many writers prefer to jump right into dialogue, arguing that a story should unfold naturally, that it should come "from the writing."

Well, that sounds good, it sounds very "writerly." And a talented few can consistently create great stories via that approach. However, I side with a writerly guy named William Goldman who, having chalked up a couple of screenwriting Oscars, has proclaimed the following: "For the most part, the public and critics have come to believe that screenplays *are* dialogue. Wrong. If movies are story, and they are, then screenplays are structure."[37]

But sitcoms aren't movies, are they? Sure they are. Just shorter and funnier. Their other differences aside, both forms are hugely dependent on story structure.

My point is that if you take the time to nail the story up front, the rest of the writing will be a breeze. (Or at least breezelike.) You will have your road map, and your story will drive forward in a purposeful fashion. There will be no wrong turns, no wasted motion.

What is more, if you create a fresh, compelling story, your producer will be very happy. He can always punch up a script's dialogue and add jokes—that's what his staff of twelve writers is paid to do. But show him that you can cough up great stories, and you might suddenly be deemed a very valuable commodity.

So, think story, study story. Read books, take classes, and analyze scripts, to enhance your story-building skills. And remember two things: Stories are driven by characters (their discoveries, decisions, and actions), and stories should remain true to the overall series premise.

NOTE: *Will you ever be asked to change a brilliantly structured story, to redesign that masterpiece that you have worked so hard to develop? Yes, always, almost without fail. With so many people involved in the creative process, expect that it will happen. But if you start out with a good story, you will (usually) receive fewer meddlesome notes. And people will remember that your original story—however much it might be changed—was crafted in a solid, professional manner.*

MOVING ON

So far, you have dreamed up story ideas, developed springboards, selected a great premise, and beaten it into a terrific story. The next step? It's time to refine your story by creating a scene outline.

Ten

Writing an Outline

An outline is a selling tool. It provides a description of your episode and aids in the writing process. It helps you to take that wonderful story that you have developed and break it down scene by scene. It forces you to pick the locations and times in which the beats of your script will unfold. Do you still have holes in the story? Loose ends to tie up? Problems integrating plot lines? It's hard to overlook these details when writing an outline.

But in addition to helping you to refine your story, or helping a producer to understand your story, an outline must also be interesting to read. And since you are writing for a sitcom, it should be funny. (Here is another instance when your efforts to incorporate humor into the story premise will pay off.) After all, you are trying to sell a producer on the idea that he should invest thousands to have you write a script, and then a million or more to produce an episode, all based on a few skimpy pages. (Which is kind of cool, when you think about it.)

If you are a freelance writer, you try to get invited to come in and pitch your ideas, your springboards, to the show's producers. If you are fortunate, they pick idea number six, and give you from two to seven days to come back with a written outline. Or they might invite you in and just dictate a story to you, or develop one with you, and then send you off to put the formal outline on paper. (Yes, you do get paid for this step.)

When you submit the outline a few days later, the producers will sometimes give you notes for changes and send you off to revise the document. Two to five days later, you submit the revised outline and, if all goes well, the producers give you more notes and tell you to "go to script." (Congratulations, now you get paid even more.) Other times, you and the staff will rewrite the outline together, and then you will be told to write the first draft. And still other times, the producers might cut you off and have someone else write a script based on your outline, either because they have already paid for that person's time or they think—based on your outline—that you are a weak writer. (So what do they know?) If you are on the staff of a show, the whole process might occur in a less formal fashion, with shorter deadlines, and it might involve group writing and rewriting efforts at different stages.

That explains how an outline fits in when you are writing a script *on assignment*. But why waste time writing an outline when working on a spec script, since no producer will ever see it? It's a fair question. As long as you have beaten out the story, as described in the last chapter, you should be in pretty good shape to begin a first draft. However, you probably still haven't translated all of the beats into individual scenes or sewn up assorted loose ends. Therefore, it would help to at least rough out an outline to clear up some final issues—scene chronology, locations, times, characters present, and a description of what transpires during each segment. Write it in crayon, in Swahili, who cares, but make those last big story decisions before diving into the first draft.

WRITING TO SELL, NOT EDUCATE

How do you make a scene outline entertaining? The outline is only four to six pages long—not much space considering all of the story information that it has to convey. How can it not seem purely functional?

Well, write it as if it were an amusing short story. Or take the approach that you would use if describing the episode to your best friend. Stick to the key story points and present them with sizzle. Bring the story to life by including *specific descriptions* of a few dramatic moments and funny situations. (Not lengthy, just specific.)

Here's a tip: *Don't be afraid to leave out less-than-critical information*. You cannot describe everything that happens in your episode in an outline. Nor should you. In fact, a sure sign of an inexperienced writer is that he feels compelled to educate the reader. He wants those producers to know every damn detail that he, the writer, has dreamed up. Because only then can the producers fully appreciate the story, and him. Right?

Wrong. Excess information slows down "the read." Sure, if you use the tiniest of type fonts, maybe you can fit every single detail into those five pages. But who wants that? The producer, who has fifty other things on her desk that require her immediate attention, will not appreciate your thoroughness. You want to sell her? Give her just enough to want more. Give her just enough to follow the beats, to get a handle on the characters, to see how the story lines end. Along the way, when you can, leave a little mystery in the air. Leave the producer hanging, let her fill in a few blanks. Make her want to see the script.

No question, writing a compelling outline is an art. How much is enough? Or too much? Developing this sense takes a lot of practice, diligent trimming, and maybe some feedback from writer friends. A helpful rule of thumb is to frequently ask "Does the reader absolutely have to know this detail in order to keep up with the story?" Every time you come back with a "No," *phhht*, dump it.

Another way to get a handle on what will sell a show's producers is to ask for copies of outlines that were written for the staff's favorite episodes. (Obviously, you should do this after the producers have heard your pitch and hired you to write an outline.) Production secretaries are usually helpful about providing such materials if they know that you have actually been hired to develop an episode of the show.

BUILDING AN OUTLINE

An outline breaks your story down into an ordered sequence of individual scenes. It should be only four to six pages long, single-spaced. (Some producers prefer eight to ten pages, *double-spaced*, as we will discuss in the next section.)

On paper, outlines are all about headings and paragraphs: headings that, in one line, identify the location and time of a scene; and, paragraphs that, sitting below each heading, describe what happens in that scene.

Usually, each scene is described in one paragraph, maybe two. Most of the space is devoted to main story lines, with subplots just getting a line or two here and there. (Some writers prefer to describe the main story developments first, then end the paragraph with a line describing any subplot developments that also occur in the scene.)

Does each scene in your outline have to feature one of the dramatic beats in your story? No. Sometimes beats are spread across scenes. Let your instincts regarding pacing of the story dictate how you divide it up among scenes.

Here are some additional points to consider when building your outline:

BROADCAST FORMAT

As mentioned earlier, a scene outline must reflect the broadcast format regularly used for the series. As you develop and order scenes, now is the time to factor in the scheduling of commercial breaks, the number of (broadcast format) acts in each episode, and whether or not the show uses cold opens or tags. Remember, the timing of commercial breaks might have little to do with how you have structured your story dramatically. Still, if you are able to position a key story moment or a clever button just before a required break, thereby leaving the audience hanging during said break, you should definitely do so. (Of course, half of the time, someone higher up will opt to insert a commercial break at a different point in the story than you had originally indicated, but there is nothing that you can do about that.)

UNIQUE ASPECTS OF THE SHOW

Now is also a good time to review any unique aspects of the series format that you discovered when you researched the show. Do the episodes always open with a scene from a B story? How long do the cold opens tend to be? Do the acts always end with a big cliff-hanger before going to commercial? Whenever possible, follow the show's lead.

HOOK THE READER QUICKLY

By the time a reader gets two or three pages into your script, he should be hooked by at least one story line. Meaning, he should know what someone is trying to accomplish, and why, and what is at stake. Jokes and clever dialogue are certainly important, but story is what keeps eyes on the screen. Take too long to establish a core conflict and the reader will become frustrated and disinterested.

You say that you can't move a story hook up because it would ruin the structure of your episode? Then, at the least, try to create an air of mystery about the soon-to-be-launched story by hinting that something big is in the works. (Better yet, realize that you probably can adjust your episode's structure and get that story moving earlier in the script.)

FORESHADOWING BEATS AND JOKES

As suggested in the previous paragraph, foreshadowing an upcoming story beat by "hinting that something big is in the works" is a great way to keep readers (and viewers) involved. Suspense holds an audience's attention, and the eventual unveiling of the foreshadowed beat provides a satisfying reward.

On a different level, foreshadowing can also aid with exposition. If the audience is to believe that Chandler's new roommate is truly a raving pyscho, it helps to foreshadow that discovery by having that character behave in an increasingly bizarre manner earlier on.

Whether dealing with a plot point or a simple bit of humor, an event sometimes carries more weight if it has been deftly foreshadowed. When that event finally occurs, it can even earn bonus points because the audience is impressed when it realizes that it has been set up.

> **NOTE:** *If you plant a seed, remember to harvest it. Otherwise it might seem that your story is cluttered with unfinished business.*

SCENE DEVELOPMENT

Most scenes develop in the same way that conventional story lines do. Short or long, they usually feature their own beginning, middle, and end. Characters enter the scene and engage in some sort of conflict or experience a revelation (dramatic acts one and two). When the scene is "resolved" (act three) and the characters move on to the next scene, the dynamics of the episode's story should somehow change. If the scene was good, either it propelled the reader forward to a new point in the story, or it somehow raised the stakes of the story. If the scene was weak, it did nothing to develop the episode's story and only served to slow down the read.

KEEP SCENE DESCRIPTIONS BRIEF

In keeping with our make-'em-want-more philosophy, each of your scene descriptions should be lean and mean. When writing for an existing sitcom, that should not be too hard to accomplish—the main characters and settings are already familiar to the reader. Simply focus on keeping the story moving and avoid bogging down in minutia. (As in, don't choreograph every detail of that food fight—just start the thing, describe the crowning moment when Frasier catches a pie in the face, and move on.)

Don't be surprised if the first few scenes of your outline come out a bit longer than the rest. Opening scenes usually contain a lot of exposition (e.g., visiting characters being introduced, the story premise being established, a new set being described, etc.) that has to be gotten out of the way at the top of your episode. Just convey the information in as entertaining and concise a manner as you can.

HOW IT SHOULD LOOK ON PAPER

It seems that every producer has a slightly different opinion of how an outline should look on paper. Fortunately, most want to see the same basic elements included in the document. It is always best to obtain actual samples from a show's staff so that your outline can look just like the ones written in-house—the familiar appearance will make your piece seem more appealing.

But in case you are unable to obtain those samples, here is generic model for writing a professional-looking outline.

FONTS, MARGINS, AND PAGE NUMBERS

Outlines should be typed in a classic serif typeface. Courier font has long been the industry standard for screenplays, so I recommend using that or something similar. For ease of reading, the type should be pica size, or twelve point, meaning that you can fit exactly ten characters into a linear inch. (Avoid using funky type styles or a variety of type sizes—the pros don't, so you shouldn't.)

As for margins, leave an inch all around—sides, top, and bottom.

As for page numbers, type them way, way up in the top right corner of every page—say, a half inch from the tip of the paper. Every page should be numbered except for the cover page (if you use one) and page one of the actual outline. Some writers also like to include identifying information directly across from each page number, in the form of a slug like [*Series Title*, "Title of Your Episode"] or ["Title of Your Episode," Your Name].

> **NOTE:** *Do not include the brackets in your slug—I am using them here only to indicate the information that you should type.*

SINGLE- VS. DOUBLE-SPACING

Some producers prefer four-to-six-page, single-spaced outlines and others prefer eight-to-ten-page, double-spaced outlines. As always, you should use whichever style is used by the producers who hired you. However, if you can't find out which they prefer, I recommend the single-spaced version; almost everything we read in life is single-spaced, so why stray from the familiar?

COVER PAGE

Some producers prefer that outlines start with a cover page and some don't—either way is fine. If you want to include a cover page, start by typing the title of the television series a third of the way down the page, centered, underlined, in all caps.

Then, skip two lines and type the phrase [OUTLINE: "Title of Your Episode"], centered, with your episode's title encased in quotes and typed in upper- and lowercase letters.

Next, skip four or five lines and type the word [by], centered, in lower case.

Then, skip a line and type your name, centered, in upper- and lowercase.

Next, skip down to the lower right corner of the cover page to insert a *block* of contact information. Start by typing the word [CONTACT:] in all caps, flush left within the block. On the four or five lines beneath that, type the name, address, and phone number of the person—either you or your agent—whom the producers should contact for follow-up; these lines should all be typed flush left *within the block*, single-spaced, in upper- and lowercase.

Lastly if you wish to include a copyright notice or a Writers Guild registration notice, type it in the lower left corner of the cover page, directly across from the lowest line in the block of contact information.

> *NOTE: See chapter 14 of this book for a discussion of copyright and Writers Guild registration issues. See appendix A for an example of a cover page used for complete scripts, which is similar to the layout used for outlines.*

BODY OF THE OUTLINE

If you are going to attach a cover page to your outline, skip to the next paragraph for instructions on how to begin writing the body of the document. If you *do not* wish to attach a cover page, your first step is to provide contact information on page one of the outline. Simply type your name, address, and phone number in an upper corner of the first page, in a single-spaced block, in upper- and lowercase letters.

Skip three or four lines and type the series title in all caps, centered, and underlined.

Then, skip one line and type [OUTLINE: "Title of Your Episode"], centered, with your episode's title encased in quotes and typed in upper- and lowercase letters.

Then, skip two lines and begin the body of your outline. As previously discussed, a sitcom script always starts with either a cold open or the first act. So type the appropriate heading—either [COLD OPEN] or [ACT ONE]— in all caps, underlined, flush left.

Then, skip one line and type the scene heading for the first scene. A *scene heading*—typed in upper- and lowercase, underlined, flush left—consists of three elements. The first element indicates whether the scene will take place indoors or outdoors; the abbreviation [Int.] is used to indicate an interior scene, while [Ext.] indicates an exterior scene. The second element identifies the scene's location—a street, a room, an elevator, a boat. And the third element, which is separated from the first two by a dash, names the day part during which the scene takes place. Traditionally, writers are supposed to designate either [Day] or [Night] here because, when it comes down to it, most scenes do not require a more specific time designation. However, there are times when you might have a compelling reason to indicate [Dawn] or [Dusk], or a specific clock time, or that the next scene is occurring [Moments Later] or, simply, [Later] than the scene that came before. If there is no gap in the time between scenes, type [Continuous] instead of a day part, or just leave that part of the scene heading blank.

Examples of scene headings? [Int. Rachel's Car—Night] means that the scene literally takes place *in* the car, at night. [Ext. City Bus—Day] means that the bus is part of the scene but is seen from the outside. [Int. Hotel Lobby—Continuous] and [Int. Hotel Lobby] mean exactly the same thing— we are in the lobby, and there is no gap in time between this scene and the previous one.

> **NOTE:** *Take a long look at the script guidelines in appendix A. They include several nuances that also apply to outlines.*

After each scene heading, skip one line and then describe the action of the scene in a paragraph or two, typed in upper- and lowercase.

When beginning the next scene, skip two lines before typing the new scene heading.

When you reach the end of a cold open, skip four lines and start your first act by typing the act heading—[ACT ONE]—in all caps, underlined, flush left. Then, proceed to the next scene.

When you reach the end of the first act, skip two lines after the last scene and type [END OF ACT ONE], in all caps, centered, and underlined. *Then, start the next act on a new page.* Indicate the new act by typing [ACT TWO] at the top of the next page, flush left, in all caps, and underlined. Then, just as before, skip a line before typing the next scene heading. This pattern is repeated if your episode also includes a third act.

If your episode includes a tag, skip four lines after writing [END OF ACT TWO]—or [END OF ACT THREE], if you have one—and type [TAG] flush left, in all caps, and underlined. Then, skip one line and describe the scene.

To indicate the end of the episode, skip two lines after the very last scene and type [END OF EPISODE] in all caps, centered, and underlined.

STYLISTIC TIPS

Here are some pointers to consider when writing your outline:

"PLAY IT, DON'T SAY IT"

This well-worn phrase suggests that one should avoid having characters enter a scene and tell us about an important event that has happened else-where. Rather, we should *see* the big stuff (e.g., confrontations, decisions, tender moments, etc.) happen. That's why we tuned in, right?

WRITE IN THE PRESENT TENSE

Outlines and scripts are written in the present tense, partly because they must be shot in the present tense. (Laws of physics.) Also, it is far more compelling to envision actions unfolding right in front of us rather than to picture them as dated events. So type that "Damon jumps for joy" rather than "Damon jumped. . . ."

". . . AND IT WILL BE REALLY FUNNY HERE"

Remember when I said that a sitcom outline should actually be amusing to read? Sorry, but pointing out where funny things *might go* does not count. Either cough up a bit of humor when needed or quickly move on, hoping that the reader himself will fill in that blank with an imagined joke.

INCLUDING DIALOGUE IN AN OUTLINE

Sometimes the best way to illustrate a story beat or lay some comedy into an outline is to include a snippet of clever dialogue. Fine, great idea. But only if the dialogue is really good—funny, true to character, just enough and no more. Many an outline has ground to a halt because a writer tossed in a big chunk of go-nowhere dialogue, serving only to give his producers second thoughts about assigning him the first draft.

DESCRIBING CHARACTERS AND SCENES

If a character or setting is a standard component of a television series, you do not need to describe him or it in your outline. Just tell us that "Drew enters his kitchen" and we'll get the picture.

When introducing a visiting character or a new setting, just give us the essentials. We only need a line or two describing appearance, quirks, attitude, etc., to catch on. The character's subsequent actions will clue us in on her personality, and superfluous details about a setting will only slow down the read.

How do you write that new character or scene description into the outline?

Smoothly. Simply integrate it into the story rather than setting it apart so that it distracts the reader. No one wants to see a separate paragraph, an asterisk, or italicized type that points out some boring, functional exposition.

Lastly, format-wise, some producers prefer that a new character's name be typed in all caps the first time that she is mentioned in an outline. Others don't care. You decide.

Avoid Using the Royal "We"

Some writers tend to describe actions and events by using phrases like "*We see* the door open" or "*We hear* a door slam." This is no crime, but it does strain the reader's suspension of disbelief by reminding him that he is reading an outline rather than witnessing live events. When possible, just go with "The door opens" or "A door slams"—no more description is needed.

Paint the Picture

An outline is supposed to be an entertaining read, right? Make it so by using active verbs and specific details to paint compelling pictures of the story's events. No, you do not want to overdramatize quiet moments or simple descriptions. And you definitely do not want to pile on purple prose (i.e., showy adjectives, adverbs, metaphors, etc.). But you can sometimes improve a line by writing "Homer inhales the donut" rather than "Homer eats the donut."

No Camera Directions

You are the writer, not the director. Unless a specific camera angle or move is absolutely necessary to your story or a featured joke, do not include it in your outline.

Any exceptions? Material written for animated series like *King of the Hill* often contains a judicious selection of camera angles, since those shows enjoy a shoot-anything-we-want flexibility. But check out several of a show's produced scripts before you start reaching for that riding crop.

Leave Lots of White Space

Producers and executives love white space. Blank areas on a page mean that there is that much less reading to do. And they make a script seem like a quick read (a good thing), since the pages fly by faster. So do not crowd your margins or forgo traditional spacing. If something doesn't quite fit at the bottom of a page, even if it will leave a bit of a gap, just move it to the next page. You will make some producer or executive very happy.

Don't Get Funky

You can have lots of fun with exotic paper stocks, funky typefaces, wacky formatting—just don't do it here. The pros don't, and you want your outline to look just like theirs, right?

Be a Perfectionist

Believe it—spelling, grammar, and punctuation matter. Sloppy writing suggests that either you don't care or are not capable. So proofread, ask others to proofread, and rewrite until you are 100 percent satisfied.

REWRITING AN OUTLINE

As noted above, producers usually ask that the first draft of an outline be rewritten, per their notes, before they will authorize a writer to begin the script. (They might do this in a meeting, or over a phone, or via notes faxed to your home.) Because you care about your work, you might find yourself becoming a tad defensive—okay, homicidal—when they ask for these changes.

Well, try to keep your cool and focus on two primary goals: You want them to let you write the script based on that outline; and you want them to enjoy working with you so much that they renew your (staff) contract or hire you to write another (freelance) script. Your job is to show that you are a professional, a can-do type of person, and that you are fun to have around. Never underestimate the value of personal chemistry when it comes to getting work.

Sure, you can lobby against changes that you think will hurt your story, but the moment that you see a producer's jaw clench or her eyes glaze over, back off. Smile while you're doing it. Get the notes, salvage what you can, and make their changes work. (Many times, as much as it will irk you, their suggestions will actually improve your story.)

What if you are writing an outline for a spec script and don't have to impress any producers? Well, unless everything you write is always brilliant the first time out, you might consider passing it around to get feedback from friends, family, and associates in the business. (Often, the most insightful comments come from people who *aren't* in the business.) And take a second look yourself, because it is a lot easier to identify and correct story problems at this phase than when you are knee-deep in dialogue.

ADVICE FROM OUR PRODUCERS

What else should you know when writing an outline?

Matt Williams: Rarely does a writer come in and pitch an episode with an A story, a B story, a runner, and lay it all out the way the staff would. So what we usually do is, we may like one element of the story, or we may say, "You know what? This B story is wonderful. It's a brilliant B story. Let's find an A story that we can wrap around this B story." And then, usually, we'll have them go off and think about it, but rarely do we have them go off, beat out the story, and then we look at the outline and send them off to write a first draft. We almost always spend at least half a day, a day, sometimes as many as three days in the room beating out the story together. . . . Usually, to actually write an outline, we'll work with them for a half a day. Then, we'll give them two days to write the outline. Again, this will vary depending on where you are in the [television] season. At the beginning of the season, you've got the time. If we're on episode twenty, we'll say, "Bring it back tomorrow." . . .

Then, what we look for in an outline is clarity. That in every scene there is some dramatic progression to the story. That it's clear what the characters are doing and what they want. . . . In a bad outline, the characters will jump from one track to another to another to accommodate the story. "I don't understand. At the beginning of the episode, he wanted to rob a bank. How come he's buying a used car? And then he's picking up a lost puppy?" . . .

In a good outline, your character will drive the story. . . .

Nine times out of ten, you get to that two-thirds mark in an outline, that sweep up to that final turning point, and that's when most outlines will fall apart, because the writer doesn't really know where they're going. They know how to set it up. They know how to complicate things. And then they get two-thirds of the way there, and they kind of peter out, and go, "Oh, I'm not sure what this episode's about or where I'm going."

Maxine Lapiduss: Generally, for that first assignment, [a freelancer's story outline] is going to be pitched out to within an inch of its life. I mean, it's got to fit into a slot between episodes five and eight, so certain things are going to have to be accomplished [in that story]. . . . We'll say, "Okay, the germ of this idea is great. We want to do this episode, and this is how we think it should go." And then the writer will go off and work on that, and come back to us with another pitch—a full-blown pitch—which would constitute the story meeting. And then we would take maybe a day or two or three, to really beat out the story [with that writer], beat by beat.

Irma Kalish: You don't want to put too much dialogue or too many jokes into the outline because by the time the producer reads the first draft, he'll be saying, "I know I've heard this joke before. This must be an old joke." So you can put a little touch here and there just to make sure that the producer knows that you can do comedy. But don't put all the jokes in.

Sandy Frank: When something happens with a character, what is his emotional reaction? You should probably even put that into your outline. He's scared. He's upset. He's annoyed. He decides he wants revenge, whatever. Because, otherwise, what happens a lot is that you force the characters to do things that don't come naturally.

Ian Gurvitz: If they pitch you a story that you really like, or some combination of your ideas and their ideas turns into a story, you talk about it for a few hours and then at some point, maybe because of time restrictions, you say, "Do you think you have enough to just bang out an outline?" And usually the person says, "Yeah. Let me go with it." (Secretly you're hoping they say yes, because you're sick of talking about it and have other work to do.) . . .

If you sit with a writer all day and you break the story, the outline you get back better reflect exactly what was said in the room. If they've added their own jokes to it or if they say, "You know, we talked about such-and-such this way, but it doesn't really seem to work. What about if we go another way," that's fine. . . .

If you short-shrift the story process you're going to be in for late hours and a nightmare production week when that story falls apart.

A SAMPLE OUTLINE FROM *HOME IMPROVEMENT*

To illustrate the points covered in this chapter, here is a copy of a story outline developed for the hit series *Home Improvement*. The episode "Nothing More Than Feelings" was written by a talented writer named Peter Tolan, whose many credits include *Murphy Brown*, *The Larry Sanders Show*, *Ellen*, *Style*

& Substance, and several series pilots. Permission to reprint this document was generously granted by writer-producer Matt Williams, a principal partner in the Wind Dancer Production Group.

Note that the following outline differs slightly from the generic format described above. For one thing, this outline is much longer than the recommended length of four to six pages. Why? Because this version includes lots of dialogue that was probably generated when the writer sat down with the staff to refine the story. While it is useful for us to see these lines, *do not include this much dialogue in your initial outline*. Follow the guidelines presented in this chapter.

Another difference in the following outline is that the scene headings are indented, and they include several elements (scene numbers, numbered days, and the names of characters appearing in the scene) that are not always included in an outline. Was the writer wrong, or sloppy, to include this material? No. His format reflected the preference of his producers, which always take precedence when writing an outline or script.

HOME IMPROVEMENT, "Nothing More Than Feelings"

Story Outline by Peter Tolan

ACT ONE

Scene One, Int. Kitchen/Living Room—Morning
(Day 1)
(Tim, Jill, Randy, Brad, Mark)

Typical morning, the boys are eating breakfast, Jill is shuttling dishes and food back and forth. Brad and Mark are engaged in verbal warfare, Jill notices that Randy is kind of quiet. She asks if he's feeling okay, he says he's fine. Tim enters and tries to figure out what he'll have for breakfast. He asks Jill what her day is going to be like. She rattles off a list of errands, including a visit to Lloyd's Service Station. Tim asks what's wrong with her car and she says it's nothing big, just some light on the

dashboard that keeps going off. Tim tenses and tells
Jill that little lights on the dashboard usually go
off for a reason. He presses for more information,
getting more and more bugged as Jill, completely
unconcerned, answers his questions. The oil light
has been on for about two weeks it turns out. Tim hits
the roof.

TIM: You don't drive around with the oil light
            on!

JILL: You're right. It's very distracting.

TIM: The whole engine could have seized up and
            fallen out. Why do you think the light's
            there in the first place? It's a warning.

JILL: Well, I thought if it was something really
            serious, the light would have gotten
            brighter. Or maybe there'd be a buzzing
            sound.

TIM: A buzzer? It's a car, Jill, not a game show.
            Was Bob Barker supposed to pop out of the
            trunk and tell you to get oil?

Jill continues to take the whole oil thing very
lightly, which only serves to drive Tim crazier. His
breakfast ruined, he goes out into the garage to
inspect the damage to the car. Brad and Mark go up to
brush their teeth and get ready for school, Randy
lingers at the table. Jill senses he has something on
his mind and she sits with him. After dismissing his
concerns as stupid, Randy tells Jill that he saw a
film at school about the environment and that he's
kind of worried about the future. Will there be
enough clean water, will there be fresh air? After
carefully drawing this information out of Randy,
Jill tells him that she shares his concerns. She
assures him that his questioning is the first step
toward making things better, and she tells him that
she's proud of him for worrying about something

other than where he put his sneakers or if they're
having fish for dinner. Jill reminds him that he can
come to either of his parents whenever he's
concerned. Randy says he didn't want to talk to Tim
about this problem for fear his father would think he
was weird. Jill tells him that his father is actually
a pretty good person to talk to about serious things.

JILL: Your dad can be pretty understanding at
           times.

Tim enters from the garage, his shirt covered in oil.
He carries an oil filter in his hands. He is so peeved
he can barely speak. He takes a few steps into the
kitchen and shakes the oil filter at Jill, choking out
a few words at a time in total frustration. He exits
back into the garage.

JILL: Of course you've got to pick those times
           very carefully.

<u>Scene Two, Int. Tool Time—Several Hours Later
(Day 1)</u>
(Tim, Al, Jim, Kyle, Vance)

Tim and Al are in the middle of welding a joint on
some pipe. Tim turns off the torch and lifts the
visor on his mask.

TIM: It's no good, Al.

AL: It looks fine, Tim. The seal is nearly
           complete. . . .

TIM: I'm not talking about the pipe, Al. It's no
           good. I can't weld when I've got a bug up my
           butt.

Tim tells everyone that they'll get back to the
welding, but first he has to get something off his
chest. He fondles the torch in his hands, admiring

its power and simple beauty. A sermonette on the
respect a man must have for his tools leads Tim
directly into recounting the story of Jill and the
oil light. Totally bent out of shape, he turns to his
audience and asks them if they know what he's talking
about. A guy in the crowd speaks up and Tim calls him
down to the stage.

TIM: What's your name?

JIM: Jim. My friends call me Jimbo.

TIM: I'm Tim. You can call me Timbo. You have
          something to say, Jimbo?

JIM: I'm a woodworker. I do a lot of carving and
          I just bought a serious set of chisels.

TIM: Bearing the Binford name?

JIM: Of course.

TIM: You're beautiful. Continue.

JIM: I bought these chisels . . . they were
          magical. And then, the other day, I come
          home and there's my wife, out in the
          garage. . . .

TIM: Be strong, Jimbo.

JIM: Prying the lid off a gallon of paint with my
          three-eighths-inch skew chisel.

(A gasp from the crowd)

TIM: Unbelievable.

JIM: And then, to make matters worse, after I
          got all upset at her, she looked at me and
          said, "So what? It's only a screwdriver."

TIM: And they wonder why we die first.

A spontaneous male forum breaks out. A fat guy named Kyle gets up and complains that his wife uses his gardening tools then leaves them out in the yard to rust. Another guy named Vance complains about all the bottles in his shower at home.

VANCE: She's got conditioners and shampoos and all kinds of voodoo potions. I've got one bottle, that's all. And my hair looks pretty damn good, doesn't it?

The crowd roars its approval. Caught up in the moment, Tim chuckles as he remembers an obscure little fact about Jill.

TIM: It's actually pretty cute. My wife drools in her sleep. Now, I'm not talking about a little spitter out the corner of the mouth. I'm talking "man the lifeboats" time. I'm talking hook up the hose, we'll water the lawn.

The crowd is loving this. Al, who's been doing his best to get Tim back to the welding job at hand during all this, finally gets Tim's attention. Tim wonders why Al isn't getting in on the discussion and asks him if there's a woman in his life. Al responds in the negative (a little foreshadowing here, folks) and Tim mocks him (gently). Something along the lines of 'Maybe when you finally get a girl, you'll know what we're talking about here.' Tim and Al go back to welding.

Scene Three, Int. Living Room—That Afternoon (Day 1)
(Jill, Brad, Randy, Mark, Tim)

The boys are running around playing some strange and violent game. Jill is dusting and tells them to settle so the dust will. She suggests they watch Tim's show . . . which they join in progress. When

they turn the set on, they see Vance talking about
his wife's shampoos. There is some confusion, they
don't know who this guy is, but then they see Tim.
Jill shakes her head in amazement.

JILL: I guess your father's become the Phil
          Donahue of the hardware set.

Jill continues to dust, then freezes when Tim starts
talking about this "cute" thing his wife does when
she's asleep. Shock turns to horror as Tim details
the drool situation. Jill snaps the television off.
The boys want to keep watching, but Jill suggests
they go out and play. Brad continues to protest until
Randy takes him by the arm.

RANDY: Better do what she says. She might drool on
          you.

Jill chases the boys out. Mark stops at the door with
a helpful suggestion.

MARK: I think you should sleep on your stomach,
          Mommy. I don't want you to drown.

Jill thanks him and he goes. The phone rings and Jill
answers it.

JILL: Hi, Linda. How are you? Oh . . . you saw
          the show. Well, yes . . . but it's not as
          bad as he painted it. He was exaggerating,
          Linda. It's not that funny.

Tim enters and Jill gets off the phone. She plays it
very coolly. Tim gives her a peck on the cheek and
looks through the mail. Jill asks him about his day.
He says it was fine. She asks about the show. He says
it was fine. She gently presses him, a great firestorm
building within her. He senses something is wrong.
He knows he's done something. Now, what can it be?

TIM: I left the seat up again?

JILL: No.

TIM: Put a wet towel in the hamper?

JILL: No.

TIM: I give up.

JILL: (Exploding) Drool, Tim! Drool! How could
            you, Tim? How could you tell everyone in
            America I drool in my sleep?

TIM: Everyone in America? Honey, I'm only
            carried by four cable systems. Probably
            nobody saw it.

JILL: I saw it. The boys saw it. Linda Weller down
            at the pharmacy saw it. She just called and
            asked if I needed a bucket.

TIM: Didn't I say it was a cute thing?

JILL: That doesn't matter. How would you like it
            if I told everyone in the metropolitan area
            about you and your toenails?

TIM: That's totally different from drooling.

JILL: You chew your toenail clippings, Tim.
            That's disgusting.

TIM: Why? Everybody chews their fingernails, why
            pass on the toenails? They happen to be the
            most flavorful nail, you know.

JILL: It's grotesque. You clip, clip, clip and
            chew, chew, chew, then spit them out on the
            bathroom floor. It makes me want to throw
            up. Of course, I can't throw up. My mouth is
            too busy drooling! At least I have an
            excuse. I'm asleep when I'm disgusting.

At this point, Jill starts to cry. Tim reacts in typical male fashion by doing everything he can to stop the flow of tears. Eventually he hugs Jill close and she cries on his shoulder. The boys enter. Tim explains that Mom's just a little upset. When Jill pulls away from Tim's shoulder, they see that his shirt is all wet.

BRAD: Dad, she drooled on you!

This sets Jill off again and she runs up the stairs. Tim looks at the boys.

TIM: Well, it looks like I'll be fixing dinner
          . . . for the rest of our lives.

          END OF ACT ONE

          ACT TWO

          Scene One, Int. Kitchen—Afternoon the Next Day
          (Day 2)
          (Tim, Jill)

Jill is on the phone with a friend. Tim is washing engine parts in the kitchen sink. Whenever he walks into the kitchen from the garage, Jill's phone conversation hushes mysteriously. He notices this and tries to catch her several times, popping in and out of the door unexpectedly. Jill finally hangs up, telling her friend that "she can't talk right now." Tim wants to know if she was talking about him. Jill ignores him and asks why he's fooling around with the car. She tells him to take it down to Lloyd's, but Tim refuses. He can save time and money if he does that

job himself. And besides, he's fixing her car as kind
of a peace offering. Tim asks Jill if she's still
upset. She tells him she was upset, she cried, she
got over it. She really wants to know why he had those
other men up talking on "Tool Time." Tim explains
that this male forum just happened and it was very
important. It was a chance for men to communicate.

JILL: All I heard was shampoo and drool. That's
          important?

TIM: We shared stuff. Thoughts. Feelings.

JILL: Oh, give me a break, Tim. That wasn't about
          sharing. That was swapping stories about
          the wives. There were no feelings there.

TIM: You weren't there.

JILL: Believe me, I feel like I was there. You
          can't honestly say you talked about how you
          felt. Men don't talk about feelings. They
          trade information. Feelings are those
          things you bottle up and soon they turn
          into a tumor.

TIM: You don't know what you're talking about.

Jill goes on to prove her point by telling Tim she was
just on the phone with Meg Harris. She considers Meg
and her husband, Jack, good friends. Tim agrees.
Jill talks to Meg once every two weeks. How often
does Tim talk to Jack? After protesting that they
talk just as often as the women do, Tim settles by
answering "Once a season." Jill knows what Meg is up
to, Tim has a vague idea of what Jack is doing. Jill
knows how Meg is feeling, Tim assumes that Jack
probably feels "like a man." Jill tells Tim that
Jack has just returned from a detox center in
Minnesota. He's a recovering alcoholic. Tim is
dumbfounded, then amazed that Meg would volunteer
this information.

```
TIM:       How can she tell you that? Being a drunk is
           a very private thing.
```

Jill tells Tim to drop it. Men don't share
intimacies, that's just the way it is. She tells him
about Randy's concern about the environment. Tim
wants to know why he didn't come to him. She tells him
that Randy thought he'd think he was weird. Tim
promises to talk to his son, telling Jill that he can
share feelings with the best of them. Jill points
into the sink.

```
JILL:      Tim, why don't you take the car to Lloyd's
           before you do some real damage?

TIM:       Honey, I know exactly what I'm doing.

JILL:      You know exactly what you're doing?

TIM:       Yes.
```

Jill lifts the rim of several plastic Tupperware
bowls out of the sink.

```
JILL:      You don't put kerosene in Tupperware.

TIM:       Okay, *now* I know exactly what I'm doing.
```

Tim takes the remains of the bowls and heads for the
backyard to toss them into the trash.

Scene Two, Ext. Backyard—Continuous
(Tim, Wilson, Randy)

Tim drops the Tupperware into the trash and hears
Wilson on the other side of the fence. Wilson is in
the middle of fixing a large bass drum (historical
significance to come). Tim wants to know if he and
Wilson share feelings. When Wilson asks why, Tim
tells him about Jill's charge that men don't share
feelings. Wilson backs her up and (straight

out of Tannen) explains that women's conversation is based on connection and intimacy, while men's is based on status and power. Tim doesn't understand. Wilson tells him that, for example, by giving him information he didn't previously know, he (Wilson) is coming from a position of power, while Tim is in the weaker position.

TIM: Well, I don't know if that's true. . . .

WILSON: You see? By saying that, you're trying to negate my authority, thereby returning an equal balance to our relationship.

This conversation continues. Everything that Tim says is interpreted by Wilson in terms of their interpersonal balance of power. Finally, Tim tells Wilson that this power thing doesn't have to get in the way between them. Tim admits that he comes to Wilson with problems a lot, but if Wilson ever has anything he wants to talk about, Tim tells him to feel free. As a matter of fact, there has been something on Wilson's mind. Wilson opens up and expresses a concern about his place in the grand scheme of things. Not a great worry, but an unsettling doubt that's been lingering. Wilson asks Tim if he ever feels that way. Confused, Tim offers to get back to Wilson real soon. Wilson thanks him as Randy comes into the yard. Tim takes him aside and as gently as he knows how, tells him if he ever has a problem, he should come to his old man. Randy says okay, and heads for the house. Tim pulls him back and asks if there's anything on his mind. Randy tells him there isn't. Tim asks him about his environmental concerns. Randy is unhappy that his mother has spilled the beans.

TIM: It's okay, son. Your mom and I were just talking and it came out. There's nothing wrong with that. Everything should be out in the open. Just don't tell your mom that I told you that she told me. That's our secret.

Tim does his best to respond to Randy's concerns, but
he takes a man's approach to the problem. Instead of
connecting with Randy, he tells him not to worry
about it.

TIM: That whole environment thing . . . you
            don't have to worry about it. Somebody
            somewhere is working on that as we speak.

RANDY: I just worry . . .

TIM: Well, you shouldn't. Okay?

RANDY: Okay.

TIM: Great. Shake it off, big guy.

Randy exits into the house.

TIM: Feels good.

   Scene Three, Int. *Tool Time*—The Next Day (Day 3)
   (Tim, Al, John, William, Chet)

Tim welcomes the audience back to *Tool Time*, and we
see three or four men sitting in chairs in a
semicircle on the stage floor. Tim incorporates what
he heard from Wilson and the great feeling he got
from talking to Randy into an enthusiastic pitch
about men sharing more than information. It's
time to prove the skeptics wrong. Men can share
feelings . . . if they want to. Tim has chosen some
regular guys from the audience. He turns to John, an
older man, and asks him how he feels.

JOHN: Hungry.

TIM: Okay . . . that's a feeling. Go with that.

JOHN: Really hungry. And thirsty. These lights
            are hot. You got anything to drink?

Tim turns to William, a great big guy in a flannel
shirt.

TIM: How about you, William? How are you
           feeling?

WILLIAM: Well, I was fine until this guy said he was
           hungry. Now I'm hungry. And that makes me
           angry.

TIM: Why?

WILLIAM: I'm hungry, I can't eat. My doctor said I
           can't have pork, it's too fatty. I used to
           grill up a big old tenderloin. . . .

JOHN: Sounds great.

WILLIAM: Now I can't have pork. What the hell is
           that? I had the bypass, why can't I have
           pork?

TIM: Okay, let's try and stay away from the meat
           products. You know, women are always saying
           that men don't cry. Women cry all the time.
           My wife's a regular waterworks.

WILLIAM: Yeah, we saw the show the other day. (To
           Chet) His wife's a drooler.

TIM: How about you guys? When was the last time
           you cried, Chet?

CHET: What do you mean? You mean cried cried, or
           cried because something heavy fell on top
           of you? One time the refrigerator tipped
           over, wham down on my left foot . . .

TIM: Let's talk about cried cried. When was the
           last time?

CHET: Pass.

TIM: William?

WILLIAM: Boy, that's a tough one. Come back to me.

TIM: Right. John?

JOHN: I'm gonna cry real soon if I don't get
          something to eat.

TIM: Guys, come on . . . don't let me down. I'm
          looking for one emotional experience.

WILLIAM: Okay. How about when the Mets won the
          pennant? That was something.

The men immediately begin talking all at once,
excitedly swapping stories about that series. Tim
quiets them and Al begins to speak. He talks about
not being in a relationship, something he's been
thinking about since Tim brought it up the other day.
He's lonely . . . and concerned that other men see
him as a loser . . . and he starts to cry softly,
turning his back to the crowd. The other men freeze
in embarrassment.

CHET: I'm going back to my seat.

The other men follow him. Tim does his best to
comfort Al, but his best is several levels below
inadequate. Tim turns back to the audience and tells
them that they'll get back to today's project. Tim
asks Al if he'll be able to go on. Al sniffles bravely
and nods his head in agreement.

Scene Four, Int. Kitchen—Early Evening (Day 3)
(Tim, Jill, Randy, Brad, Mark)

It's after dinner, and Tim's taking everyone out for
ice cream cones. They head for the garage. Tim stops
Randy and gives him a paper bag with a small book

inside. He mumbles that it's something they might
want to read together. Randy looks inside the bag and
smiles, a little embarrassed but grateful. Jill asks
Tim what it was. Just a book . . . *100 Things You Can
Do to Help Mother Earth*. Jill realizes that men and
women communicate differently . . . but there's
hope. They head out to the garage. We hear car doors
close. The engine starts . . . then we hear a loud
bang . . . and then silence. Jill and Tim enter. She
wants to know what that big thing on the garage floor
is. He tells her it's the engine. Tim guesses he
didn't tighten a few bolts . . . a few critical
ones. Jill presses him as to why he didn't take the
car to Lloyd's, and after coming up with a litany of
excuses, he admits that he didn't want Lloyd to think
he couldn't take care of his own car. He admits that
this is stupid . . . and that it's going to cost him
a lot of money . . . but he didn't want to look weak
in front of Lloyd. Lloyd will talk and soon Tim will
be a laughingstock. (I have no idea where this goes
from here.)

END OF ACT TWO

TAG

Int. Garage—The Next Day (Day 4)
(Tim, Jill, Lloyd)

Lloyd surveys the damage as Tim explains. Lloyd
wants to know what went wrong. Jill jumps in and
covers for her man, explaining that she ignored the
oil light and it's all her fault. No, Tim wants the
truth to be told. He tells Lloyd that he was afraid
that if he didn't fix his own car, Lloyd would think

less of him. Tim tells him he can laugh if he wants,
but that's the truth. Lloyd is understanding and
tells Tim that it takes a real man to admit that he's
gone and done something he shouldn't have. Tim is
relieved and Lloyd heads off to confer with the tow
truck operator.

LLOYD: Taylor took his engine out and forgot to
          bolt it back in!

And as the two men laugh, we fade out.

<u>END OF SHOW</u>

ABOUT THIS OUTLINE

The writer, Peter Tolan, knows his stuff. The story lines develop nicely
and are true to the series premise. The writing style is tight and entertaining.
The dialogue is funny and true to the show's characters. (Though again, remember: You should include very little dialogue in an *initial* outline.)

If you have half an hour to invest in an exercise, I have a suggestion.
Examine the above outline in terms of the elements discussed in the last two
chapters. Your time will be well spent.

Eleven

Writing the First Draft

Once your outline is done, and redone, congratulations—you are finally ready to tackle that first draft. If you are working on an actual assignment, your producers will usually give you one to two weeks for this step. That's seven to fourteen days to write about fifty pages (if writing in tape format) of quality prime-time television. Where do you start?

JUST DO IT

Start writing. You have done all of the prep work. Now let the creative half of your brain cut loose and crank out a rough draft. Naturally, you should consult your outline regarding story development and scene structure. And you can use the same page layout that you saw when you studied scripts from the show. Just mark this page of the book and set it aside, turn off the editor in your head, and come back with fifty (tape format) pages. Then use the information in this chapter, and the script format guidelines in appendix A, to clean up your rough draft.

You don't feel ready to dive in just yet? That is fine too. This a creative process and we all create differently. If you prefer, read the rest of this chapter first and then tackle your script.

What if, halfway through the first draft, you come up with a new story direction or some different scenes that would greatly improve the script? If you are writing a spec script, then great, run with it. The Sitcom Police won't arrest you if you stray from your original outline. However, if you are writing a script on assignment, check with your producers before you make any radical changes; they don't usually like to receive huge surprises when reading a first draft.

If you do decide to make big changes halfway through a draft, my only advice is that you should take the time to sort out your new story beats before plunging ahead. Otherwise you might wreak havoc on your episode's structure.

WRITING SCENES

Here are some thoughts to consider when writing the scenes of your script. Linda Seger, in her book *Making a Good Script Great*, makes the following points:

> Through the use of images and dialogue, a great scene advances the story, reveals character, explores an idea, and builds an image. A great scene will do all of these. A good scene will do more than one. . . . Film is dimensional. A scene can accomplish many purposes, all at the same time. The background might be showing an image. The actions might reveal character. A piece of dialogue might advance the story. And the combination of all of these can explore the theme.[38]

> **Maxine Lapiduss:** You sometimes only have four or five days to write a first draft. Now, my sister, who's a comedy writer too, once worked on a show with a gentleman named Robert Blair. And so he, we, have something that we call the "Blair System." The first day, when I'm sitting down and I have to get the script out, rather than craft the first page, and make sure that the descriptions are perfect, and that there are five really sharp jokes on that page—now, I "Blair" through the script. I try to write two to three scenes, a whole first act, the first day. Because it's much easier to go back and rewrite later. It's not just a blank page.

While not all scenes can accomplish all of the above goals, each scene should be unique and have purpose. Being funny, by itself, is not enough. Here are some other thoughts to consider when writing scenes:

FIRST SCENES ARE CRITICAL

Agents, writers, producers, and executives are busy people. If your first few scenes are weak (i.e., slow, not funny, clichéd), none of these folks will keep reading long enough to discover that "the story really picks up in the second act." By then, the script will have been tossed onto the "don't call us, we'll never call you" pile.

Avoid this by grabbing your reader immediately—in the first few pages. How? By opening with a neat story hook and fresh humor. Remember, sitcom scripts average two to three solid jokes per page, starting with the *first* page.

SCENE LENGTH

Sitcom scenes can range in length from an eighth of a page to five or more pages. Follow whatever patterns or trends are used by the show you are writing for. (You probably noticed such patterns when you first studied the series.) While there are no formal rules regarding lengths of scenes, most probably run two to four pages (when writing in film format). Longer scenes are fine, but once you go beyond five pages, you might want to consider how that scene affects the overall pacing of your script.

START LATE, FINISH EARLY

Today's audiences are so sophisticated, having watched thousands of hours of television and film, that they require very little orientation when viewing a program. Open a scene with two characters in the middle of a raging argument and viewers will catch right on—they don't need to start out by seeing two minutes of a conversation turning hostile. If you start a scene too early, it will seem drawn out and dull. Start a scene as late as you can, and it will open with momentum and sweep the viewer right along with the story.

Similarly, once a scene is done, once the story points have been covered, end it. Allow its momentum to carry us into the next scene. Don't linger to rehash an issue or squeeze in extra jokes.

> **NOTE:** *For some great examples of how little scene information an audience requires, rent a copy of* Pulp Fiction. *The Oscar-winning screenplay for this film required the audience to fill in numerous blanks concerning everything from locations to character back-stories.*

How do you judge too early versus too late? Use the old exposition test— "Does the audience *really* need to know this stuff? And does it need to know it *now?*"

Any exceptions to this start-late-finish-early maxim? Of course. You might deliberately prolong a segment to establish a particular mood (e.g., young lovers struggling through a first dinner date). Or to build dramatic tension (e.g., young lovers struggling through a first dinner date, at *her folks' house*). Sometimes a more languorous approach is just the ticket, though you are more likely to see it used in straight drama than in modern, keep-it-moving sitcomedy.

CHARACTER ENTRANCES AND EXITS

How many times have you seen this: One character says his good-byes and exits a scene, just as another character oh-so-conveniently enters through a second door to pick up the conversation. The obviousness of this maneuver reminds viewers that they are watching a staged (poorly staged, in fact) show.

Characters should have a good reason to enter or exit a scene. If you will need them later but want to avoid an awkward entrance, give them a good reason to be present at the beginning of the scene and then engage them when the time is right.

END WITH A BUTTON

A *button* is a clever line or small dramatic twist located at the very end of a scene. It is sometimes used to provide a touch of closure before moving on to the next story segment. Buttons can range in weight from a simple punch line for a joke to a minor revelation that affects the story.

Buttons are clever, compact things—a big story beat that ends a scene is not the same animal. While most writers always aspire to be clever (and compact), it is not always possible or desirable to end scenes with a button. Sometimes it is better to close with a big story beat, a cliff-hanger, a note of mystery, a quiet moment, or a simple reaction line.

USING A MONTAGE SEQUENCE

A *montage* is a string of very short scenes—three, five, or more—that provides a quick view of someone going through a sequence of steps. In sitcoms, you might see a montage of *Drew Carey* stumbling through an exercise program, or *Friends*'s Joey blowing a series of acting auditions, or *3rd Rock*'s Sally being brainwashed by an alien race of supermodels. While a writer shouldn't overuse this device, it can be a remarkable tool for compressing time and actions. Most montage sequences incorporate very little, if any, dialogue, and all (sitcom versions) feature a healthy dose of visual humor. One or two montage sequences in a script are fine, but it might seem distracting—unless you are intentionally repeating a funny pattern—to incorporate more. (Details regarding the page layout of a montage sequence are provided in appendix A.)

PACING OF SCENES

If you have developed a well-structured story and kept your scenes lean and mean, you should be in pretty good shape regarding the pacing of your script. Otherwise it's a matter of just going with what feels right. Sometimes you will want to trim here or indulge in a moment there. As long as you give preference to decisions that serve the overall script rather than those that favor merely one scene, you will probably do just fine.

Don't Overdo Visual Humor in a Spec

I believe that it is a mistake to base too much of a spec script's comedy on *visual* humor. Many writers would disagree with me, but my reasoning is this: Visual humor is meant to be seen, right? Producers and execs giving your spec script a ten-minute read are more likely to catch dialogue jokes than funny imagery crammed into a scene description. In my experience, a surprising number of "pros" aren't even able to appreciate visual jokes (in a script) because they just don't have an aptitude for translating written type into images. (This is not a dig, just a different-people-have-different-strengths thing.) So unless a series revolves around physical gags, I advise against writing a spec script that relies too heavily on visual humor. Once you get the job and have more leeway, you can go wild with the pratfalls.

HARVESTING COMEDY BUILT INTO THE PREMISE AND SCENE LEVELS

Guess what—you've already done the hard part. You have created a funny story, composed of funny scenes, and you have studied the art of writing seamless jokes. The humor is all there—just write the words. And have fun. This phase of the job is the reason people get into sitcom writing.

What if you hit a bump and the jokes just aren't coming? Flip back to chapter 6, ". . . Comedy in Dialogue and Actions," for a quick review, and see if that gets you going. Also, think back to the elements that made the episode premise seem funny to you in the first place.

PROFESSIONAL SCRIPT FORMAT

For details of how a professional script looks on paper, turn to appendix A, where you will find instructions for writing in three different styles, tape format, film format, and animation format. (You should know, from your earlier research, which style your show uses.)

Please understand that script format is very important. If your script doesn't look just like a professional's, the reader will be reminded, on every page, that you are not a professional. Who wants that? Sure, once you have racked up a few Emmys and are producing your own show, you can get creative. But until then, why take the risk?

For now, all that you need to know about format is that live-action sitcom scripts are about thirty pages long if written in film format, and forty-five to fifty pages long if written in (the more loosely spaced) tape format. Animation scripts for shows like *King of the Hill* are written in sort of a mix of the two formats, and usually run forty to fifty pages.

Whichever format is used, the two primary elements that appear on a script page are scene descriptions and character dialogue, as described below.

WRITING SCENE DESCRIPTIONS

Scene descriptions are very brief paragraphs that depict the setting of a scene. They describe the physical layout of the space, the characters who are present, and any important actions that occur. While scene descriptions found in movie scripts are often lengthy and dramatic, those featured in sitcom scripts tend to be short and sweet. They frequently consist of no more than a single line like "Raymond enters and plops down on the couch." Why the minimalist approach? Most of a sitcom's scenes take place in a finite number of familiar sets and involve limited doses of physical action, so there is little need for elaborate descriptions. (And, of course, viewers at home will never read or hear a script's scene descriptions.)

Scene descriptions are usually found immediately following each scene heading in a script, because readers need at least some information about the setting of the coming scene. Additional descriptions are inserted between dialogue segments whenever the story requires them—a new character enters the room, the phone rings, two characters start wrestling, smoke pours out of the oven, etc.

Here are a few stylistic points to consider when writing scene descriptions (you will remember some of these from our discussion regarding story outlines):

WRITE SCENE DESCRIPTIONS IN THE PRESENT TENSE

. . . for the same reasons previously mentioned.

PAINT THE PICTURE

Though scene descriptions are supposed to be brief and functional, they should not be boring. When appropriate, use active verbs and specific details to describe the action in a scene.

AVOID USING THE ROYAL "WE"

. . . for the same reasons previously mentioned.

GRAMMAR AND PUNCTUATION

Use proper grammar and punctuation in your scene descriptions unless you are deliberately writing in a loose conversational style. Which approach is better? Both work. But if your attempts at conversational prose occasionally seem stilted or forced, because you haven't yet found that "voice" in your writing, stick with the more formal approach. Plenty of pros do, and it is better to be safe than awkward. (Naturally, dialogue should be written in a conversational style—make that a variety of conversational styles—because each character speaks in a unique voice.)

NO CAMERA DIRECTIONS

Unless you *absolutely must* indicate camera angles in order to describe a joke or moment, do not include them in your script. A good writer can accomplish the same goal by directing the reader's attention through artful scene descriptions. If you want a close-up to show Joey's surprised face when he opens that door, write "Joey's eyes bug out" when you describe his reaction. The reader will picture Joey's face *in close-up*. Mission accomplished, without camera angles.

CHOREOGRAPHING BIG ACTION SCENES

As with camera directions, it is not your job to choreograph every little detail of a big action scene. Just launch us into the food fight or the mud-wrestling match, describe the key moments, and tell us how the scene comes out. Trust the director and his actors to connect the dots, or you will end up with a thirty-second scene that takes up three pages of your script.

NO MAPS, PICTURES, OR BLUEPRINTS

Do not draw on your script. If you can't describe the essence of a location or an action via a scene description, it's time to find a new career.

INDICATING A PAUSE

There will be many times when you will want to indicate a brief pause in a scene. Perhaps you want to suggest an awkward moment between characters, or that a character is taking a beat to react to something that another has said or done. Or perhaps you just want to leave a little breathing room after a punch line. To indicate such a pause, simply type either [Pause.] or [Beat.] as a line in the scene description. (In fact, that one-word sentence, by itself, often serves as the *entire* scene description.) Then resume the action or dialogue.

> **NOTE:** *Obviously, this new meaning of the word* beat—*as in, "she takes a beat to respond"—is not to be confused with a* story beat.

INDICATING A REACTION

There will be times when you will want to indicate that a character gives just the reaction that one would expect—she looks stunned, frustrated, dismayed, whatever. But said reaction seems so obvious that it would be lame to actually describe the thing. To indicate that the (obvious) reaction does occur, simply type a line of scene description that reads [*Character's name* reacts.]. As with [Pause.] or [Beat.], this two-word sentence often serves as the entire scene description.

WRITING DIALOGUE

On paper, a character's dialogue is written as a block of sentences positioned directly beneath his name. As described more fully in appendix A, his speech might begin with or include a *dialogue cue*—a word or a couple of words that describe the character's mood or an action that he performs while speaking.

If you have studied the characters in a series and have a good ear, your dialogue should ring true. If you don't quite feel that you have captured a character's voice, you might find it useful to look at two things: speech patterns unique to that character, and ways in which that character's emotions affect his speech.

UNIQUE SPEECH PATTERNS

Everybody speaks in a unique voice. To get a handle on how a particular character talks, try looking for patterns in his . . .

Sentence structure. Does he use proper grammar, or talk in double negatives and mismatched verbs? Does he describe himself in the third person ("George is not happy!")? Does he speak in complex sentences, thick with subordinate clauses (as *Frasier* might)? Or is he a short-sentence, monosyllabic type of guy (such as *Seinfeld*'s Puddy)?

Vocabulary. Does the character use big words, small words, right words, or wrong words? (At the extreme, characters such as *Friends*'s Joey frequently get laughs by mangling words or using malapropisms.) Does the character swear or use vulgar language? Are his words appropriate for his age, education, and cultural background? (How many times have you seen a kid walk on stage and start talking like a grownup?) Does he use a unique vernacular inspired by his interests, career, or environment? (*Home Improvement*'s Tim Taylor describes many things in terms of muscle cars and power tools.) Does he concoct his own words or labels? (Many a love-struck character addresses his romantic interest by using cuddly, made-up names.)

Pronunciation. Some characters regularly mispronounce words, either because they lack a strong vocabulary (*The Simpsons*'s Homer) or English is not their native tongue (*Wings*'s Antonio). Others, such as *Murphy Brown*'s Jim Dial, are distinguished by the pains that they take to pronounce every syllable clearly. Similarly, some characters tend to use contractions ("he's," "they're," "don't," etc.) while others give each word its full due.

> **Note:** *When writing for characters that speak with an accent, avoid slowing down the read by including too many corrupted spellings in your dialogue. Just insert a funky mispronunciation every sentence or so and the reader will remember that the character talks in fractured English.*

How Emotions Affect Speech

Not only does every character speak with a unique voice but his emotions affect his speech in unique ways. Depending on the context of a particular scene, you might find it helpful to consider how your characters would act if they were . . .

Arguing. When arguing, people tend to yell, stumble over words, omit words, swear, and start slamming things. But that's the norm. How would your characters act? Do they grow quiet? Become martyrlike? Babble incoherently?

Depressed. Depressed people often become monosyllabic, speak negatively, talk in short sentences, reach for chocolate. Your characters?

Happy. Happy people tend to talk exuberantly, use glowing adjectives, view everything in a positive manner, and speak in run-on sentences.

Fearful. Frightened people tend to use short sentences, curse, exclaim, call for help or mercy, and try to bargain.

Anxious. Anxious people often chatter about their concerns, seek reassurance, focus on negative consequences, and overanalyze comments made by others.

Other emotional dynamics that affect speech include a desire to seduce, placate, manipulate, impress, terrorize, and so on. An artfully honed character will act differently in each circumstance, and his speech will be affected accordingly.

COMEDIC NUANCES

One thing that every writer wants to hear a producer say is "You really nailed the characters' voices." Part of the trick to achieving that feat is to develop a feel for the little comedic nuances that distinguish a particular character's dialogue. Here are just a few examples of the *many* little quirks that might shape a character's voice:

Nervous babbling. When the going got rough, *Ellen* got babbling. Rather than beating a hasty retreat, as most people would, her character generated laughs by going into dialogue overdrive. This amusing trait was also shared by several of Mary Tyler Moore's sitcom characters.

The understated response. As long as we're flashing back, think Bob Newhart, king of the low-key response. The house could be burning, thugs threatening, the sky falling, but characters like Bob (and *Drew*, and *Seinfeld*'s Puddy) meet every event with the same understated response. Their incongruous reactions almost guarantee a laugh.

Exaggerated response. Think characters like *Seinfeld*'s Kramer or *Ellen*'s friend Barrett. Outrageous, flamboyant, sometimes a touch wacko, these types generate laughs by overreacting to even the most ordinary of events. (Another incongruous response.)

Answers questions with questions. Some characters get an occasional laugh by trying to deflect an angry question with a question. Example: *Mad About You*'s Jamie discovers that she is being blamed for something, she asks husband Paul if he is the guilty party, and Paul responds with "Was that bad, was that a bad thing to do?"

Spaceshot POV. Some characters see the universe from such a different point of view that their comments and responses frequently consist of twisted but funny logic. Their words make sense, but only if you live in a different dimension. Half of the lines spoken by *Friends*'s Phoebe fall into this category.

Irony. Some characters love to play the caustic commentator or misunderstood martyr. Their speeches often feature dry irony, which Webster's defines as the "use of words to convey a meaning that is the opposite of its literal meaning." Think *Caroline in the City*'s Richard, reacting after accidently being hit with spaghetti: "Don't apologize. It's not like I can't just buy another silk tie . . . handwoven by blind monks . . . blessed by Mother Teresa."

Wordplay. Jerry Seinfeld is an example of a performer who can get a string of laughs just by juggling a word, or several words, for an entire speech. Wordplay involves repetition, juxtaposition, and playing off different meanings of a word. For instance:

> How do they do it? How? Do they know people I don't know? Or do I know
> the people they know, but I don't know it . . . because I know the right people,
> but those people are holding out on me. I don't know![39]

Double entendre. Some characters are always on the make. Their own speeches frequently feature a sexual connotation and they often interpret other characters' lines as having a second, risqué meaning.

Catch phrases. Some characters are distinguished by their fondness for catch phrases, phrases that generate laughs every time the character misuses or over-uses them. On *Seinfeld*, this idea was carried to an extreme; entire story lines were launched by simple phrases such as "to get hand," "master of my do-main," and "close-talkers."

Again, these are just a few of the many ways that a character's dialogue might be distinguished by comedic nuances. Obviously, the best way to de-velop a feel for an existing character's voice is to watch episodes and read scripts from his show.

MISCELLANEOUS TIPS

Here are a few more points to consider when writing dialogue:

SPEECH LENGTH

The average character's speech—in a sitcom, not Shakespeare—probably ranges from one to five sentences in length. If a character is lecturing, ranting, or emoting, it might go on for half of a page, maybe three-quarters of a page. If that character is still speaking after a full page, shoot him. Or at least, trim his speech, or have another character interrupt his speech with questions or comments. Though the dialogue might be enthralling, it will cause a break in pacing that will call the audience's attention to the fact that they are watching a show. (Make that a soliloquy.) Usually, the only times that such overlong speeches make it to the screen are when an Emmy-lusting star has bullied the producers into waxing dramatic, or the show is a hit and suddenly the head writer thinks that he *is* Shakespeare.

SUPERFLUOUS DIALOGUE CUES

Unskilled writers often include far too many dialogue cues in their scripts, which slows down the read. If the dialogue is good, the reader doesn't need any help in figuring out what moods the characters are experiencing when they deliver their lines. And the writer should trust the director and his actors to interpret the script; often, they will put a fresh spin on the material that gives it a whole new dimension.

OVERUSING CHARACTER NAMES IN DIALOGUE

Avoid having characters say another character's name every time they address that character. They only need to say the name once or twice early on in order for the audience to remember it. The exception is if you are writing for a character whose nature is such that she frequently addresses other people by their names when she speaks.

OFFENSIVE LANGUAGE

Adult sitcoms, particularly on nonbroadcast television, sometimes include a lot of coarse language in character dialogue. No sweat, as long as that language is true to character—witness the brilliant series *The Larry Sanders Show*. However, language and moral views *included in scene descriptions* reflect on the writer, not the characters. Unless you wish to risk offending a sensitive producer or executive—some are more conservative than you might think—you might want to keep your scene descriptions clean. (Hey, I am not your mother or the Sitcom Censor—I only mention this because I want to see you employed.)

SIGNATURE LINES

Some characters are distinguished by a signature phrase that they frequently use (e.g., Tim Taylor's "More power!" followed by barking-monkey sounds). These phrases wear thin quickly, so use them once or twice in your script, if you must, to demonstrate familiarity with the show's character, then take evasive action.

PLANTING EXPOSITION

Exposition can be defined as information that an audience needs to know in order to keep up with a story. As always, less is more—your job is to entertain, not educate. You can't go too far wrong if you remember the writer's mantra: "Does the audience *really* need to know this stuff? And does it need to know it *now*?"

When you choose to reveal exposition, it should be seamlessly integrated into your story. Avoid having a character run in to tell us about some critical event that happened elsewhere. Instead, *show us* the event—that's why we tuned in.

Hollywood screenwriting guru Robert McKee points out that exposition can sometimes be served up as a plot point, thereby performing double duty. His example, from the film *The Empire Strikes Back*: "You can't kill me, Luke. I am your father." By using a piece of exposition to drive the story forward, the writers created a very powerful moment; the audience must deal with both a huge revelation about a primary character and the impact that this news will certainly have on the rest of the film's plot.

McKee also points out that one can sometimes disguise exposition with jokes or an argument. The audience still gets the information, but is too involved in the material to notice.

Another technique deals with characters or actions that seem too incredible to believe, such as a three-year-old who knows karate or a horse that talks. A writer has a better chance of selling an outrageous idea if he has one of his characters proclaim that "That's crazy!" The fact that someone has acknowledged the outrageousness of the idea reassures viewers, helping them to maintain their suspension of disbelief. (This used to be referred to as *hanging a lantern* on an implausible piece of information.)

Similarly, an unlikely idea goes down a lot easier if you foreshadow the information. You want *Drew Carey* and his pals to suspect that a new chum might be dangerously psychotic? When you introduce the newcomer, start by creating a little mystery about his background. Then, reveal a string of increasingly ominous facts as you go, so that it later seems reasonable to accept the idea that this chum is actually a homicidal maniac. The audience will usually go along with a fantastic notion as long as you don't just spring it on them at the last moment.

Another (very important) type of exposition involves *characters expressing their emotions and beliefs*. Some writers shy away from having characters state how they feel about other characters or emotionally charged situations. True, such deeply personal dialogue can be difficult to write without getting gooey or lapsing into clichés. However, viewers want to see these moments—they represent the heart of a story's conflict. And viewers need to hear characters express their feelings in order to keep track of where the story is heading. So be bold and reveal your characters' emotions and beliefs through dialogue. As long as you keep an eye out for clichés and stay true to the characters' voices, the clarity of these statements will strengthen your story.

On a more functional level, *characters should also state their goals.* You're the writer, so you know what the character wants to accomplish. But if someone doesn't clarify those goals for the audience, your story might appear unfocused. Of course, if you can't figure out what words a character should say to describe his goal, then you have a bigger problem—your story *is* unfocused. If even you can't explain what your characters want, there is no way that an audience will be able to keep up.

ADVICE FROM OUR PRODUCERS

What are producers hoping to see in a spec script, or in the first draft of an assigned script?

Matt Williams: I look for three things. First, is the voice true to the series? In other words, are the voices those of the characters in the series? In a really good spec script, you read the first three, five pages, and you know instantly that the writer has captured the voice of the regular characters. There's a certain tone, a certain world that's established with each sitcom, and the first thing is, has the writer tapped into that world?

Secondly, I look to see if the story is moving along. For a lack of a better word, does the plot work? Sometimes what will happen is that we stop for a scene or two to do a bunch of jokes about toast or something, and you go, "This doesn't have anything to do with the story." . . . I want a story that's driven by character motivation. I want to understand why characters are doing something. I think one of the big things that happens in spec scripts is that you have characters doing incredibly wacky things, but you stop and go, "But why would they ever do that?" And the writer's answer usually is, "Well, it's funny." [Wrong answer.] You have to be real within the parameters set up in the sitcom. . . .

The third thing I look for is just—I guess the best label would be "punch." Are there any really funny, unexpected moments, situations, or lines? Anything that surprises me? Because, after you've done this for a while, you kind of know the rhythm. You know there's going to be a setup, setup, punch. You kind of know what Tim Allen is going to do. You kind of know what Roseanne's going to say and do. If you can surprise the reader—keep it within the world, keep it truthful—but surprise the reader a little bit by exposing something new, especially in the lead characters, then you've really done something. . . .

I'm less concerned about individual jokes or moments. Is the story working? Are the characters clear? Because if the structure's right and the story's working, you can rewrite every line of dialogue in four hours. . . . If you get to a Monday table reading and you're up there trying to figure out what act two is about, you're going to be there [rewriting] until four in the morning.

Maxine Lapiduss: The one thing that's very important for a comedy spec script is that it's really funny and that it really makes me laugh. Any script that comes across my desk that makes me laugh out loud more than once, I'm generally going to call that writer in for a meeting. . . . It's also important that the characters' voices are really clear and clean. If you're reading a *Seinfeld* script, the jokes should sound very different than if you're reading a *Friends* script. . . .

A lot of writers don't even do a spell check. You know, they don't even take the time to check grammar, to see if the periods are in place, the commas are in place. I think, at the very least, that a script should look like a script, be written in the correct format, and have a professional appearance. . . .

Recently, a guy sent me a bunch of spec scripts. And they were all really mediocre. And his whole thing was, "Well, I've got this and this, and if you don't like this, I've got this." [Your career] shouldn't be a car dealership. If you're going to put the time into four spec scripts, it's much smarter to take that time and put it all into one spec script, and really hone it and make it fantastic.

Irma Kalish: I would hope they would have studied the show and know that we don't have such and such characters in it because they died two years ago, or that we would never in a million years go to someone's house (because we never had before), or that we can't have twenty acts in a half hour, or seven changes of scenery and six changes of wardrobe. . . .

I always asked to see first drafts. That's where a writer's work is best represented. If you look at a produced script, you're looking at the work of a staff or a rewrite by another person who didn't get credit. You have no idea. So, you ask to see a first draft. . . .

When you turn in what's called a first draft, it should never be *your* first draft. You should always go over that first draft and do your own rewriting before you're given notes on it. Be your own worst critic. Go over it again. . . .

Sometimes you are disappointed that a writer whom you had in, because you liked the previous scripts he or she had done, does not deliver on the first draft. And you have to suspect, one, that they didn't put the time into it or, two, that they were busy doing a lot of other scripts and they just gave this one short shrift.

Lawrence Konner: If you have a pile of a hundred [spec scripts] on your desk, which you often have, there are liable to be twenty that are just clearly unprofessional. Just people who don't really have a clue. Wrong format, sloppiness . . . I mean, it seems silly, but . . . it's got to look like it's a professional script, cleanly typed and spell-checked. (I have read more than one spec script in which leading characters' names were misspelled.) And then you have probably forty or fifty scripts that feel like they've been transcribed from an already existing episode. They feel like last week's leftovers. Properly done but no spark. That makes about 70 percent. (And don't forget, these are the hundred scripts that made it in through agents or some other recommendation. These are presumably the best of what's out there.) So then, of the 30 percent that are left, these now are pretty good. These have met the first requirement, which is that they're professionally done. And they meet the second requirement, which is that they have a new idea, they feel fresh. This is the group that you look at. . . . [Out of the hundred scripts, you end up with] two or three that have an inexplicable shine. . . .

Number one, and underline this: I want the work that the writer does when they leave my office to reflect what we talked about in the office. I don't want them to go home and have a new idea. And this is a very difficult thing because often the new idea is better. Certainly the writer thinks it is better. But, generally speaking, I'd rather you call me and say, "You know, I did what we said. But it occurred to me that if we take the grandmother out of the show, it could be a lot better. Let me tell you why." That I can work with. I can look at the decision we made, which was to give this business to the grandmother, and then at your new suggestion, which is to take the grandmother out, and I can weigh it. But don't take the grandmother out without telling us. . . . [When you call to point out a problem,] the producer might say, "You're right." Or he might say, "No, you're wrong. Here's a quick, simple fix." Don't forget, he's been doing this for twenty years. . . .

And number two, which might seem like a contradictory note, I wouldn't mind being surprised a little bit in the script. No big surprises, little surprises. Little-big surprises . . .

It's not your job to change the show. It's not your job to improve the show. It's not your job to be the savior of the show. You know, "If only I was the guy in charge, boy, this would be a whole lot better." You can think that, but you can't behave as though you think that. When you're doing an episodic job, you defer to the bosses. You give them what they want and you try to make it the best you can make it even if you think the story shouldn't include the grandmother. If he said put the grandmother in, you do the best job you can of putting the grandmother in. . . .

[If you come back two weeks later with a script] that simply doesn't reflect what was discussed in the room, that's the worst sin you can commit. Because now it's useless to me. Now I have thirty pages that I can put in the shredder, and a guy whose name I'm going to cross off my list.

Sandy Frank: Most spec scripts are not very good. But most scripts are not very good. I just read about forty pilots that were produced this year. These were the produced pilots—the best, the cream of the crop. And most of them were quite dull. Some will look better when they're produced, because the actors will do something good and the sets will look nice, etc. But in general, it's very hard to write a good sitcom. . . .

If the jokes in a script actually make me laugh, that's a good thing. Because most of them are just, "Yeah, yeah. Okay, I've seen jokes like that before. Okay, that one, that one, that one." . . .

The plots you see are usually like those from that list of the hundred most common plots, in that big, pink book about sitcoms. You know, two dates for the prom, or the high school reunion, or someone is hit by lightning and becomes just like some other character. You see them all the time. . . . You don't want to have any weird logic bumps in your story, where it's like, "Wait a minute. Why did . . . Huh?"

Avoid including a lot of internal direction—you know, like "slyly" or "quietly." That's stuff for the actor and the director to figure out. And, you know, a lot of people [executives and producers included] don't read action cues. So don't put many in. . . .

I read someone's spec script recently—a friend of a friend asked me to—and it was in this weird format that I had never seen before. The margins were a little bit weird and such. And it threw me. And I know it shouldn't. I know it's not that big a deal, but . . . You just don't want to throw the person who's reading your script. You don't want the person for one second to think, "Huh?" . . .

I once read a *Cheers* spec script where the title was spelled *C-h-e-a-r-s*. I'm not usually much of a stickler for spelling, but I thought that was a bad sign.

WHEN THAT FIRST DRAFT IS FINISHED

Once you have completed the first draft of your script, you should pause and pat yourself on the back. What human on the planet hasn't said, "Aw, I could write a better show than that"? Well, you just did. And, whether it ever gets produced or not, whether it's your first script or fiftieth, you have accomplished something that most others just talk about. You have written. You are a writer. Neat, huh?

Of course, your work isn't quite finished yet. Before collecting that Emmy, there's one more step that every writer has to go through.

REWRITING THE SCRIPT

As discussed in the first section of this book, an unfortunate truth of the sitcom world is that three-quarters of all writing is rewriting. If you are a staff writer, you are expected to participate in many rewrites of many scripts. If you are a freelancer, writing one episode for a series, your (industry standard) contract obligates you to write both a first *and a second draft* of your script. The process runs something like this: You get one to two weeks to write a first draft. You submit the script and, usually within a day or two, the producers meet with you or call you to discuss their notes for revisions. (Or you and the show's staff might decide on changes during a group rewrite session.) You are given two days, five days, maybe a week to do the rewrite—less time than for a first draft since most of the story is already laid out. You submit the second draft, they say thanks, and then they shoot your script word for word.

Okay, I'm lying. They take your second draft and, as often as not, rewrite the heck out of it. It might be handed to a staff writer for the first overhaul or it might go straight into *the room*. The room is a conference room where some or all of the show's writing staff meet to work on scripts. (This group effort is referred to as *roundtable writing* or even *gang-banging* a script.) These sessions consist of five, ten, or fifteen writers and writer-producers sitting around the room, rewriting a script line by line. Everyone tosses out script fixes and jokes, the senior producer decides which go into the new draft, and someone—a producer, script secretary, or low-level writer—writes down the changes. An assistant prints up a hundred copies of the new script, circulates those for additional notes, and then that draft is rewritten. And rewritten again. It is not uncommon for the staff of a show to rewrite a script five or more times.

Are they doing this just to torment you? At times, you will be convinced that they are. But their goal is simply to make your episode the best that it can be. To complicate their efforts, they must address mountains of script notes from executives at the production company, the studio, and the network. Plus notes from the cast, the star's girlfriend, his agent, her agent, and Carl the caterer. In Hollywood, everyone thinks that he's a writer. And giving notes is just like writing, except that you aren't the one who has to stay up until three A.M., trying to fix that second act.

Naturally, different producers operate in different ways. On some shows, producers strive to preserve a writer's creative vision by putting tremendous effort into guiding her work on the story outline and the first two drafts. On other shows, a producer might take a writer's first draft but not require a second—though he will still pay for one—because he prefers to have his staff do all of the rewrites. On still other shows, the producers will sometimes have different staff writers rewrite different scenes of a script and then patch those scenes together. Whatever the dynamics, many writers consider themselves fortunate if half of their original dialogue makes it into the final shooting script. Of course, if you are a member of the show's staff, you are in a better position to defend your material than a freelancer is, because you are right there, part of the team.

Just what types of script notes are given?

VAGUE NOTES

Some people are not very good at identifying and describing script problems. (Not surprising, since many of the people who are empowered to give notes are not, and could never be, writers.) The worst of them will dish out some power-lunch clichés like "You need more of that whole contra-oedipal, boy-hates-Dad-loves-Mom-but-*is*-Dad type of thing, you know? Go there, that's the fix. And it's *true*."

Uh-huh. What??

You've got a scene in a basement and they're telling you that it's not funny. But some people can't just say "needs more jokes here." And most people can't see that the real problem is located *three scenes earlier*, when you failed to establish the predicament that is supposed to get paid off in the basement scene. Oh, well. Smile, nod, and listen. Though vague notes can be frustrating, they do sometimes point toward a flaw in the script. It's up to you to identify the real problem and fix it.

NOTES REQUIRED BY BUDGET LIMITATIONS

On occasion, producers will give notes designed to reduce a script's production costs. They might ask you to move the scene on the ski slopes to the interior of a chalet. Or to have the argument that occurs in the courthouse take place in the lead character's kitchen. Or to replace a proposed expensive guest star with a celebrity-blocked-from-view-by-his-entourage. Hey, fair is fair. Not only do your producers have an obligation to keep costs in line, but you, as a professional writer, should avoid putting costly elements into your script.

GOOD MATERIAL GONE STALE

As previously discussed, once the surprise of a joke is lost, it just doesn't seem as funny. One unfortunate byproduct of extensive rewriting is that good material is often tossed out because, after twelve readings, it no longer gets a laugh. An added frustration is that its replacement sometimes creates other script problems; while the new joke might be just as funny, the wrong choice can screw up some other part of the story. Which means more rewriting.

What can you do? Not much. You can try to convince your producer that the original material is worth saving but, if you push too hard, she might conclude that you are either difficult to work with or short of ideas. A professional writes, and rewrites, as required.

REWRITE MANIACS

Some writers are so prolific that they can come up with a joke anytime, anywhere, on any subject. As impressive as this is, if that writer is also a producer, he can make other writers' lives hell. It is so easy for these talented people to cough up new jokes that some of them tend to change script material at the drop of a hat. Unfortunately, the new jokes that they come up with—or ask you to come up with—do not always improve the script. Sometimes they are just new, not better. And sometimes the substitution creates new story problems, which someone—you?—then has to fix.

Of course, other times, these comedic volcanoes are the geniuses who drive the funniest, best-written shows on air. What to do? Grab hold, hang on, and try to learn from these people. For as much as rewrite maniacs might burn through your best material, working with them is a tremendous way to hone your own comedy-writing skills.

Sandy Frank: A lot of times, when you're down on the stage and you're shooting the episode, some people are still trying to punch up every joke. And it actually has a big psychological effect; everyone thinks it's really making the episode so much better. But in reality, the script is 98 percent done. You're really just killing yourself for that extra 1 or 2 percent. But performers, especially if they're stand-up comedians, really like it when you give them a new joke because that is a laugh and therefore good. And executives tend to like the frenetic activity and the fear; it makes them feel like you're earning your money. And it's also the nature of sitcoms today—they tend to be very jokey. So throw in an extra joke at the end, and people go, "Oh, oh, that's great. There's an extra joke"—even though it may just be edited out later.

CONFLICTING NOTES FROM DIFFERENT BOSSES

Once, when I was writing a freelance episode for a CBS series, my boss was replaced midstream. I had gone off to write the first draft after getting outline notes from the executive producer. When I showed up to get notes for the second draft—gulp!—a different producer was now in charge. (The first one had gotten a development deal, or been killed or something.)

Unfortunately, but predictably, my new boss just didn't see things the way the other producer had. This meant that I had to do a *page-one rewrite*. Meaning, the entire script had to be drastically rewritten, from the first page. And, as is usually the case, the new draft was due in half the time allotted for the first draft. Yippee. But the new boss had a right to his creative viewpoint, and it was my job to make the changes.

A bigger problem occurs when you receive conflicting notes from different bosses who are both still on staff. Say a co-producer instructs you to change a scene even though you distinctly heard the executive producer declare, in an earlier discussion, that said scene was perfect. You've got a problem. Piss off either the big boss or the lesser guy by ignoring his notes and you might create an enemy who sees that you never get more work on that show. Probably the best solution is to get on the phone to one or both parties and be honest—point out that you have received conflicting input and ask for a final ruling. (Even better, suggest a brilliant compromise.) Then, proceed per your instructions and try to keep your head down. If someone confronts you later, apologize, explain the confusion, and offer to rewrite the scene again.

The most confounding script notes of all? The notes you get most often? A producer will have the nerve to suggest changes A, B, and C, and much to your dismay—she's right. They all work, they greatly improve the script, and, dammit, why didn't you think of them?

Oh, well. You'll get good notes and bad notes, notes that fix and notes that create havoc. The one silver lining is that even if the show's staff completely rewrites your script, you usually get full credit for the finished teleplay. This is a traditional courtesy paid to writers, partly in recognition of the fact that they have limited control over what happens to their work. Why do you care? Because your reputation is built on script credits, and the amount of residuals that you collect from reruns of an episode are determined by your credit.

POINTERS ON REWRITING

Here are some pointers regarding rewrites:

- Fight for the really big points but let the others go. Professionals don't get bogged down in minutiae.

- Follow orders graciously. If you have made your point but the producer still says to make a change, smile and do so. Often, you will discover that she is right. And you do not want to alienate a producer who thought enough of your writing samples to hire you, and who might hire you again.

- Don't offer to do more rewrites than are required by your contract. Your gesture is likely to come off as a desperate effort to curry favor rather than an earnest desire to improve the script. (Plus, the Writers Guild of America frowns on free drafts because they undercut industry rules regarding the amount of work that can be demanded of writers.)

- If someone offers notes on your script but is not paying you to write it, you should not feel compelled to incorporate his ideas. At the same time, if a reader suggests changes and you do choose to incorporate them, that does not entitle that person to part ownership of your script. Some unscrupulous types might claim that it does, in a very loud voice, but if you haven't entered into a legal agreement with them, and they didn't type out portions of the new draft, then you owe them nothing. And, in view of their behavior, you would be wise to avoid them in the future.

- If one of your producers gives you a note that you absolutely cannot live with, even if you might alienate that person by ignoring the input, there is a little trick that you might try. When next you see that producer, thank him for his terrific idea and point out how it *blah, blah, blah* the whole *blah, blah, blah*. (Insert some impressive film school jargon in the place of *blah, blah, blah*.) The producer might be so impressed with the brilliance of his contribution that he fails to notice that you never changed a word of the section in question. He's happy, you're happy, and the script is saved. (This trick is risky, to say the least, but *I've heard* that some writers have found it useful.)

WHEN REWRITING BY YOURSELF

The above section describes the rewriting process involved when you are writing a freelance assignment or working on staff. But what if you are working on a spec script all by yourself? The good news is that you don't have to deal with reams of script notes. The bad news is that you don't have ten to twenty seasoned professionals offering advice on how to improve your script.

What should you do? First, be a perfectionist. If you can't honestly say that a draft is the very best that you are capable of writing at this point in your career, then it's back to the keyboard. Find the flaws, explore the moments, make the script sing. Because that script is the ultimate proof of your writing talent. You usually get just one chance to impress a producer or executive, so the sample that you hand her had better be the best that it can be.

Even at that, expect that you will skim through the thing in four months and see room for improvement. If the script is still fresh enough to use as a work sample, rewrite it again, and again, for as long as you keep circulating it.

Are you doing all of this in a vacuum? You don't have to. Solicit feedback from friends, family, teachers, and other writers. While few of them are likely to have a professional sitcom writing background, "civilians" are often good at locating weak points in a story, even if they can't articulate why an element doesn't work. Conversely, they can be just as helpful in identifying script strengths that you might want to explore in greater depth.

When receiving their input, try not to get defensive. Try not to talk, period. Instead, listen, take notes, and then discuss their points *after* they have finished listing them. If you interrupt their thoughts to defend your creative decisions—as most writers instinctively want to do—your readers might forget to mention other points or become reluctant to speak further. For that matter, if you have to defend or explain a creative decision, it probably needs a second look anyway—because you certainly won't be around to defend or explain that decision when some producer is reading your script.

When reviewing other people's notes, avoid letting your pride get in the way. If you can't take constructive criticism, you should not waste other people's time by asking them to evaluate your scripts. If all you want are ego strokes, then offer copies to Mom and assorted doting relatives, and pray that the producers you approach are as easily impressed.

At the same time, always take other people's notes with a big grain of salt. If you still feel that an original decision was valid, don't change it. It's your work, your call.

If you or your readers find numerous faults in the writing, have the strength (and wisdom) to do a major rewrite. Preserving flawed material might save you some short-term effort, but it can also ruin your chances of getting work. (A real shame, after all of the time that you have already invested.) The first step in making big changes is to reevaluate your beat sheet and outline. Fix the broad story beats *before* rewriting dialogue. Otherwise you risk becoming so focused on punching up lines that you overlook fatal structure flaws. Or you might become so enamored of a scene or some jokes that you can't see that they should be cut.

In other words, your rewriting priorities should be story first, then sequences, scenes, moments, and dialogue. And, at every step, comedy, comedy, comedy. Reverse the order of your priorities and you risk ending up with a bad patch job; yeah, you sort of fixed everything, but the read seems uneven and the script feels weak.

ADVICE FROM OUR PRODUCERS

What else do producers want to see during a rewrite?

Sandy Frank: When you're given a note, you basically have to do it. Now, you may think, "All right, this is a terrible note." It's a good thing to say, "Well, wait a minute. If you change A, isn't that going to change B, C, and D? And now the ending won't really work if we make that change." That's fine. You should say that. It's your job to say that. But if the producer then says, "No, it's okay," you just have to shut up and basically do it. Because if you continue to fight—first of all you may be wrong, the other person may be right—if you continue to fight, it will not be good for you. You become an annoyance.

Maxine Lapiduss: You might have the most brilliant idea in the world, and you might have executed it in the most brilliant way possible, but if the executive producer thinks it should go a different way, then you have to be flexible enough to let go of your idea and accept the changes that are being made. . . . The hardest thing for me as an executive producer is if somebody's being really resistant and holding on to something that I know either I can't sell to my actor—because they absolutely don't want to wear the funny hat that day or dress up like a chicken or whatever—and I'm saying, "It's not going to happen," but they're fighting and fighting and fighting to hold on to that idea. All they accomplish is that they make it tougher, I think, to get recommendations for their next job.

Ian Gurvitz: There's a reason why you have seven to ten people in a room and going to run-throughs every day. It's not just to constantly walk around going, "This is a great script. Boy, is it great. It's still great." It's to constantly be thinking and making it better. . . .

If you go to the shoot to see your episode and it bears no resemblance to what you wrote, or if there are, maybe, two jokes left from what you wrote, it's going to sting. Be prepared for the experience. In the course of the week, drafts get changed and rewritten. It's not always that they didn't like what you did. More often than not, it's just that that's the nature of it. . . . You're going to feel like, "I didn't do a good job." But if they say you did a great job, accept it.

Lawrence Konner: Laziness shows in rewriting. If the worst surprise of the first draft is to turn in a completely different story [than was discussed], then the worst of the second draft is to demonstrate laziness. You do token changes, a line here, a line there. Okay, the producer said to put the grandmother in, and so you write, "Grandmother enters, says 'Hello,' and leaves." That's not what he meant. . . . You should use the second draft notes as an opportunity to rethink things. Remember that once you've gotten the first job, your goal is to get another job. And one of the things that's going to impress people is your willingness to put some effort into the second draft.

Irma Kalish: There's no point in saying—because they've all heard this before—"Do you want it good or do you want it tomorrow?" Forget it. Make it good and hand it in when you promised.

Matt Williams: There are two extremes that you don't want to go to as a beginning writer. One is the give-it-up mode. Those writers just give up on everything. They have no point of view. The room says paint it green, "Okay, it'll be green." And the other one is holding on to every word you've written. Somewhere in between those two extremes is the ideal. Express your opinion. Justify why you think something works, and if the room is still resisting and the head writer says, "I'm sorry, I don't see it," give it up. And then listen. Listen, listen. Because in sitcom writing, in the ideal world, the room becomes one mind. Not a collection of minds; it becomes one mind. As the outside writer coming into the group, listen and try to tap into what that single mind is so that you can understand what the room is trying to do.

ONCE THE SCRIPT IS FINISHED

Writing a sitcom script requires that a million and one creative decisions be made, and all in the course of three to five weeks! Here is the average schedule for a freelance script assignment:

two to five days to prepare a verbal pitch;

two days to a week to write an outline;

two to five days to rewrite the outline;

one to two weeks to write the first draft of the script;

two days to a week to write the second draft.

If you are working on the staff of a show, you might be given less time, depending on production deadlines. If you are writing a spec script, you get to determine the schedule.

Once your latest writing sample is finally finished, polished, the absolute best that it can be, you are ready to send it out into the marketplace. But what exactly does that mean? How do you land work as a sitcom writer?

You get work by selling, by taking aggressive action. If you are serious about making your living as a sitcom writer, you have to get up from the keyboard and make something happen. If you do it right, it's a little bit like going to war. . . .

Part Three

A Battle Plan for Launching Your Career

Twelve

Step One—Developing a Strategy

Most writers absolutely hate to sell, but selling is how a writer gets work. Because there is no avoiding the process, the best alternative is to attack it head-on. The following chapters present an aggressive, focused, take-no-prisoners strategy—the quickest way to get a writer employed, and back at the keyboard where she belongs. This strategy is broken up into a series of finite, doable steps to make the job search less overwhelming.

THE JOB MARKET—IT'S NOT 1995 ANYMORE

First, it helps to understand how the network development process works, because it dictates what writing jobs become available.

In the old days—say, up through the late eighties—almost all sitcoms aired on the big broadcast networks (ABC, CBS, NBC, and, later, FOX). The networks rarely produced these shows themselves, due to government regulations that limited their right to own shows that they aired. Instead, networks would pay "license fees" to outside producers in exchange for the right to air selected shows that they, the outsiders, agreed to produce. (The outside producers, who actually owned the shows, could later exploit them by rerunning them in syndication.) Occasionally, some syndicators and station groups would band together to launch an original series in syndication, and the cable networks managed to put a few original shows on air. But back then, everyone pretty much conformed to a traditional series development schedule that runs something like this:

- From fall to midwinter, pilot scripts for new series are commissioned and developed.

- From January to April, a handful of the best scripts are produced as pilot episodes.

- In May, the networks announce which shows, old and new, will be given production orders for the coming year.

- In August and September, new series premiere and old series return with new episodes.

- In midwinter, failing series are replaced with *midseason* entries that had been held in reserve.

If a show seemed very promising and its producers or star had leverage, it might be given a full year's order of twenty-two or twenty-four episodes. (Repeats and preemptions occupied the remaining twenty-eight to thirty weeks of the year.) If a show seemed weak or its principals didn't have leverage, it might receive a short order of only four, six, or thirteen episodes. And it might be relegated to midseason replacement status—meaning, it might never make it onto the network's program schedule. If a short-ordered series got on the schedule and proved successful, the network would give it a *pickup* order requiring that additional episodes be produced, to carry it through the full broadcast season.

That was then. Nowadays, all bets are off. The broadcast networks still stick mostly to the traditional development schedule. However, original sitcoms are now being produced by and for a host of pay cable, basic cable, syndication, and satellite networks. (Which means more jobs for you.) Series are being developed and launched at all times of the year. In fact, some cable and pay cable programmers prefer to premiere their shows in early summer, to take advantage of the less appealing reruns that air during those months.

Additional changes that have occurred more recently, during the mid- to late nineties, include the following:

- The (previously mentioned) regulations restricting network ownership of programming have been, for the most part, eliminated. In response, the broadcast networks have started to produce a number of TV series in-house in order to maximize their control of, and profits from, the shows that they air. (This was a wise move, because the recent proliferation of media channels has greatly reduced the broadcast networks' access to a previously captive television audience.) The in-house network production divisions also supply shows to rival television networks, because profits are profits, however they might be generated. Predictably, each network seems to favor its own in-house productions when it comes to scheduling and renewal decisions, though all would vigorously deny the charge.

- When a network orders a series from an outside producer, it now sometimes demands that it be given a piece of the show (partial ownership) as part of the deal. Because the network then has a greater financial stake in the project, it takes a more aggressive role in controlling its development and production.

- On another front, since more networks are now competing for the services of top producers and stars, the series development process has become more "deal driven" than in the past. Meaning, many new shows are given a production order or granted a time slot on a network schedule simply because that network owes someone a deal. Usually, such deals are made in order to lock up some top talent's future services or to entice a top talent into participating in a different project. Whatever the reason, the result is that many network time slots are being sacrificed to satisfy business obligations rather than being allocated based on program quality.

- Another change in this increasingly competitive business is that new shows are given even less time to find an audience. More and more series start out with very short production orders—four episodes is not uncommon—and some have been pulled off the air after only one or two airings. If this strategy was applied years ago, we never would have had *Cheers* or *Seinfeld*, series that took months or even an entire season to establish themselves. But such is progress, right?

What does all of this have to do with you getting work as a writer?

First, the traditional network development process described above has created several different *hiring windows* for writers. We will identify these and explore ways to capitalize on them later, in chapter 14.

Next, the proliferation of visual media has spawned new networks, which means more shows, which means more jobs. The competition for talented sitcom writers has grown such that, today, many untested writers land a staff position as their very first job. In ancient times—pre-1995?—writers usually had to earn their stripes first by landing a couple of freelance assignments.

On the downside, while there are more jobs for sitcom writers, job tenure can be fleeting. (Make that "more fleeting.") The faster turnover rate for new shows has an obvious impact on writing staffs. In addition, producers of new shows prefer to hire writers whom they know and trust when assembling a new staff; understandably, they are reluctant to deal with unknown talent when struggling to get a series up and running. This, combined with the accelerated turnover rate for shows, can make it more difficult for some writers to find regular employment; personal connections and endorsements from network executives often count more than writing ability.

In summary, today's market seems to offer more jobs and better entry-level jobs, but less job stability, than in recent years. And as for the material being written? You've seen *The Larry Sanders Show* and *South Park*. The creation of new media outlets has given writers the opportunity to explore all types of subject matter, from profound to lurid.

HOW THE WRITER FITS IN

The great thing about the television industry is that *the writers run the show*. Okay, yes, they get loads of input, pressure, and—many would say—interference from the executives who control the money. (The network suits, studio suits, and production company suits.) But happily, the executive producers of a sitcom, the individuals who have the most creative control, are usually *writers*. (Unlike in the movie industry, in which creative control is usually held by the director or, sometimes, the star.)

Producers who are deemed capable enough to turn out a network-quality television series are called *show runners*. This is an exalted, highly paid position, achieved by very few. (An executive producer title does not automatically qualify one as a show runner; that honor usually goes to producers who have previously held *primary* responsibility for delivering a show, preferably a hit show, week after week.) A show runner might create a new series or be brought in as a hired gun to help with someone else's project. If a lesser writer-producer creates a new series but has not, in a network's eyes, achieved show runner status, he will be forced to work with an established show runner if he wants to see his series produced. With so much money at stake, sometimes millions of dollars per episode, network executives are understandably reluctant to trust unproven talent with their investment.

How do you get to be a show runner, so that you can see your own series ideas become a reality? How do you get any job as a staff writer?

The hiring-and-promotion sequence for staff writers usually goes something like this, working up from the bottom of the ladder: term writer, story editor, executive story editor, story consultant, executive story consultant, co-producer, producer, supervising producer, co-executive producer, executive producer.

A sitcom might employ anywhere from five to twenty writers and writer-producers, though most shows probably average a staff of eight to twelve. Not all job titles are used on all shows, and a writer being promoted might skip several titles—say, go from story editor to coproducer—if she is a hot commodity. As a writer climbs the ladder, she gains a greater say in creative decisions and is eventually given responsibility for aspects of the show's production. Otherwise, job duties vary widely from job to job, and show to show. The few constants are that all staff writers write scripts, join in group writing sessions, and attend read-throughs, run-throughs, and final shoots.

If most of a show's producers are writers rather than production types, who takes care of the technical stuff? Titles vary, but each show employs technically proficient producers whose job is to manage the facilities and crew needed to produce the series. (Most of these producers have little to do with creative issues such as scripts, casting, and direction.) From high to low, their titles might be producer, line producer, unit production manager, and associate producer. They are assisted by production coordinators and production assistants, and, of course, a large production crew.

A WRITER'S WORK WEEK

As romantic as the title of Hollywood writer sounds, exactly how do you spend the hours of the day? Is it all ego-boosting meetings with fawning executives, chatty lunches at overpriced bistros, basking at the beach as you pound away on a laptop? Not quite.

You already know the routine for a freelance writer, from our discussion in part 2 of this book. A script assignment means three to five weeks of intense writing. You pitch, write, get notes, rewrite, and pray—because if you do a great job, you might get another assignment or land a staff job. (Most freelance writers want to join a show because staff jobs pay more, offer longer terms of employment, and are the only route to eventually achieving some level of creative control, via a producer's rank.)

If you are a staff writer, you probably put in sixty, seventy, or more hours per week. You work in the show's production offices on a studio lot, crammed into one of many small writers' offices. (In fact, it is usually a production company or studio, not a television network, that pays your checks.)

On most sitcoms, one episode is produced each week, with a week taken off here and there to allow for catch-up. Traditionally, the actual production season lasts nine to ten months; producers prep and staff a show during early summer, start producing episodes in July or August, and shoot until the following March or April. Most shows shoot the final versions of their episodes on either Tuesday or Friday nights. The five days preceding a final shoot might break down as follows:

- *Day one* often starts with a *table reading*, attended by producers, writers, cast members, department heads (from the crew), and assorted programming executives. Everyone sits around a large table, or a circle of tables, as the cast reads through a draft of the script being produced that week. Notes are given and the writers go off to rewrite the script (again) while the director and department heads start prepping all of the physical elements needed to produce the show. If the script looks bad, the writers face a very long night.

- *Day two* often features another reading and more notes. If the script looks good, the director starts plotting camera moves and rehearsing the cast. Some producers schedule a regular rewrite night on this day, regardless of what shape their scripts are in.

- On *days three and four*, the actors get serious about memorizing lines as the script settles into its final form. The director rehearses the cast and blocks out camera movements. More notes are given, and more rewriting is done.

- *Day five*, the shooting day, might culminate in two run-throughs of the episode: first, a formal dress rehearsal, followed by notes, last minute changes, and perhaps dinner; and then, the final shoot. Afterwards, it's off to editing, where the best elements of both run-throughs are combined to create the finished episode.

The above steps describe just one of several five-day models used to produce sitcoms. Some shows use multiple (three or four) cameras to shoot an entire episode straight through, pausing only to redo a scene or move to a different set; others use a single camera to *block and shoot* the scenes of an episode over the course of several days. Some shows shoot on film, which provides a rich look but can be more difficult to produce; others shoot on videotape, which is easier to use but results in a flatter look. Some shows shoot before a studio audience and others—primarily single-camera operations—do not. Some shows record dress rehearsals and others only record the final performance. Some smother their audio tracks with canned laughter, others do not.

Every production team runs its show differently, but all engage in read-throughs, rewrites, rehearsals, blocking, and shooting.

When not helping to repair or punch up the script currently being shot, a staff writer is usually busy performing other writing functions. Perhaps she is generating new story ideas to pitch to the writing staff. Or she is writing the first draft of an episode that she has been assigned, or rewriting someone else's script. Or she is joining other staff writers in the room to *break a story* (meaning, to figure out the story beats of a future episode). Or she and the other writers are punching up the script that is scheduled to be produced next week, or the week after. Or she is sitting with a producer while a freelancer makes a pitch, or helping to beat out a story that the freelancer will then write.

Did I say "or"? Make that "and." Because that writer will probably do most of these tasks during the course of a week.

It can be tons of work but it's also exciting. Being a staff writer means driving onto a studio lot every day, bumping elbows with celebrities, earning big bucks, and getting paid to sit with funny people, creating funny stories. And getting to see your words come out of actors' mouths, on camera, en route to an audience of millions. (Including Mom, Dad, and that jerk who dumped you in college.)

WRITING IS A BUSINESS

As glamorous as it might seem, sitcom writing is a business. If you want to succeed, you must treat it as *your* business. Yes, you must have talent. And you must produce consistently, writing script after script. But you also need to attack the sitcom-writing job market as you would any other highly competitive career field. Many a talented writer has failed to get work because it was just so much safer and easier to stay at home, typing away.

That behavior doesn't cut it in a field where

formal education means little;

employers erect barriers to deflect job applicants;

hiring decisions are often based on personal friendships;

thousands of talented, charming people are competing for a handful of jobs.

If you are serious about launching a writing career, a big chunk of your day should be spent thinking in terms of meetings, schedules, deadlines, contacts, and follow-up. You must sell your material and yourself.

It helps to have a master plan of sorts, which is why the following chapters were written. Assuming that you already have at least one terrific spec script in hand, your next goals are as follows:

1. Keep writing. "Writers write." And it might be the next script you create that finally gets you hired.

2. Land the right agent.

3. Get your spec scripts to the right people.

4. Turn pitch meetings into jobs.

5. Turn jobs into a career.

Those are the broad goals. But before you plunge ahead, there are three important matters that we should discuss: the age factor, how to keep eating, and moving to Los Angeles.

AGEISM

Remember when I mentioned, at the beginning of the book, that a surprising number of sitcoms are run by thirty- and thirty-five-year-old producers? And perhaps I mentioned that many television executives are that age and younger? It's true. And to be frank, that is bad news for those of us over forty. Why? Because young producers do not always feel comfortable giving orders to people who are older than they are. And TV execs seem convinced that anyone over thirty is out of touch with the latest trends. (And therefore can't relate to the youthful audience demographic that television advertisers seek.)

What can you do, if those gray hairs are starting to come in? Besides going the Nice 'n Easy, Grecian Formula route? Well, if you are already an established writer who thinks and looks young, you're probably in pretty good shape. For a while.

But if you are forty years old and just starting out, the going could be rough. If you feel a tremendous drive to write sitcoms, do it anyway, take a shot. Life is short, so go for it. You can always try something else if this doesn't work out.

On the other hand, if you don't think it wise to buck the age bias, there are alternatives. You want to write comedy? Write comedic screenplays—age is barely a factor. Or write books, or articles, or plays, or short stories. Nobody ever said that sitcoms were the only road to a writer's fulfillment.

It's your call, and I regret tossing out a wet blanket. But I did promise that this would be your comprehensive, all-in-one guide to the field.

PUTTING FOOD ON THE TABLE

Unless you are rich, you will probably need a job to put food on the table. Launching a writing career can take many months, even years—and that is assuming that you are eventually successful. How will you eat during that time?

Your options? Marry a very rich, very old person. (Just a thought.) Or get a proverbial "day job," if you don't already have one. There are two basic types of jobs. First, if you live in Los Angeles, you can get a job *in the industry*—working as a production assistant, an executive's assistant, a producer's assistant, a tape librarian, a runner, or in some other entry-level capacity. The advantages? You are right there, as part of a production team, rubbing shoulders with people in the business. You can make contacts, learn the production process, show people your work, and maybe even impress someone enough to be given an assignment.

The disadvantages? You're not really rubbing shoulders with those people—you bring them coffee. And you type, deliver scripts, type, place calls, order Thai food, pick up dry-cleaning, and type. And, because everyone wants to work in show biz, you work very long hours for very little pay. Which leaves you little energy to keep writing the scripts that you need to write.

The dilemma is that a job in the industry can give you access, but it can eat up all of your free time.

How about an undemanding job in another field, just to pay the bills while you write? The advantages are that you will probably work fewer hours and make more money. But you are out of the loop. While you are playing receptionist in some lawyer's office or waiting tables at the Ivy, you might miss out on an important connection that you would otherwise have made while working as a lowly PA.

What to do? As long as you can find a way to keep writing and circulating your material, either path can serve you well. An ideal compromise is to get a job as an assistant to someone who works in the business but isn't a slave driver—maybe a producer who is between shows or an executive who blows out of the office at six every night.

Or some people land jobs as *floaters*, employed either at a studio or a network, or via referrals from a specialized temp agency. Working as fill-in secretaries and gophers, floaters are sent to help out when needed at different shows. This enables them to develop a large circle of contacts. At the same time, their temp status usually means that they get decent pay without having to face all of the job pressures that their full-time counterparts face.

In short, the ideal day job provides you with industry access and leaves you time to write.

If you live in Los Angeles, how do you land one of these food-on-the-table industry gigs? That's a whole other book. Fortunately, there are already a number of publications that address that subject—check your local bookstore. Just to toss in my two cents, I will suggest the following:

CHECK THE TRADE PAPERS

Every week, Hollywood's daily trades, such as *Daily Variety* and *The Hollywood Reporter*, list projects that are starting production. Grab a phone book, call the companies involved, and talk your way into an interview for any job that they might have available.

CALL THE BIG COMPANIES

Networks, studios, and large production companies usually have a human resources (or personnel) department. While these departments have no say regarding which writers, producers, or other creative types are hired, they sometimes do fill secretarial positions within the company. Call and get an interview.

CHECK THE INDUSTRY DIRECTORIES

Several publishers put out industry directories that list everything from production companies to animal trainers. Sold at entertainment-oriented bookstores (like the Samuel French chain or Larry Edmund's Books), at standard bookstores, through the mail and through the internet, these guides are available to everyone. (See appendix B for the names of several popular directories.) Buy a couple and start dialing. Call every company that seems to be connected to the sitcom world and ask who hires their secretaries, runners, PAs, whatever.

CALL YOUR COUSIN'S WIFE'S BROTHER

Everybody knows somebody in Hollywood. Call that person and ask that she keep her ear to the ground. My advice is to *canvas everybody*. As for style of approach, I suggest the following:

1. *Use the phone* rather than mail out a ton of résumés. It might be scarier to just call people out of the blue, but it prevents them from cutting you off with a standard rejection letter.

2. *Be polite and prepared*. When you call, have your thoughts in order. And know what type of job they might have available rather than blurting out "Gee, I'll take anything!"

3. It is usually better to *frame a cold call as a request for an "informational meeting"* rather than a plea for a job. Don't worry—if an employer has an opening, she won't be shy about mentioning it if she thinks that

you'd be a good candidate. Also, be prepared to ask intelligent questions when you call to request that meeting; the employer might put you on the spot to see if "information" is what you're really after.

4. *Do your homework.* People are always flattered and impressed when you bother to learn who they are and what they have done.

5. *Start at* A *and go to* Z, and keep calling until someone says, "You're hired." Do not let someone's words of encouragement slow you down. The best thing that could happen is that you suddenly end up with three job offers, putting you in the driver's seat.

6. *Keep good records.* Names, job titles, phone numbers, dates that you called, dates that they said to call back, strategies that occurred to you, etc. Think that you'll remember everything? Think again. And no, those scraps of paper piling up on your bureau don't count.

In the end, it all comes down to knocking on doors until someone hires you.

On a related subject, you probably noticed that I keep referring to industry day jobs *located in Hollywood*. Which brings up the last big question . . .

MUST YOU LIVE IN LOS ANGELES?

Yes. Sorry.

Not that Los Angeles is a bad place to live—it is known for its balmy weather, sunny beaches, and friendly folks. But balmy and friendly aren't for everyone.

Unfortunately, if you want to write network sitcoms for a living, you may not have a choice. Hollywood is where almost all sitcoms are produced. Yes, a couple are done in New York City, but they represent very few jobs. And many of the writers on those shows came from L.A., and none of them is anxious to hand his coveted spot over to you.

True, some established writers manage to land occasional freelance assignments from out of state. And an extraordinarily successful writer-producer like Matt Williams (creator of *Roseanne* and *Home Improvement*) can live just about anywhere he wants to. But unless you already have that type of clout, it would be a mistake to think that you could charm producers into making such exceptions just for you.

The good news is that *you do not have to move to Hollywood right away*. In fact, I strongly recommend against it. First, find out if the work is for you, and if you have a legitimate shot at earning a living as a sitcom writer. How? We will discuss a strategy for testing the waters, long distance, in the following chapter.

Let's move on to the next phase of your job search—landing an agent.

Thirteen

Step Two—Landing an Agent

DO YOU HAVE TO HAVE AN AGENT?

You betcha. Most producers and executives won't read your writing samples unless they come through an agent. Why? It's a weeding process. If you are a psycho, you probably can't get an agent, which means that you can't get to the producers and executives. If you are untalented or lack drive, you probably can't get an agent. If you are a gold digger looking to sue someone for stealing your ideas, you are less likely to get an agent. In short, agents screen out a large portion of the bad writing samples and weak writers that would otherwise end up in the offices of those producers and executives.

Exactly who are these agents and how do they work? An agent is primarily a salesperson. He might work for a big multinational outfit headquartered in expensive Beverly Hills digs, or a specialized boutique agency employing ten or thirty people, or a one-person company (his) operating out of an apartment bedroom. An agent spends the day canvasing the industry for information regarding job opportunities, and pitching his clients to prospective employers. He does most of his work on the phone but also frequently gets out for meetings, business meals, and production run-throughs. When he closes a deal, he usually negotiates the basic terms himself, and then either he or a lawyer drafts the formal agreement.

Agents live by their contacts and the quality of their client lists. They usually specialize, focusing in one area like feature films or television series. (Agents who handle writers are called literary, or *lit*, agents.) Sometimes, especially at a big agency, different specialists team up to service a client. You might have one agent for TV, another for film, and so on—though, usually, one member of that team is your primary agent, the person whom you deal with most often. Sometimes an agency will assign particular agents to deal with particular networks, studios, and production companies, so that those companies aren't constantly being deluged with calls from twenty agents at the same firm.

What does an agent get for his troubles? Ten percent of your up-front writing fees. Agents who are affiliated with the Writers Guild of America work strictly on commission—they do not charge you money in advance and they do not get a cut of your residuals (i.e., additional money paid to you if a show is distributed after its initial airing). If you never earn money as a writer, you owe your agent nothing. If a prospective agent tries to charge you an up-front fee in exchange for representing you, pass him by; such deals are forbidden by the Writers Guild and the guy cannot be legitimate.

Lawrence Konner: The cliché is that your agent works for you, that your agent is your employee. It's just not true. You need to relate to them as another employer. You need to be in their good graces.... Take every meeting that they get you seriously. Don't show up unprepared. The last thing you want is for the producer to call your agent and say, "The guy came in here and he had nothing to say." Then your agent will stop sending you out.... Your agent has to believe in the future of your career, because 10 percent of [a new writer's income] is not enough to justify their time. They actually call new people *development clients*—as in "research and development"—because it's, "Well, this person could pay off in five years, so I'm willing to take this chance." So you have to present yourself to the agent as *that* person, the one who's going to eventually become a million-dollar-a-year client.

NOTE: An agent might earn fees in addition to the standard 10 percent if a deal involves more than basic writing services—such as agency packaging or a complex production financing arrangement. And an agent might be due additional money if he has negotiated above-scale fees for the writer. However, newer sitcom writers are rarely involved in such deals, and those who are rarely begrudge the fees since they mean that the writer is making more money.

Are agents worth 10 percent of your earnings? Most are. In addition to helping you to find work, good agents also do the following: negotiate your compensation, job title, and working conditions; go after fees that are owed to you; provide career guidance; dig up background information on people that you will meet; provide you with produced scripts and tapes; and serve as a buffer between you and your producers when there is a problem.

Note that I did *not* say that a good agent also serves as a writing coach and a shoulder to cry on. While some are very helpful in these respects, it is a bad idea to waste their valuable selling time by asking them to play coach-therapist. That's what friends and families (and coaches and therapists) are for. You need your agent to be on the phone, all of the time, trying to get you work.

What is the difference between agents and managers? Managers, rather than hunting jobs for a client list of twenty to forty people, focus on honing the careers of a handful of clients. They provide much more personal attention than an agent can, doing everything from generating networking opportunities to managing finances, to hiring household help, to offering that shoulder to cry on. In exchange for 10 to 15 percent of the client's earnings, they attempt to groom her for success. Though the law prohibits managers from seeking jobs for their clients, they do so all of the time, frequently working hand in hand with the client's agent. (Of course, there are also cases in which a writer's agent and manager are constantly battling over which paths the shared client should take.)

Should you get a manager, in addition to an agent, if you are just starting out? If you do, 20 to 25 percent of your earnings will be going out the door. You should not. And you probably couldn't anyway, because a good manager wouldn't be interested in you unless you were already making enough money to justify his investment of time. But if you become successful, and *your* time is at a premium, it might one day seem wise.

What about the differences between agents and lawyers? After all, some entertainment attorneys will agree to work on a deferred commission basis.

While you should probably retain a lawyer if you are closing a complicated deal, or if that lawyer can provide unique access to someone needed for a high-profile project, a lawyer is no substitute for an agent. Lawyers spend their days doing law things—drafting contracts, taking depositions, negotiating deals, going to court. Agents spend their days calling producers and executives, and pushing clients. Which do you want working for you?

DEVELOPING AN AGENT HIT LIST

Okay, you want an agent. How do you get one? Better yet, how do you get the right one? Well, while you can't be too picky if just starting out, there are a few criteria that your agent should meet:

- *She should be a signatory to the Writers Guild of America.* Most legitimate film and television agents sign an agreement with the Writers Guild of America, the screenwriters' primary union, that requires them to conform to certain standards that protect writers. (For details about the WGA, see chapter 14.) Ask the agent if she is a Guild signatory and call the WGA's agency department at (323) 782-4502 to check.

• *She should specialize in sitcom writers or, at least, television series writers.* Some agents who specialize in a different form, like feature films, are happy to sign television writers even though they (the agents) have no television connections themselves. They hope that you will find your own work so that they can collect a commission for merely closing the deal, or that you will help to open up some television doors for them— thanks for nothing! Unless you are desperate to have *any* agent just so that producers will read the stuff that you submit, keep looking.

NOTE: If an agent's office is not located in or near Los Angeles or, at the least, New York City, it is doubtful that he has any influence in the sitcom industry. Investigate further before you sign.

• *Some of her clients should have staff jobs.* The best test of an agent's abilities is to ask which of her clients are now working, particularly in staff positions. On a related note, if some of her clients have attained producer status, they themselves might be in a position to hire some of her other clients (like you); the advantage here is that since they too want to keep their agent happy, they are predisposed to favor any writers whom she recommends.

• *Should she work at a big agency or a small agency?* Hard to say. The big agents at any firm are not likely to take on new writers—they've got their hands full, servicing established clients. You might benefit by signing with a newer agent at a big firm because she has access to that firm's massive network, and your work will be associated with a very successful company's name; of course, an agent at a large firm might feel so much pressure to produce that she is quick to drop any client who doesn't immediately find work. Many believe that you are more likely to get personal attention and loyalty from agents at a small firm, and that you will face less competition from that firm's other clients; on the other hand, a small firm might lack the leverage of having a bunch of clients already ensconced as producers around town, who are predisposed to favor their own agency's clients. In reality, if you are fortunate enough to have a choice between an agent at a big firm and one at a small firm, you should base your decision on who best meets the following requirement.

• *She should love your work.* Here's a news flash: If an agent isn't knocked out by your writing, she will not push you as hard as she will her other clients. Who needs that?

Now that you know what to look for in an agent, how do you find these people? You might start by simply gathering names.

• *Get a copy of the WGA's Agency List.* This is a *partial* listing of the agencies that have become signatories to the Writers Guild of America. (Some firms opt to keep their names off the list to cut down on the number of would-be clients who contact them.) The list contains basic office addresses and phone numbers, but not the names of individual agents. It indicates which agencies have said that they would be willing to accept unsolicited scripts from writers and it is updated every two months. You can find this list published on the Web, at the WGA (west's) home page at "www.wga.org," or you can get a copy by contacting the WGA,w's agency department at (323) 782-4502.

NOTE: *There are two branches of the Writers Guild of America—"WGA, west" (based in Los Angeles) and "WGA, east" (based in New York City). Each is an independent organization and the two branches don't always agree on every issue, but both try to act in concert when it comes to big issues such as industry-wide negotiations on writers' contracts. Usually, if you live west of the Mississippi, you are expected join the WGA,w, and if you live east, the WGA,e. Of course, if you want to write sitcoms, a form produced mainly in Los Angeles, you will probably end up in the WGA,w. Requirements for joining both branches of the Guild are discussed in chapter 14.*

• *Check industry directories.* As previously mentioned, a number of industry directories are available at your corner bookstore. Some are even devoted specifically to identifying which agents do what, and some are updated every three or four months (an important point, in view of the rapid job turnover in Hollywood). No one directory is all-inclusive, so buy or borrow several to cover all bets.

• *Read the trades.* I recommend either *Daily Variety* or *The Hollywood Reporter*. In addition to informing you about what is going on in the industry, which is important to know, the trades often report on agents being hired and who is representing whom.

• *Track down your favorite writers.* This one is a bit harder, but worth the effort if you are trying to impress a desirable agent. The idea is that you should jot down the names of the writers who work on your favorite shows. (These names are listed in the shows' on-air credits.) Then, find out who represents those writers, either through resources such as those noted above or by calling the WGA,w's agency department at (323) 782-4502 (or you can pick up a copy of the WGA's membership directory). The goal is to get the names of specific agents, not just the names of their firms. Having this information serves two purposes: You have identified agents who apparently appreciate writing tastes similar to yours, because they represent writers whose work you like. And when you call to seek representation, you can impress their assistants and them by showing that you do your homework; meaning, you can flatter each of these agents by explaining that you have specifically sought him out because he represents great writers like so-and-so (his client). It doesn't always work, but it certainly does improve the odds that an agent will consider taking you on or giving you a referral to someone else.

- *Investigate possible referrals.* Do you know *anyone* in the business, or anyone even remotely associated with the business? Cruise through your Rolodex, check your college yearbook, ask friends and family. You might be surprised to find out that Aunt Sally's friend Bob's wife once dated an agent, and she'd be happy to make a call on your behalf. (Don't be shy—people in the entertainment industry rely on personal referrals all of the time.)

Once you have taken the above steps, you will have a long list of legitimate agents from which to pick. However, as discussed, not all of these people will be right for you. I suggest that you winnow the names down to create, let's call it, an *agent hit list*.

Not that there's much winnowing. Any agent who is a Guild signatory and who represents sitcom writers should be on your list. Avoid the temptation to rule out agents because they seem too small or don't have a fancy address— you might be desperate for them to represent you if bigger names don't work out. Also, though the WGA list and several directories indicate that some agencies will only respond to query letters or personal referrals, *ignore these restrictions* and add those agencies to your list. (When calling these firms, you will often connect with someone who isn't aware of or doesn't bother to enforce such policies.)

Then I suggest that you prioritize the hit list in order of your preferences, from most desired agent to least. While doing this, don't be timid. If the guy you'd most like to have as an agent is some hot shot who probably won't even return your calls, *put him down anyway*. Take the shot. Because what if he did return the call? And became your agent? Hey, it happens. But it can't happen for you if you won't even call, right?

Once you have gotten your agent hit list in order, and have at least one great spec script under your arm, you are ready to start dialing. But first . . .

BEFORE PICKING UP THE PHONE

Landing an agent can be an arduous process, sometimes taking months and months. Are these people waiting for your call? Do they even want you to call? Not really, because hundreds of other writers are already banging on their door.

You should do a little homework. Be prepared before reaching for the phone.

- *Know your goal.* You have only one mission when contacting an agent's office: You want her to read a sample of your work. Period, that's all. Sure, a meeting would be great, but nobody is going to sign you until that person has read your material. So keep focused on your goal. Once they say that they'll read something, get off the phone and send over a script.

- *Use the phone.* Notice that I keep saying "phone." While it might seem easier to just mail out a bunch of query letters, *don't do it*. At many talent agencies, part of an assistant's job is to respond to unsolicited query letters by mailing back a standard letter that says, "Thanks, sorry, no can do." It is much harder for them to turn away a pleasant, intelligent human being (you) speaking on the other end of a telephone line. Yes, agents prefer that you send query letters—it's easier on them. But making their lives easier is not your job; your job is to get one of these guys to represent you.

   If you're worried that they'll get offended if you call, don't be. How do you think agents get their business done? They use the phone because it is a much stronger sales tool than the mail. In truth, any agent who turns someone down simply because she called the agent's office wasn't going to sign that person anyway. So, nothing lost.

   Still too pushy for you? If you are serious about launching your career, you need every advantage you can get. The sooner you land an agent, the sooner you can stop chasing agents. So, use the phone.

NOTE: What's a query letter? *Many times, agents and producers will ask that you send a query letter describing your script, rather than the script itself, before they will consider you further. One or two pages long, these letters consist of a brief introduction that outlines your credentials, and a synopsis of your script's story.*

- *Don't send unsolicited scripts to an agent's office.* Some writers, desperate to land an agent, will send a writing sample to an agent before being invited to do so. This is considered rude and is usually a waste of time, because the agent's assistant probably has standing instructions to return such scripts unopened or simply toss them in the trash. Not only does your ploy fail, but they are likely to remember your name—in a bad way—should you contact them again in the future.

- *Prepare a phone spiel.* Once an agent gets on the line, you've only got a few seconds to win him over. He's busy, you're nervous, there's a lot at stake—why leave things to chance? Figure out what you should say *before* you pick up the phone. Prepare a clever little spiel that quickly introduces you and the purpose of your call. Create five or so sentences that will spark the agent's interest enough so that he asks for additional information or says the magic words, "Okay, send it over."

What goes into this pitch? The answer is different for everyone because it has to sound completely natural. If someone the agent knows referred you to him, obviously those should be the first words out of your mouth ("Hi, I'm Evan Smith. Joe Bigshot over at Paramount suggested that I call you. . . ."). Or you might hit on a personal connection that you discovered when researching the agent, such as graduating from the same college, coming from the same area, or having a mutual acquaintance. Or you might mention, as discussed above, that you are approaching the agent because you are a big fan of another client's writing; of course, you better then be able to discuss some of that writer's recent work.

If you can't come up with some sort of connection, then a clever but unassuming pitch might do the trick. There is a lot to be said for simply being earnest, passionate, determined, and articulate. If you can also be amusing—after all, you are selling yourself as a comedy writer—so much the better.

If you don't feel comfortable winging the pitch, write out the points that you want to hit and practice on someone. If any elements seem false, awkward, or pretentious, change them—the last thing you want is to have your phone spiel sound like a rehearsed speech.

- *Don't call until you have something great to show them.* Agents do not sign clients just because they have a great personality or they have a script in the works. If you haven't got one ready to go, don't call. Otherwise, the agent will think that you are either a rank amateur or a nut, or both.

MAKING THE CALL

Your agent hit list in hand, your phone spiel at the tip of your tongue, you pick up the phone and start dialing. When a person answers, try to sound polite, confident, and pleased to be talking with that individual. (Don't call if you're not feeling upbeat—you need to sound like a winner.)

You might have to go through an agency's receptionist to get to an agent or his assistant. If you don't have a specific agent's name, and the receptionist refuses to forward you to "an agent who handles sitcom writers," then politely end the conversation. Do more research, get a specific name, and call back another day.

Once you reach an agent's assistant, ask if you might speak to the agent whom you are pursuing. Unless the assistant is incompetent, he or she will ask if they can help you instead. Do you blow them off and insist on speaking with the agent? Of course not. That assistant is a powerful gatekeeper; alienate him and he will shut you down, charm him and he might champion your cause. (Plus, the guy is a person too and deserves some courtesy.) Instead of being pushy, just say, "Yes, absolutely," and then proceed to make your phone pitch *to the assistant*.

At this point, any of several things might happen:

- If you are very fortunate, the assistant might interrupt you to say, "Please hold"—and the next thing you know, the agent is on the line. What do you do? Just start your phone pitch over from the top, remembering that you have only one goal—to get the agent to agree to read your material.

- The assistant might simply invite you to send the script in, without checking with the agent. Great! Get the assistant's name, express your gratitude, and follow through ASAP. There'll be plenty of time to talk to the agent later, *if* she likes your material.

- The assistant might shut you down with a blanket "Sorry, we're not taking on any new clients right now." Or, "Sorry, but we only sign clients who are already established writers." Or, "Sorry, we only see people who have been referred by someone we know." You have several options here: You can try to small-talk your way into getting the assistant to make an exception in your case. Alternatively, you might ask if the agent would be willing to meet so that you can ask a few questions about how to get started in the business; a pleasant informational chat might lead to the agent reading your script or offering you a referral to another agent. Another option is to ask the assistant if *he* would look at a script; he might be so flattered that he ends up forwarding it to his boss.

- The assistant might insist that you submit a query letter before they will consider reading your spec script. Try to talk your way out of this one—it is far better that they read a polished script than a brief summary of your story. (Plus, submitting a letter only gives them an easier way of passing on you, via a return letter.) If the assistant insists, send a very brief, very good query letter; just cover the highlights of your script and leave them wanting more. Then, call in a week to (ostensibly) see if the assistant received the letter, and again try to talk him into letting you submit a complete script. (It doesn't matter if they ever read the query letter.)

- The assistant might just blow you off. Big deal, it happens. Call back in three weeks and you might catch him in a more receptive frame of mind. Or someone else might pick up the phone.

Start at the top of your agent hit list and keep calling until you reach the last candidate. Then update the list and go through it again. Keep calling until an agent signs you. Do not slow down just because ten people are reading your scripts—it might be number fifteen that does the trick. And nothing could be better than to suddenly get calls from five agents who want to represent you; whoever signs you would work harder on your behalf because you seem to be a hot property.

If you are having trouble getting agents to read your material, revise your pitch.

If you are having trouble getting past an agent's assistant, try calling after 6:00 P.M. Sometimes the assistant will have already gone home and the agent herself will pick up the phone.

Keep calling, keep honing your pitch, and remember that your only goal is to have that agent read the script. Once she says yes, get off the phone before she changes her mind, and deliver the script pronto.

SUBMITTING YOUR MATERIAL

When an agent agrees to read one of your scripts, there are certain steps that you should take:

- *Send your best work.* You've only got one shot at impressing this person, so submit your strongest writing sample.

- *Signing a legal release.* Many agents will insist that you sign a one- or two-page legal release before they will read your material. This protects them, to some extent, in case you later try to sue because they profited from a project that seems very similar to yours. Do you sign the release? You have to or else they won't even consider you. But don't worry too much—agents aren't in the business of stealing material. And if you do run into an infringement problem, you can still pursue the matter through the Writers Guild and the courts.

- *The package.* The script should be a clean, new copy, enclosed in a standard manila envelope. (See appendix A for professional script format guidelines.) Include a brief, two- or three-sentence cover letter that thanks the agent for agreeing to take a look at the script. This note, another sample of your writing, might reiterate something said in your phone conversation or a highlight from your phone pitch. Keep it short. Make it engaging, or at least mercifully concise.

  Many people prefer to hand-write such notes on personalized note cards—small (3x7-inch), blank cards, cut from standard "card stock," with your name printed in one corner. I recommend that you have your own batch printed up; they are very handy when it comes to submissions and follow-up letters.

- *Enclose a stamped, self-addressed return envelope.* Agents have no wish to pay return postage on the scripts that they have rejected. In fact, if you don't include a proper return envelope in your script package, some will even toss the script into the trash, unread. After all, if you don't know enough to do them that courtesy, you're not likely to be a worthy client. One positive note is that, while you will want to mail your scripts to the agent via first class mail, you can select fourth class (book rate) for return postage—it's much cheaper.

  An increasingly popular alternative to having "used" scripts returned is to ask, in your cover letter, that the script be recycled if the agent chooses to pass on you. (After all, you probably won't use the script again once someone has bent its corners and spilled coffee on it.) While you might lose the miniscule psychological edge of showing that you value your work by paying for its return, you will save a tree or two. The only true disadvantage is that, occasionally, an assistant who doesn't check your cover letter might think that your submission lacks a SASE, and toss the thing out. But, if you keep track of your submissions, you will discover the screw-up and can resubmit.

- *Deliver it in person.* Mailing a package can take a lot less energy than driving it over. *However,* if you deliver the package yourself, you might luck into some very valuable face time. You could get another chance to chat up the assistant, or the agent herself might cruise through the reception area while you are standing there. Bingo! Now you are a real person to these folks rather than merely a disembodied voice on the phone. Well worth the drive over, huh?

Of course, it's hard to hand deliver scripts if your home is three thousand miles away. What do you do if you don't live in L.A.?

TESTING THE WATERS IF YOU DON'T LIVE IN L.A.

As mentioned before, I strongly recommend that you test the waters before packing up to move west. There are several steps that you can take to help you make an informed decision.

- *Write those spec scripts first!* You can write anywhere. And it's far easier to write when the rest of your life is settled. So don't get on a plane unless you already have a couple of dynamite spec scripts in hand. If you find it difficult to buckle down and write in your current (comfortable, familiar) environment, you should ask yourself how productive you'll be when you have just moved to a new city and acquired new financial burdens. (Frankly, you might find, after cranking out a couple of scripts, that you really don't enjoy the work—it's better to learn that now rather than after you have already moved to L.A.)

- *Try to land an L.A. agent via long distance.* Use the same techniques as described above to launch an agent search. Many of the people you contact won't realize that you are calling from out of town. If someone does question you about your location, be honest, but at the same time, if you have decided to move to L.A., be sure to mention that you are in the process of relocating. Because the competition in Hollywood is intense, if you aren't passionate enough about the work to move out there, it is just as easy to find someone else who is. Plus, television writing involves a lot of face-to-face meetings and group effort—what agent needs the hassle of pushing someone from out of town?
    Some out-of-town writers, believing that their location is hampering their agent search, go so far as to create an L.A. presence for themselves. How does this work? You funnel calls and mail through a friend's or relative's home in Los Angeles. A call comes in, they take a message, they alert you, and you call back from your location. Mail comes to you at their address and they forward it to you, and you use their address as

the return on outgoing mail. Sound like a hassle? Definitely. But if money is scarce, it might be a temporary fix. Another alternative is to sign up with an answering service and rent a post office box, both in L.A. This is less of a hassle but it's a more costly option.

- *They want to meet.* If an agent loves your material, she *might* be willing to sign you up sight unseen, with the understanding that you will soon be arriving in L.A. so that you are available for work. However, the odds are greater that the agent will insist on meeting you before offering representation. Should you ask her to finance a flight out? Don't even think about it.

    In either case, if you manage to sign with an agent, you have arrived at the crossroads of that big move-to-L.A. decision. An agent is not likely to circulate your material until you actually move to town. How would she look if a producer asked to see you the next day, but you were living in Wisconsin? You might plead that you would gladly fly out but, honestly, how often could you spring for a last-minute plane ticket that costs five hundred bucks, a thousand, fifteen hundred? Just for an introductory "hello" meeting? Sure, you can *try* to schedule a bunch of meetings together to make a trip cost effective, but the odds of several producers all wanting to see you during the same few days are pretty slim. Sorry, but as discussed, producers are not going to hire you from out of town, so that you can then feel justified in moving to L.A.

Bottom line, you need to make a decision. At least, by going through the steps of writing scripts and securing an agent, you are in a much better position to make an informed decision. If prospects look good and your responsibilities are few, perhaps you should take the shot; you can always hop a plane back home, satisfied that you gave it a try. But if Hollywood has given you a lukewarm reception or other barriers stand in your way, think twice; you can always write in a form other than sitcoms, without disrupting your present existence.

FOLLOWING UP

Once you have submitted a script to an agent, what next? You wait. Give her about three weeks before calling the assistant "just to make sure that they received the script." Be pleasant, not pushy, and use this opportunity to chat up whoever answers. Odds are that they have received the script but haven't read it—agents often take one to three months to get to a new submission. Fine, say thanks and good-bye, and call back in two weeks if you haven't heard. And again two weeks after that, and two weeks after that, until you get a response. Don't fret about the time frame; good agents have stacks of scripts to get through. Of course, sometimes a writer will call after waiting for weeks, only to hear that—oops—they lost his submission. Oh, well. Graciously tell them "No problem" and rush a new copy over. Sometimes their goof works in your favor because they then feel obligated to give you more attention.

> **NOTE:** *You should probably know that even when someone in Hollywood swears that he will read your script, that sometimes means that his assistant or a professional reader will do the reading. Then, if that person thinks that the submission is brilliant, the agent/producer/executive himself will read it. It might be disheartening to hear but this is how people get through the mountains of scripts sitting on their credenzas.*

Remember, be a charmer during all of your discussions with the agent and her assistant. Be sharp, courteous, clever, prepared, fun and/or funny. Most of all, try to appear confident. If you seem desperate or needy, people in Hollywood tend to run the other way.

Keep detailed records. Start a contact file, on paper or via a computer program. Create a tickler system that reminds you to touch base with *all* of your contacts once in a while. (You never know who might point you to a job.) Write down anything that might help you to connect with a person, from mutual acquaintances to shared gripes. Keep track of names (correctly spelled), job titles (some people are very touchy about these), phone numbers, fax numbers, addresses, dates that you called, dates that they said to call back, strategies for following up, etc.

IF YOU FAIL TO LAND AN AGENT

One after another, your scripts come back, some preceded by an agent calling to let you down gently and others accompanied by a friendly pass letter. You've been through your entire agent hit list three times but nobody has offered to represent you. What can you do?

You regroup. First, take a hard look at the quality of your scripts. Are your samples good enough? Get some feedback from people whose opinions you trust. And try sending out different samples. And, as always, keep writing new samples.

> **Lawrence Konner:** Avoid bitterness. Avoid the kind of negativity that sometimes swirls around this town and around this industry, including envy and jealousy. It simply doesn't serve you well. It doesn't serve your mental health or your professional health, because you're just focused on the wrong things.

Then, though you should have already done this, revise your phone pitch. Are you getting enough agents to agree to read your material? Are the *right* agents reading your material?

When an agent does pass on you, here are a few tactics that you might try:

- *Ask if you can submit more samples down the road.* Many agents, anxious to avoid being negative, will cheerfully agree. Which means that you get another shot at them once you have written a new spec.

  NOTE: *The more times your scripts hit someone's desk, the better. After a while, that person—the agent, producer, or executive—will recognize your name and perceive you as someone who is serious about writing. If your scripts are good, your perseverance will usually make him more inclined to take you on.*

- *Ask for a referral.* Though this agent has decided to pass on you, he might know of other agents who are looking for new clients. If you don't ask, you don't get.

- *Strike a deal for passive representation.* If a desirable agent is encouraging but does not feel that he can sign you on at this time, ask if you can use his name to get your material read. The agent won't have to do anything but, if you land a job on your own, he gets to close the deal and collect 10 percent. And, hopefully, he will then be interested enough to sign you as a full-fledged client.

  Give away 10 percent when the agent hasn't done anything? Yes. By letting you say that he represents you—something many agents would not feel comfortable doing—he is making it much easier for you to get your material to producers and executives. Plus, if it only costs you one commission to get a good agent, it is well worth the price.

- *Approach an agent with a deal in hand.* If a desirable agent is encouraging but refuses to represent you, you might land him by returning with a deal in hand. Meaning, you use other methods to land a job and then offer to let that agent close the deal, *if* he agrees to sign you as a regular client. Sometimes the agent will be impressed enough to do so, and everything works out wonderfully. Other times, an agent will say no. And occasionally, an agent might agree, just to get the commission, but then do little to get you more work. Obviously, this last arrangement is not what you bargained for. But there are no guarantees that any agent will perform and, at the least, you can use the guy's name until you find a better agent.

YOU GET AN OFFER!

Finally, you get the call. An agent has read one sample, maybe two, and likes the work. He invites you in for an introductory meeting—*the* meeting. If all goes well, you will have an offer of representation before you leave his office.

Though the agent will try to make the meeting comfortable for everyone (you, him, and possibly another agent or two), treat it like a big job interview. You are out to make a sale, to get the offer. He is evaluating the way that you present yourself, to see if he thinks that you will impress producers and be pleasant to work with. What image should you present? Dress in casual clothes that look expensive, the type of things that you might wear to a nice brunch rather than an office job. (Think polo shirts and loafers rather than ties and pantsuits.) Be prompt. Be engaging. Be confident. And ask intelligent questions.

- Who are his other clients, and which of them are currently working?
- Who else works at the agency, and will you be dealing with them?
- What are his agency's strengths?
- What strategy would he recommend for you?
- How often does he brief his clients regarding the status of submissions?
- What are the odds of you getting work quickly?
- Does he have any thoughts on what you should be writing now?

Ask about his background, about how he got into the business. Show a personal interest in the man, to flatter him and to get a sense of how he really operates.

Take any promises of instant employment with a grain of salt. The key questions are: Does this person have the right connections, and will he aggressively circulate your material?

If the meeting goes well, he will formally offer to represent you. If you like what you see and don't have any other offers to consider, you can either shake hands on the deal or ask that he let you sleep on it overnight (so as not to seem too desperate). If you have other offers on the table, tell him so; unless you rub his nose in them, they will only enhance your appeal. Name names and ask him why it would be better to go with his agency.

If you get an offer but are waiting to hear from a different agency that you like better, ask the first agent if you can sleep on the offer and immediately call the preferred agent. Without appearing pushy, explain your situation and ask if the second agent has any interest in representing you. If and only if the preferred agent *pursues you aggressively*, sign with him and send your regrets to the first agent. But if you get a halfhearted response from the second agent, you would be wise to go with the person who has shown more interest.

One last thought: Remember that, when signing with an agent, you are not hiring a new best friend. If a friendship does develop, terrific. But writing is a business, your business, and what you need most is an agent who can sell you and your work.

SIGNING THE CONTRACT

What do you actually sign when signing with an agent? They will offer you a brief contract, probably anywhere from one to ten pages long. If the agent is a signatory to the WGA, his contracts must include a number of standard provisions that protect you, the writer. These provisions include:

- *Term of the agreement.* An agent may only sign you for up to two years. If you are both happy after that time period has passed, you can renew. If not, you are free to move on.

- *The ninety-day clause.* If you "do not receive a bona fide and appropriate offer of employment for an aggregate of at least [~$35,000—call the WGA for the current figure], during any period of ninety consecutive days, you can terminate your contract with your agent."[40] All you have to do is give him written notice and in ten days you're done. Of course, this clause works both ways—if your earnings fall short of the current cutoff figure, your agent can also terminate the contract.

- *Rider W.* Every signatory agent's contract is subject to a WGA-approved rider referred to as *Rider W.* This thirteen-page rider (it's often much longer than the agent's contract) presents a long list of standard provisions that govern agreements between agents and writers. If an agent's contract includes a provision that contradicts a provision in this rider, the rider always prevails; that is good for you, since most of the rider's provisions are designed to protect the writer.

While it is always wise to run a contract by an attorney before signing it, agreements with agents who are WGA signatories are so closely regulated that they usually can't do much harm. Of course, you should study the documents and you might even elect to ask for a change or two. For example, some contracts state that the agent gets a commission from nonscriptwriting earnings such as lectures, recitals, concerts, novels, etc. Unless the agent is prepared to seek work for you in these areas, you might ask that they be deleted from the agreement. (If the agent wants to keep them in, put him on the spot—ask him to explain what efforts he plans to make to land you those types of work.)

Lastly, there are two secondary agreements that deserve mention, both of which might be included in the primary contract or presented to you as separate documents. These documents grant the agent *power of attorney* to do the following: the first gives your agent the right to sign employment agreements on your behalf; and the second allows your agent to collect your writing fees, deduct his commission, and then forward the remaining money to you. Should you sign these agreements? Personally, I don't care to sign the first; I feel uncomfortable giving someone else the right to commit me to a job before I have read the contract myself. As for the second agreement, which allows the agent to collect my fees and deduct his commission, I gladly sign that because I want my agent to know that I trust him and want him to get paid promptly. (Conversely, to not sign the second will irritate your agent by suggesting that you do not trust him—a bad start for the relationship.)

ONCE YOU HAVE THE AGENT

Congratulations, you landed an agent! But has anybody hired you yet? Ninety percent of nothing is still nothing. Your next step is to get potential employers to read your work.

Fourteen

Step Three—Getting Your Work Out There

Any new writer who merely sits back and waits for his agent to generate work is likely to go hungry. Your success depends on getting your writing samples out to as many potential employers as possible. That means that you and your agent should both be trying to reach these people.

SCOUTING THE MARKET

Forget about selling those wonderful spec scripts that you wrote. When circulating those scripts, their only purpose is to land you an entry-level staff job or a freelance script assignment.

Staff jobs are likely to open up any time that a new show gets picked up or an existing show receives an order for additional episodes. As for freelance script assignments, the WGA requires the producers of every show to assign several episodes to outside writers every season; the exact number depends on how many episodes of that series have been ordered. Of course, many of these freelance assignments go to people who have an inside track: a deserving member of the production staff, a friend of a producer, the studio exec's nephew, a bored star who thinks he's a writer. (Once I lost a promised assignment to a pair of attractive women whom the producer met in traffic school; they had never written a word before but thought it would be neat to write an episode, and the producer thought they were neat, so . . .) Certainly it is irritating when favoritism robs you of an opportunity to work but, once you get going, personal connections might just as easily work in your favor.

How do you land a job? Your first priority is to get your spec scripts read by producers who currently have a show in production, or who have just received a production order. Then, your second priority is to target programming executives at studios and networks; they don't hire staff writers directly, as producers do, but they do recommend writers to the producers of their shows. (Actually, executives will often force a producer to hire a writer, but they usually do so only when the writer is already a hot commodity.) While it is best to catch these people when they have shows in production or heading into production, there is also a long-term benefit to making contact in their off season; two months later, that executive might recommend you to a producer, who three months later has an opening on a show. (This also illustrates why you should stay in touch with old contacts.)

Your third priority is to find people who can connect you with your first and second priorities, those producers and executives. Perhaps your friend, a gardener, mows a producer's lawn, or your cousin, the CPA, does an executive's taxes.

Yes, your agent should already know many of these people and should have a good idea of what jobs are currently open; he and his partners are, no doubt, constantly trying to sniff out new opportunities. But two or more heads are better than one. And on some occasions, as is only reasonable, your agent will push other clients instead of you. So gather your own intelligence: read the papers, read the trades, talk to neighbors, join your college alumni club, join industry organizations, start a writers' group, participate in team sports, join community organizations, go to church or temple or mosque. Develop an active social life that not only keeps you sane but also continually expands your network (and makes you a more well-rounded writer).

But don't you risk irritating your agent, by inadvertently contacting someone whom he is already pursuing? The trick is to consult regularly with your agent so that that doesn't happen. And if it does, big deal. Now that producer has *two* copies of your script. Plus, your efforts will reap a side benefit—most agents will work harder for a client if they see that he is working hard.

While trying to get producers and execs to read your material, what if you trip over an actual job opening that your agent hasn't heard of? You have two options. As it is, many writers usually ask their agent's assistant to send over a script once the writer has convinced someone to take a look; that way, the script looks more official because it bears the agent's script cover, and the writer doesn't have to play secretary. However, if you uncover an actual job opening and alert your agent to it, she will probably pitch a couple of other clients, in addition to you, for that job—you have just created competition for yourself. If you trust your agent, you can ask that she not submit other clients unless and until the producer passes on you. (Well, you can *ask*. . . .) Or your second option is to just send the script over yourself, with a brief cover letter identifying your agent (her name, firm's name, and direct dial number) for follow-up purposes. In fact, many agents, to save themselves delivery costs, are happy to give their clients some of their agency's mailing labels, so that the writers' direct submissions look more official. (Ask for a bunch so that you have them when you need them.)

HIRING WINDOWS

A few chapters back, I mentioned that the big broadcast networks tend to develop and air shows in a seasonal fashion. To reiterate, the traditional schedule runs roughly like this:

- From fall to midwinter, pilot scripts for new series are commissioned and developed;

- from January to April, a handful of the best scripts are produced as pilot episodes;

- in May, the networks announce which shows, old and new, will be given production orders for the coming year;

- in August and September, new series premiere and old series return with new episodes;

- in midwinter, failing series are replaced with *midseason* entries that had been held in reserve.

It seems that all networks, including the big broadcast networks, develop and premiere shows at all times of the year. However, many series are still produced per the traditional schedule outlined above. Because production dates dictate when writers are likely to be hired, a smart writer and her agent try to capitalize on the resulting hiring windows in the following manner:

1. *Midfall to midwinter.* You and your agent should focus on getting writing samples to network and studio executives *months before* the networks decide which series pilots to order. That is the time when these people have the time to read the material. The hope is that the executives, if they are impressed, will later recommend you to those producers who are asked to produce pilots.

2. *January through April.* The second that a pilot production order is announced, your agent should try to get your material to that pilot's producers. (Actually, some producers will receive orders for multiple

episodes at this point.) Reaching these people is a difficult task, because they are extremely busy with their make-it-or-break-it pilots. While they are usually not interested in hearing directly from an unknown writer at this time, they will often accept an agent's submission. (Of course, if your agent won't make these calls, then you should try.)

3. *May through July.* This is the prime *staffing season.* The second that series orders for the coming television season are announced, you and your agent should pounce on the producers. After all, one of their first goals will be to lock up a strong writing staff.

4. *July through the fall.* Most staff assignments are filled by now, but many shows give out their freelance assignments during this period.

5. *Fall to midwinter.* As shows start to succeed or fail in the ratings, additional episode orders will be given out. Both staff and freelance assignments will open up.

Again, all networks produce shows at all times of the year and you never know when the next contact might result in a job. So, while you will want to take advantage of these traditional hiring windows, you should be applying maximum effort at all times. Until you are employed.

WORKING WITH YOUR AGENT

Your agent's time is valuable—to you. Call regularly, every couple of weeks, if you aren't hearing from her. When you call, be efficient. Have your updates and questions ready. Sure, a little pleasant chatter is healthy for your relationship, but try to follow her lead regarding the amount.

A great side benefit of being an organized and efficient client is that when the agent talks to you, she feels an added incentive to be organized and efficient herself. At the same time, some agents don't like to "waste time" by keeping their clients updated on current submissions and news of job openings. That doesn't help you, because you need to know if your material is being sent out. If your agent tries to blow you off, persist, amicably. If she doesn't have the information handy, make an appointment to call back for a "quick chat regarding strategy." If your agent continues to blow you off and months go by without any indication that your material is going out, have a frank, friendly talk with her. If you still don't get any results, then it's time to start looking for a new agent.

My first agent introduced me to a very productive practice: Prior to peak hiring windows, we would meet in her office for an hour or two to go over every opportunity that was currently available. She would interrupt the discussion to call producers as I sat there, tying up any loose ends that we uncovered. (And yes, she had to take a call or two while I sat there—a small price to pay.) I highly recommend that you try these sit-downs with your agent. If you both come prepared, they are a great way to get a lot done, quickly. Plus, it's a chance for you and your agent to bond.

It is also helpful for you to act as your agent's *tickler file*. Every time your agent mentions a new job opportunity or a place where she has submitted your material, write down the details. When you talk to the agent two weeks later, ask what came of that situation. If she has forgotten to follow up (it happens) or hasn't heard, nudge her, gently, to take action. Then check back on the matter again when next you speak.

WHICH SCRIPTS TO SEND

Sometimes you or your agent might not be sure *which* of your samples will most impress a particular producer or executive. A *South Park* producer might like your *Frasier* script but feel that it is too "old and conservative" to prove that you can write for him. A *Frasier* producer might like your *South Park* script but feel that it is too "broad and sophomoric" to prove that you can write for her. When possible, ask the contact which of your specs he would like to read. Otherwise, all you and your agent can do is submit whatever seems best in each case. Sometimes you win, sometimes you lose.

A related problem involves circulating spec scripts based on old, canceled, or already-off-the-air shows. Usually it is considered a mistake to submit scripts written for shows that no longer air. (They're old news, who wants to read them?) Even if an aging show is still getting good ratings, it might be better to send samples based on newer series. Why? Because producers and executives have to go through hundreds of scripts; after a while, they get tired of reading episodes from the same old shows.

Of course, everyone has his favorite shows and you can't always crystal-ball someone's reaction. I once got a job for an hour series by submitting a spec (my only one-hour spec) written for the long-dead *Magnum* series. Go figure.

BEING PICKY ABOUT JOBS

Unless you are independently wealthy and don't care if you antagonize your agent, you should probably take whatever legitimate writing jobs come your way. A producer wants to hire you but you hate his show? So what. Just focus on your episode. Write thirty minutes of television that would make your mom proud. Get the credit and the money, and then move on to shows that you *want* to write for. Get picky later, when you have the leverage to call your own shots.

COLD-CALLING PRODUCERS

How do you cold-call producers to get your material read? First, you need names and numbers. In addition to the many ways of gathering intelligence that we have already discussed, you might want to get a copy of *Written By*, the WGA's monthly journal, and start calling every sitcom office named in its Television Market List. (*Written By* can be bought for five dollars an issue, or forty dollars for an annual subscription; WGA members receive it for free.) You can supplement this list with the weekly production updates posted in the trades.

What should you do when you call? Just ask to speak to the person whose name you dug up. When you get that person, or if you get blocked by that person's assistant, cheerfully plunge ahead with your pitch. Using some of the very same spin that went into your get-an-agent spiel, quickly identify yourself, explain why you are calling, and ask if your agent may submit a script for their review. The responses you will get will vary; some people will cut you off, some will invite you to submit, and some will insist that your agent call first. If you get blocked, make a note and try again later—who knows if the same person will answer? If they invite you to submit, do so promptly, remembering to include a brief cover letter that identifies your agent and thanks the contact person for authorizing you to send in your material.

> **NOTE:** *If an agent has agreed to a* passive representation *arrangement, thereby allowing you to use her name even though she isn't actually seeking work for you, what do you do when a producer says, "Have your agent send us the script"? Simple. Send it yourself, with a cover letter that thanks the contact for agreeing to read the script and identifies your agent for follow-up purposes. (If your passive agent will let you use some of her firm's mailing labels, even better.)*
>
> *The only downside to this arrangement? A few weeks after meeting you, a busy agent will probably forget your name. If someone calls to ask about you, he is likely to be greeted with "Who?" But no big deal. Just try to cover your bases by alerting the agent or her assistant when it is likely that an interested contact will call. It's not a foolproof system, but it's better than having no agent at all.*

Whenever you have a choice of people to call regarding a job opening, try to get to the real decision maker. We have discussed how the producer hierarchy breaks down, but what about those programming executives? Generally they are based at a network, a studio, or a large production company. Some are *development* executives, the people who supervise the creation of new series, and some are *current programming* executives, the people who supervise the ongoing production of existing series. Some executives handle both functions, depending on their company's needs. As for job titles, most executives work in departments that include a vice president, a director, a manager, and maybe a general programming executive.

How do these people spend their days? Taking pitches (if they work in series development), reading scripts, giving script notes, attending runthroughs, screening program footage, attending production meetings, working on program scheduling, supervising advertising and publicity efforts, and performing various administrative functions. Many executives have the authority to veto new projects, but very few can actually authorize expenditures related to scripts and production—which is why you should aim as high up the ladder as possible.

That said, let me mention one job-hunting strategy that does not involve aiming high up the ladder. Sometimes, if you can't get through to a primary producer on a show, it might be possible to make contact with a secondary producer. Every week, the primary producers are getting calls from all of the agents and half of the writers in town, hounding them for work. An up-and-coming co-producer doesn't get those calls, but is very well connected to the decision makers on the show. If you can find a connection—perhaps you loved the last episode he wrote?—you might call to introduce yourself. (Production secretaries don't screen as rigorously when calls come in for lesser staff members.) See if he would be willing to read a spec script or even meet with you. If he is receptive to your approach, you could end up with a well-placed champion on that show's writing staff or even a new writing mentor.

KEEP WRITING

The best job-hunting strategy of all is to keep writing. Writing improves your writing. What's more, producing script after script gives you and your agent an excuse to keep calling producers. After a while, those producers will start to remember your name and the fact that you are very productive (a good thing). If your writing is strong, many will eventually become inclined to hire you—if only to keep from having to read more of your spec scripts.

On another level, being productive also keeps your agent interested in you. Even if work isn't coming your way, he sees that you are still making things happen. Which encourages him to follow suit.

If you start running out of steam and find it difficult to keep writing, do something proactive. Take a screenwriting class, change your work habits, join or form a writers' group. Try to get one of the writers' internships occasionally sponsored by organizations like Warner Brothers, Disney, and the Academy of Television Arts and Sciences (see appendix B); not only are these a great way to learn the craft, they frequently lead to personal connections that can launch a career.

Do whatever it takes to keep those scripts coming. After all, you never know which script will be the one that lands you that next job.

> **Ian Gurvitz:** If someone's new and they haven't any credits and they have one great spec script, it really begs the question, did they shoot their wad on this? Did it take them ten years to write it? Did a bunch of friends help them punch it up? These are all stories you hear. So, often, you'll want to see a second sample. And more than that, you want to meet them to see whether they come off in a room like the person who wrote the script.

> **Lawrence Konner:** Print a sign that says Sit Back Down, and paste it over your computer. Keep writing. There's no substitute for writing. I think that young people have a tendency to focus too much on agents, deals, and whom you know. But I think that good writing wins. Good writing always wins.

> **Irma Kalish:** Don't live or die with one script. Some people write a spec script and they keep sending it out, and sending it out, and sending it out, and they never write another script. Go on, do another one. Then another and another. And don't just think, "Well, I want to be a writer, so make me a writer." No one is going to make you a writer. You're not going to be a writer unless you actually write. That sounds simplistic, but a lot of would-be writers [have exactly that attitude].

WRITING IN TEAMS

Many sitcom writers embrace the two-heads-are-better-than-one theory—they work in teams. There are definitely some advantages to the idea. Comedy writing is very demanding and subjective—some days, it is a huge relief to be able to share the load.

Ideally, each partner complements the other. Maybe one is good with story structure and the other is a walking joke machine. Or one partner is the real writer of the pair but the other can sell anything to anybody. Writing teams usually make producers happy because they can often get two bodies for the price of one. And the odds are good that, out of two people, one of them has to be funny.

Of course, there are disadvantages too. Unless you and your partner are in great demand, you will have to split script fees and staff salaries. And there will be two names on the scripts that you write; if the team dissolves, most producers and execs will want to see writing samples and credits that only bear your name before they will hire you. (For all they know, the other guy was the talented half of the team.)

Still, half a fee is better than none. If you know someone who shares your sense of humor and complements your writing strengths, and you would feel more comfortable working with a partner, give it a shot. Allow yourselves a little time to develop a comfortable routine and see what you can come up with.

REJECTION

Rejection stinks. But all writers encounter it. If someone says that your material isn't funny, just remember that comedy is extremely subjective. That is why attracting a mere 20-percent share of the TV audience makes a sitcom a hit, and why blockbuster comedies produced in England and Canada (similar cultures, similar speech) don't play in middle America. It is also why many comedy writers opt to work in teams, depending on their partners to keep their humor on track. So the next time someone pans one of your sitcom scripts, chalk it up to different sensibilities. And remember that if it was easy to get work as a television writer, everyone would do it.

> **Lawrence Konner:** The only true test of comedy is whether people laugh or not. There are a lot of situations where I and others say, "That's funny. Why aren't they laughing?" But they're not wrong. They're always right. If they're not laughing, it's not funny.

Of course, if everybody you approach thinks that your last ten scripts are horrible, then you might have a problem. Time to seek some input on how to improve your writing, or reconsider med school.

DEALING WITH WRITER'S BLOCK

Entire books have been written about how to deal with writer's block. Frankly, professional sitcom writers don't really have the luxury of succumbing to this problem. The script is due in five days? Then you had better deliver. (A hard deadline does wonders for getting a writer unstuck.)

The little bit of advice that I can offer on this subject would be the following:

- *Set easy goals.* If you break the work up into manageable tasks, it won't seem so daunting. You don't have to write the whole script in one day. Tackle the opening scene first. Start that by outlining the beats of the scene. Decide who will be in the scene. Play with ways to open the scene. Pick one and just write a page. The next thing you know, you're three pages in and you know how the rest of the scene should go. Problem solved, you're on your way.

- *Check your story.* Sometimes you might have trouble getting into a script because a part of your brain knows that there is a problem with the story. If work grinds to a halt, step back to see if you have overlooked something that needs fixing. If so, fix it, and see if that loosens things enough so that you can get back to the script.

- *Fill some pages.* It is better to write badly than never to have written at all. (According to some of my students.) To get the creative juices flowing, force yourself to quickly write a hack version of the scene you're working on. As often as not, some of what you create will be useable. Or it might help you to trip over an alternative approach that works.

If you still feel blocked, buy a book on the subject. Or save the money and *just do the work.*

PROTECTING YOUR WORK

Probably all writers worry at one time or another that their work might be stolen. It does happen, rarely, but more times than not a perceived infringement is merely a coincidence—two writers living in the same universe, struck by similar thoughts at the same time. The only way to ensure that your material won't be stolen is to stop circulating it. Of course, then you won't be getting any work either. Can't you do anything to protect your ideas? "Ideas," no; you cannot own, via copyright, a simple idea. However, you can protect " 'original works of authorship' that are fixed in a tangible form of expression."[41] Meaning, a script or even a detailed treatment. How? You have two options, one good and one not so good.

First, you can register your script with the U.S. Copyright Office in Washington, D.C. According to current copyright law, an original work of fiction is automatically copyrighted the moment you put words down on paper. However, who besides you knows that it exists if all you do is print it out? To get full copyright protection, you must register the script through the U.S. Copyright Office. Not only does this establish a public record of your claim to ownership, it also entitles you to sue for additional types of compensation if someone does infringe upon your copyright.

Sounds too complicated? Not at all. Just call the Copyright Office at (202) 707-3000 and ask them to mail you an instructional pamphlet and the proper application form for a fictional teleplay. Currently, the correct form is designated "Form PA," which covers materials related to the performing arts; you can fill out a one-page short-form version or a more detailed two-page version, the latter designed to accommodate multiple copyright owners.

To register your copyright, simply fill out the brief application form and send it back, accompanied by an unbound copy of your script and a check for twenty dollars. (Send it as registered mail with return receipt requested so that you will know that it has been received.) As long as the Copyright Office doesn't stumble over some conflict regarding the application, you will eventually receive a formal certificate of registration via return mail. Once it arrives, type an official registration notice in the lower left corner of your script's title page and you are done. (The proper notice consists of three elements: the copyright owner's name, the year in which the copyright was registered, and either the word "Copyright" or the symbol "©." Examples might include "Copyright 2001 Evan Smith" and "Evan Smith © 2001.")[42]

> **NOTE:** *It can take months for the Copyright Office to process your application and send you a certificate of registration. However, do not worry— the registration is deemed effective on the date that the government "receives all of the required elements in acceptable form." If you want an idea of how long the wait might be, call and ask an operator for their current estimate when you make your submission.*
>
> *Some people believe that they can gain full copyright protection by mailing a script to themselves in a sealed envelope. Sorry, this is only a myth— started, no doubt, by some guy at the post office.*

Copyright registration is one way to protect a script. The second option is to register it with the script registration department at either the WGA, west or the WGA, east. (See below for contact information.) This process is very similar to the copyright registration process. First, type identifying information—such as your name, address, social security number, and project title—on the script's title page or a cover letter. Then, submit an unbound copy of the script and a check, via mail or personal delivery. How much does Guild registration cost? Call and ask to be sure, but current fees are as follows:

twenty dollars for non-Guild members and ten dollars for Guild members if you are registering with the WGA,w; or, twenty-two dollars for nonmembers and ten dollars for members if you are registering with the WGA,e. Once your submission has been received by the WGA, you will be assigned a script registration notice that you should type in the lower left corner of your script's title page; the official notice will consist of "WGA Reg. #" followed by the number assigned to your script.[43]

As indicated earlier, I do not recommend registering your scripts with the WGA. While doing so is better than taking no action, even the Guild acknowledges that WGA registration is "not a substitute for filing with the U.S. Copyright Office."[44] One key difference is that you can't sue for the additional types of compensation previously mentioned if you don't register the copyright. Another difference is that the Guild throws out your script in either five years (WGA, west) or ten years (WGA, east) if you don't pay to renew the registration, whereas a copyright filing lasts for as long as your rights in the script last.

Should you register the script both ways, just to be safe? No. Planting both notices on the title page will just make you look paranoid or amateurish, or both, because both registration services serve the same basic purpose of establishing a claim of ownership.

Unfortunately, even registering a script with the U.S. Copyright Office does not, by itself, guarantee compensation or justice if someone else steals your work. Its primary purpose is to supply you with vital supporting evidence in case you decide to file a lawsuit against someone who has infringed on your rights.

If you do believe that another party has injured you, pause to consider the pros and cons before charging off to file suit. If you sue and win, what compensation might you actually receive? Is it enough to warrant the effort and expense involved? Also, what impact might the negative publicity of a suit have on your other potential employers? Or on your relationship with your agent, who might have to keep dealing with the infringing party in the future? Bottom line, is a lawsuit worth all of the hassle? Many times, it is not. But if the answer seems to be yes, talk to a lawyer who specializes in copyright law.

NOTE: *I am not a lawyer. The practical advice that I present in this book is intended to point you in the right directions rather than substitute for proper legal counsel. If you have an infringement problem, or any other legal concern, talk to a pro.*

Is it even worth bothering to register a sitcom script, if there are so many obstacles to enforcing your rights? In my opinion, yes, you should register scripts with the U.S. Copyright Office. But I do not recommend registering a mere sitcom outline; because those documents consist primarily of story *ideas* (which do not qualify for copyright protection) and elements of a series premise (characters, settings, etc.) that belong to the show's producers, it might be very difficult to prove an infringement involving such scanty material.

Ultimately, the best way to protect your work is to see that it only goes out to people who have legitimate connections to the sitcom world. But beyond that, limiting its circulation means that you are also lessening your chances of landing work.

For more information about protecting your work, contact the following:

Copyright Office
Library of Congress
101 Independence Ave., S.E.
Washington, DC 20559-6000
(202) 707-3000

Writers Guild of America, west
Script Registration Dept.
7000 W. Third Street
Los Angeles, CA 90048
(323) 782-4540

Writers Guild of America, east
Script Registration Dept.
555 W. 57th St.
New York, NY 10019
(212) 767-7801

WHO KEEPS THE COPYRIGHT?

Since it is not likely that anyone will ever buy a spec sitcom script that you have written, lucky you, you get to keep the copyright. However, if you are hired to write an episode of a television series, the producer who hires you gets to own the copyright because it's written into your contract for the job. To protect the producer's investment in your episode, which might cost a million dollars or more to produce, it is important that she secure the underlying creative rights to the story. That way, if you suddenly object to her interpretation of the material, or you go insane and start insisting on bizarre changes, she doesn't have to worry. She owns and completely controls the property, and you no longer have a say in the matter.

A script written under this arrangement is called a *work for hire* or *work made for hire*. (You will see this phrase in the contract provision that describes who retains the copyright.) While it might seem illogical or even unfair that an employer, in effect, gets to proclaim herself the author of something that she didn't write, do not fret about this issue. It is a standard provision of script deals, and Writers Guild regulations ensure that it doesn't cause writers undue harm. More to the point, if you don't agree to let the producer acquire the copyright, she will not hire you. Which leaves you with 100 percent ownership of a never-to-be-produced script.

JOINING THE WRITERS GUILD OF AMERICA

Just what is the Writers Guild of America, this wonderful organization that protects hardworking film and television writers from the evils of Hollywood? The WGA, west and east branches, is the official screenwriters union. (It also serves interactive writers, animation writers, and other media writing types.) The WGA does not find jobs for its members, but it does provide many useful services, including the following:

- Negotiates the industry-wide agreements that protect writers' interests regarding compensation, working conditions, and creative rights

- Collects residual payments for its members

- Provides contact information to those who want to reach a writer or his agent

- Provides free legal advice regarding union- or contract-related problems

- Provides a home base for numerous writers' committees that explore everything from ageism to new technologies

- Provides an excellent health insurance plan for those who earn enough to be eligible

- Provides pension benefits for eligible members

- Governs writing credits and provides a process for arbitrating credit disputes

- Encourages networking by sponsoring seminars and business functions

- Publishes an informative monthly journal titled *Written By*
  . . . and much more.

Sounds great! How do you join? Well, the bad news is that, as with many unions, you have to land some work before you are allowed to join the WGA. And that work must consist of legitimate writing assignments handed out by Guild-signatory producers, not your uncle Leo.

But how can you get Guild-sanctioned work if you aren't even *in* the Guild? That's the good news. Producers don't care—and probably won't even ask—if you are a Guild member when they interview you for a job. If they love your writing samples and you, that's all that matters. Guild membership, once you qualify, comes later.

How much work must you get before you can join the Guild? Requirements are different for the WGA, west and the WGA, east; it's easier to get into the eastern branch but, because almost all sitcoms are produced in Los Angeles, geography dictates that most sitcom writers must join the western branch. (As previously mentioned, membership is supposed to be determined by which side of the Mississippi you live on.) To become eligible for membership in the WGA,west, you must first obtain a minimum number of "employment units." The current requirement for *full* membership in the WGA,w is twenty-four units, meaning that (Guild-signatory) producers have hired you to write at least two complete sitcom episodes or "the equivalent." If a writer gets some work but not enough to qualify for full membership, she may elect to become an associate member of the WGA,w; this would entitle her to receive mailings and many benefits of Guild membership, but she could not vote on Guild matters or run for office.

The membership requirements for both branches are somewhat confusing. If you start to get work as a film or television writer, call the nearest Guild's membership department to get information on current requirements for full membership or details of how to become an associate member. (WGA,w's department can be reached at (323) 782-4532, and WGA,e's at (212) 767-7800.)

Or do nothing. Because—more good news—once you have landed enough Guild-sanctioned sitcom work to qualify for full membership, you are automatically admitted! You don't have to audition, or know somebody, or bribe somebody. In fact, the WGA will contact you without your having to do a thing. Based on hiring information that your producers must regularly supply to the Guild, it knows when you become eligible. At that point, the membership department will send you a delightful "Welcome to the WGA" letter—and a bill for twenty-five hundred dollars in initial dues. Then you will receive a copy of the Guild manual and a continuing stream of useful mailings, and you are on your way.

To sustain a full membership in the WGA,w, you will be required to pay quarterly dues of twenty-five dollars plus 1.5 percent of your gross earnings as a writer. The bookkeeping is easy; you receive regular statements and invoices.[45]

Is it worth the cost? What if you don't want to pay these fees? It is worth it, considering the many benefits of WGA membership. And you don't really have a choice about paying if you want to keep working as a sitcom writer, because Guild-signatory producers are prohibited from hiring anyone who has qualified for membership but does not pay the required dues.

> **NOTE:** *At this point, I should also mention that if you become a WGA member you are prohibited from writing for producers who are not signatories to the WGA. If the Guild discovers that a member has written for a nonsignatory producer, it has the option of subjecting that writer to disciplinary actions, including a fine that can equal up to 100 percent of the amount that the writer earned from that job.*

MOVING ON

You've got an agent and you are getting your work out to the people who count. Finally, the call comes in—a producer loved your spec script and wants to meet you. You're close, but how do you land the job?

Fifteen

Step Four—Pitching for Assignments

Until just a few years ago, sitcom writers usually started their careers by landing a couple of freelance script assignments. Then, if they proved themselves, they moved on to low-level staff jobs and began working their way up.

Today, thanks to the expanding job market, many new writers land a staff job right out of the gate. And some do so based on having written *only one (strong) spec script*. How come? Competition for talented writers has become so intense that producers have to grab hot prospects wherever they can find them. On the one hand, that's great news for those seeking entry-level jobs. On the other, it means that many new writers aren't getting a chance to learn their craft before being thrown into a group writing environment. Either route, pitching for a freelance assignment or competing for a staff position, can lead to your first job—we'll discuss both, starting with freelance assignments.

Matt Williams: [Today,] people are thrown into positions before they've had time to serve their apprenticeships. Somebody comes in and is really funny at the table, and in two years, all of a sudden they're a co-executive producer and they're asked to run a show. And they don't have the slightest idea of how to supervise an editing session, a sweetening session, or how to beat out three stories at once, or make sure that their stories are building properly. . . . You have to learn the basic building blocks of storytelling. There are certain dramaturgical elements that exist in one-act plays, full-length screenplays, Broadway musicals, and half-hour sitcoms. They're like molecules. The essence of storytelling.

THE CALL COMES IN!

You and your agent have been circulating your samples like mad. Finally, the call comes in. Your agent informs you that a producer of *Show X*—your new favorite show—loves your work and wants you to pitch for a freelance script assignment. This means one of three things: either the producer is counting on you to bring in the world's best idea for an episode; or she wants to hear what types of ideas you can come up with (to get a sense of your talent) but ultimately plans to assign you one of their ideas; or she doesn't even require that you bring in ideas because, if she likes you, she intends to just hand you one of theirs.

PREPARING FOR THE PITCH

When your agent calls to schedule the pitch, try to get a date that gives you at least two to three days to prepare. Use all of that time to get ready. Pitches are hard to come by and these people are already predisposed to hire you.

Most of what you need to do was already covered in part 2 of this book. The first step in developing ideas for a show is to study that show. Get several tapes and scripts, and take a hard look at them.

Then create your springboards. How many? Some successful writers believe that half a dozen are plenty. I don't. Often, a show's producers will quickly eliminate one or two of your ideas because they think that they have already been done elsewhere. Then they might cross off one or two because they themselves have done or are about to do similar stories. That leaves you with only a couple of shots at making a sale. Why play those odds?

My philosophy is that, having worked so hard to get invited in for a pitch, it's worth my effort to generate *ten to fifteen solid ideas*. If the producers immediately dismiss four or five for assorted reasons, no problem—I've got plenty more. Not only do I increase my odds of hitting on a premise that the producers love, but I impress them by showing that I have tons of good ideas.

Pitch meetings usually run thirty to forty-five minutes so there isn't enough time to fully describe ten to fifteen stories. That's why you start out with those three-to-five-sentence springboards. If they don't like an idea, you can quickly go on to the next.

When an idea does catch the producers' interest, they will stop you and ask that you fill in some blanks. Quickly run through the key story beats. Answer the producers' questions. Adjust the story to their tastes if they see it going a different way. (Remember, the client is always right.)

Preparing these concepts sounds like a lot of work. Do you have to be able to fully explain all of those story ideas? No, not all. Some stories, especially high-concept ideas, are so clear (when you pitch the springboard) that you don't really need to fill in any gaps. For other stories, yes, you should be prepared to lay out the key beats, to quickly outline a beginning-middle-end, if a producer asks for details. (Figure a couple of paragraphs' worth of description, max.) Of course, again, if the producers see a story heading in a different direction, don't fight them; adapt to their vision *without complaint*.

If a producer asks for details that you haven't figured out yet, don't panic. If a workable answer pops into mind, toss it out. Or simply say, "Gee, I don't know. Could I get back to you on that this afternoon?" The producers will probably tell you not to bother, or promptly come up with an answer themselves. No problem; they know that all stories have elements that need to be worked out. What matters is that you aren't thrown by the question and that you have demonstrated an eagerness to solve problems.

Here are some other points to consider when preparing for a pitch:

- As you create your springboards and flesh out the story beats to back them up, remember that *your goal is to sell, not educate*.

- Because producers sometimes mull over a pitch before deciding on an assignment, some writers like to supply them with *leave-behinds*. These are simply copies of the springboards (not lengthy story descriptions) that were pitched, each neatly typed on a separate page, with the writer's name at the top. The thinking here is that a writer's carefully honed springboard can probably do a better job of selling the producers than can their own vague recollections of what he pitched; so why not leave written copies of the ideas that the producers thought were worth considering? Of course, there are two caveats: Don't annoy the producers by leaving behind those springboards that they already passed on, and make sure that what you leave behind is very well written.

- After you have developed your ideas, *practice your pitch*. Do it out loud, in front of a mirror or your roommate, bouncing off the sofa, throwing in sound effects, whatever. Find a style of presentation that works for you and rehearse until you are comfortable with the material. Yes, some people hardly prepare at all but always manage to wow their listeners. And yes, you should avoid reading to your listeners or memorizing a pitch. However, practicing a bit, so that you can focus more on where the meeting is heading than on what happened in which story, is always a good idea.

- *Try to pitch funny*—you're supposed to be a comedy writer.

- *Research the pitchees.* Find out what you can about the people to whom you will be pitching. You never know when a personal connection might tilt a hiring decision in your favor. And you might uncover information that clues you in to what types of stories the producers want to see.

THE PITCH

On the day of the pitch, dress the part of a successful, easygoing comedy writer. As previously mentioned, think casual clothes that look expensive—polo shirts and loafers rather than ties or pantsuits. Maybe a hip skirt from Melrose Ave., or nice jeans and sneakers if they look really good.

Take a note pad when you go. You might want to jot down someone's comments or the producers might end up dictating five pages of story outline to you. Also, it's a place to tuck leave-behinds, if you bring any.

Give yourself plenty of time to get to the meeting. (Being late is not an option.) Sometimes it will take place in an office building, which means that your only concern is finding a parking space. Most of the time, it will take place at a studio lot, which means that you'll face a whole chain of time-consuming barriers. First, the guard at the studio gate will stop you while he searches for your "drive-on pass," which is supposed to have been arranged for by one of the producers' assistants; half the time, he can't find the pass and you have to wait while he calls someone to get clearance for you to enter the studio. Then, inevitably, you are instructed to park in a space located as far from your meeting's location as is geographically possible. After a brisk jog across the lot, you find that you have been directed to the wrong building and must now double back. Finally, you locate the correct structure and make your way to the office. (By now, you can forget about that relaxed bathroom check.)

You will probably be asked to wait in an outer office. Be pleasant to any assistants that you meet; a couple of nice words from one of them might greatly improve your chances of getting hired, just as a few pointed barbs could lessen those chances.

Eventually, you will be ushered into an office or conference room. You will probably meet with one to four people—usually a couple of producers and an assistant who will take notes. (No, your agent will not attend.) Try to relax and enjoy the moment. You are the guest; these people want you to feel comfortable. After all, they loved your writing samples and they know what it's like to pitch to a bunch of strangers. If they are up for a little small talk before getting down to business, go with the flow. If they offer coffee, sure, have a cup, but only if they're having some too. Cigarettes? Chewing gum? No. Too many people find them offensive.

Bottom line, the whole key to a successful pitch is to *always follow their lead*. Most particularly, the lead of whoever seems to be in charge.

Okay, that's not the *whole* key to a successful pitch. There's one other maxim: *Never appear desperate or needy*. Hollywood is a billion-dollar business built on whimsical ideas. If you seem insecure, you won't get hired; how can an employer believe in you if you don't? So even if your knees are knocking and your car is being repossessed as you walk into the pitch meeting, put on your best glad-to-be-here-but-I-won't-die-if-I-don't-get-this-job face when you arrive.

At some point after everyone in the room has gotten settled, someone will cue you to begin your pitch. Put on your happy face and crank your energy up a notch. You worked hard on these ideas, they're good, and these people are lucky to be hearing them. Start going through your springboards, pausing after each to get a verdict. Sometimes a producer will cut you off because she can tell early on that an idea won't work; if you don't have the perfect solution for her problem, smile, toss the idea, and move on. Occasionally a producer will interrupt to ask a question. And sometimes an assistant or a phone call will interrupt. Don't let these events throw you—get the pitch back on track.

As you go through your ideas, remember that you are *selling*. Show some passion and excitement. Try to make the meeting fun for all involved.

At the same time, *listen and watch*. Look for cues—nodding heads and amused grunts that indicate interest, crossed arms and traveling eyes that indicate boredom. Make eye contact with everyone, particularly the person in charge. If someone seems unhappy with an idea, don't argue with that person. If someone suggests that a story should go a different route, and that someone is a senior person, try to go with her idea. If someone seems very interested in a particular springboard, stop pitching and try to make the sale.

Sometimes the producers will interrupt your pitch to get your reaction to a story concept that they have generated. Here's your response, whatever the idea—you love it! (Only, try to seem sincere when you say it.) They pitched the idea because they are sold on you and it. You are mere moments from landing an assignment. However, if you express strong reservations about the concept, no sale. It's not that you can't have questions about how to develop the idea—that's fine, it's part of the writing process. But if you don't *like* the idea, they would be foolish to assign it to you. (And of course, once you have rejected their idea—their thinking, *them*—you might find it a degree more difficult to sell them one of your own ideas.)

ADVICE FROM OUR PRODUCERS

More thoughts on the subject of pitching:

Irma Kalish: The main thing is enthusiasm. If you come in and you just say, "Well, I don't know. You may not like this, but . . ." [That's not good.] You've got to really sell it. . . .

One person came in to me saying, "Have you done the one about? . . ." Well, if anyone says, "Have you done the one about? . . ." I'm not going to listen to whatever else he or she might have to say. . . .

A producer, believe it or not, is not thrown off if a writer comes in with an idea that's already been done on the show. Because I, as a producer, would not believe that they would deliberately see that we had done a particular story and just come in with the same idea. What you would think is that, "Well, they've got the idea. They know what our characters would do or what we would like to do on the show." So, I would say, "Well, we've done that already. What else do you have?" . . .

It's almost like the cliché saying, "I know what I like when I see it." You know? I know what I like when I *hear* it.

Matt Williams: When pitching, there's a saying—pitch the sizzle, not the steak. I think the biggest mistake with pitching is [that some writers] get too bogged down in details. You should have those answers in your head but, for instance, if [a producer asks], "Well, gosh, how did they get . . . ," [don't answer] "Well, they took the bus across town, then he got on the elevator. He went up to the fifty-fifth floor, he waited for half an hour. . . ." We don't care. Just say, "He went across town and he's in the office." Get to the essence and pitch the two or three key moments in the story. If you embrace the major turning points or the two or three funniest moments in the script, then I'm hooked, and I'll say, "But, I don't understand. How did he get to the office?" "Well, he took a bus, he went up to the fifty-fifth floor. . . ." Lay the details in *if* you're asked about them. . . .

The big deciding factor [when hiring a freelancer] is the confidence of the writer. [He should] know exactly what this episode is about. It's not a collection of scenes where you're chasing jokes that have nothing to do with the story.

Ian Gurvitz: The hardest thing about pitching from the outside is coming up with a fresh take on a show that the people on the inside have been thinking about every day for years. How are you going to think of something they haven't? . . .

I did a *Frasier* episode where part of a pitch, a one-line part, happened to attach to a story arc that the producers were thinking of doing. It was just one little one-line idea for something—I think it was "what if Maris was missing?"—and that led to them say, "Well, we were thinking of going down that road where they separate, and this could be the catalyst." And from there, it became that episode.

Maxine Lapiduss: I think the best thing that you can do when you go in is to try to get as much information as possible from someone on staff before the meeting. Do sort of a pre-pitch, if you can. Call a low-level writer on the staff, a story editor or co-producer, and say, "I'm sort of thinking..." That way, if you have five great ideas but they're the ones that they're already doing that season, you can avoid spinning your wheels [by perfecting a doomed pitch].

Lawrence Konner: I always feel like I want to tell stories when I pitch and I want to hear stories when I'm listening to pitches. Stories that show that this person understands the series. Show the producers that you're smart enough and entertaining enough, and that you understand their show enough, and they will want to be in business with you. They need people to write this show more than they need ideas for new episodes....

Don't get so focused on trying to impress them with your story ideas that you fail to impress them with yourself. A smart producer would rather be in business with a talented writer who didn't pitch him the world's greatest idea, than with a less talented writer who did....

Remember that the person whom you're pitching to is controlling the room. If they want a lot of small talk, be ready for a lot of small talk. If they want little small talk and then straight to business, you're ready to go straight to business....

Remember that the guy sitting behind the desk has probably had ten writers in ahead of you and will have ten writers in behind you that day, and that he has fifty other problems, as well. If you come in with any kind of attitude like, "I'm here to bail you out. This is the greatest idea for *Caroline in the City* anybody's ever had," then you've already turned them off. The producer has probably already heard every permutation of Caroline's problems that can be imagined....

When you come to Hollywood, no matter how good you are, the industry doesn't need you. They will do just fine without you. They've done okay without you up to now, and if you never show up here and never get in, they'll keep going. And I think you have to sort of suggest [to the producers] that you understand that. You understand that this is a big factory kind of operation and you want to be a cog. You're happy to be a cog and you want to be a cog.

Sandy Frank: Let's say you're up for a new show. You'll generally be given a chance to watch the pilot [as part of your introductory meeting]. Sometimes you'll be in a room down the hall, watching the pilot, and you've got to think of something good to say about it—which is not always easy. I've had the experience, when hiring, of showing a writer the pilot and coming in and just seeing by the expression on her face that she hated it. And, you know, she pretended that she didn't hate the pilot, but I didn't hire her because I knew her heart was not going to be in it. It's not that different from other jobs, where you have to pretend, "Oh, I love your toilets. I love the toilets that you manufacture, or the air freshener you distribute." You're expected to be reasonably enthusiastic. . . . You know, when you tell someone that their ugly baby is the most beautiful baby in the history of the world, they will smile and agree with you. They will not think, "What a ridiculous thing to say." So, in general, when you say, "Your pilot was really, really funny," they will think so, too. So it's hard to go too far in that direction with most people. . . .

You may think that you know who the most important person in that room is, and you might figure that someone else must be a secretary or something. But that may not be the case. So treat everyone nicely. Be courteous and don't interrupt people when they're talking. I once was sort of interrupting Jim Brooks in a pitch meeting, and one of the people in the room motioned to me and made a . . . sign. And he smiled when he did it, but I think he was serious. . . .

You also have to realize that it's not really within your control. We all think, if we go to a job interview or whatever, that if we do and say exactly the right thing, things will work out. That may not be the case. It may work out no matter what you do, and it may not work out no matter what you do. So just relax and try to be as much of a normal human being as possible under the circumstances.

WHAT MIGHT HAPPEN

How does a pitch meeting usually end up? Generally, if you are up for a freelance script assignment, one of three things happens:

THEY WANT TIME TO DECIDE

The producers might like a couple of your ideas but need time to confer with each other or—horrors—to take pitches from other writers competing for the same assignment. If they end the meeting with "We'll get back to you," offer up the leave-behinds for stories they liked (if you brought any leave-behinds) and make a graceful exit. Then run to a phone and call your agent. Fill him in on the details so that he can call the producers to press for a sale. (If he doesn't volunteer to do so, suggest it yourself. Strongly.)

THEY PASS ON ALL OF YOUR IDEAS

Not good. But it happens all the time, for all sorts of reasons. Still, you have one chance to salvage the situation. It's a long shot, but ask if you can come back for another pitch in two days. Explain that you now have a better idea of what they're looking for, or something like that, and lobby for a return date. If they say no, you lose nothing. If they say yes, do your very best to come up with a better pitch. Because two strikes will leave a bad taste in their mouths.

THEY SAY "GO WRITE AN OUTLINE"

Congratulations! You made the sale! Now stop pitching before they change their minds.

At this point, the producers might just give you some notes on the story and tell you to go home and write the outline. Or they might sit down with you for a while to sort out the big beats and then send you off to put the outline on paper. Or they or the entire writing staff might meet with you a couple of times, over a couple of days, to beat out the story together. Before you compose the official outline, ask a producer's assistant for copies of past outlines so that you can format yours in the same manner.

As soon as you can after making the sale, call your agent so that she can sew up the deal. Then, all you have to do is write the thing. Do a good job and they'll assign you the script. Do a great job and they might put you on staff.

THE CONTRACT

Once a WGA-signatory producer tells you to write an outline, you've got a deal. And, unless you are a very hot writer who can command overscale payments, there usually isn't much to negotiate. The production company will send your agent (or you, if you are agentless) their standard contract for what is called a writer's *step deal*. Step deals are so named because they allow a producer to terminate a writer's employment once certain steps of the deal have been completed, if the producer does not wish the writer to finish the project; in sitcoms, the only cutoff point occurs after the writer's delivery of a story outline. (Fortunately, few sitcom producers actually cut writers off, and they still have to pay you for any work done before a cutoff point.)

What sorts of provisions go into these standard contracts? A typical agreement is just a few pages long and it includes elements such as the following:

- introductory paragraphs that identify you, your agent, the production company, and the material that you are being hired to write;

- clarification that you are being hired to write either a "story and teleplay" or a "story with option for teleplay." The latter pays a little more because that's the option that enables a producer to cut you off after the first step, if he chooses to;

- details of how much you will be paid, at what points. Again, these figures are usually the standard minimum rates that must be paid to all Writers Guild members for this type of work. (These fees are dictated by an industry-wide collective bargaining agreement known as the writers' MBA, or Minimum Basic Agreement.) In sitcoms, your fee is usually paid in two or three installments—following delivery of the outline, the first draft, and the "final" draft;

- language stating that you are required to deliver work on a schedule dictated by the producers;

- language stating that the copyright in the script will belong to the production company, because you are being hired to create a "work for hire" (as such, the production company is free to make any changes to the material that it wishes to);

- language stating that the production company is not obligated to produce the script that they are hiring you to write (though they still have to pay you for your work);

- warranties from you stating that the work you will furnish will be your own original creation and that your employment will in no way infringe upon a third party's rights;

- a description of the writing credit that you can expect to receive, barring a credit dispute.

While every company has its own standard contracts, the meat of these agreements doesn't change much from show to show. The primary reason is that all must conform to the provisions dictated by the above-mentioned writers' MBA.

That said, you should still read the agreement. And you should talk with your agent if you have any questions. If she is unable to satisfy your concerns, consult with an attorney who specializes in entertainment law. Or if you belong to the WGA, seek the free legal advice that that organization makes available to its members.

THE MONEY

Before getting paid, a producer's assistant will probably ask you to fill out a tax form and provide proof of U.S. citizenship. If you have granted your agent power of attorney to collect your fees, your checks will be funneled through him; his office will take 10 percent off the top and then send you the rest. (Yes, taxes are usually deducted up front, even though you are clearly operating as a freelance employee.)

So, how much will you make? Below are a couple of the Writers Guild minimums that have been negotiated to date. These fees are for a complete "story and teleplay" of a half-hour prime-time sitcom episode being produced either for a broadcast network (ABC, CBS, NBC, or FBC) or a pay-cable network (like HBO or ShowTime):

From 5/2/99 to 5/1/2000: $17,588
From 5/2/2000 to 5/1/2001: $18,116

Script fees for a syndicated or basic cable show are less, a bit more than half of the standard network fees:

From 5/2/99 to 5/1/2000: $9,338
From 5/2/2000 to 5/1/2001: $9,665[46]

Again, if you eventually become a writer in great demand, your agent might be able to negotiate overscale fees for you. And, in addition to these up-front fees, you will receive more money (called *residuals*) if the show is rerun or distributed in other media. If the series is a big hit, those additional fees might eventually add up to *more than your original payment*.

If you want more information regarding writing fees, order a copy of the WGA,w's current "Schedule of Minimums" by contacting its operations office at (323) 782-4520. It costs two dollars to have the pamphlet mailed to you if you are not a member of the Guild.

MOVING ON

Today, fewer and fewer sitcom writers start their careers by pitching for freelance assignments. Let's examine the alternative—landing a lucrative staff job.

Sixteen

Step Five—Landing a Staff Job

Some sitcom writers have no desire to work on the staff of a show. They prefer the freedom of coming in to do freelance episodes here and there rather than being chained to a seventy-hour-a-week job. Unfortunately, there aren't a lot of freelance episodes to go around. The WGA requires producers to dish out a few assignments every season, but a lot of those are handed out as favors to friends or assigned to hot writers who have more work than they can handle. Another reality of freelancing is that you have little say over what happens to your work; you hand in the second draft, get a check, and you're done—though you're welcome to attend the final taping. And then there's the money. While you can make a good living as a freelancer, if you can land an entry-level staff job, you could make six figures in your first year.

Which is why many people aspire to become staff writers. Though others are quite happy to keep freelancing. If you're one of the former, how do you get started?

LANDING A STAFF WRITING JOB

Sometimes it's as easy as falling off a log. You write some great spec scripts and they generate a buzz (thanks in no small part to you and your agent pushing them like mad). It comes around to staffing season and, suddenly, several different producers are asking if they can meet you. You go in, say some hellos, and the next thing you know, your agent has two job offers on the table. She uses the competing offers to negotiate a great deal with one of the producers, and bingo—you've got a staff job.

No pitching, no writing freelance episodes. And not much chance to learn your craft either. You jump straight into a group writing environment and either swim or sink.

Other times, it's not quite so easy. You might have to write a couple of freelance assignments before someone deems you a candidate for a staff job. Or you might be asked to pitch for a freelance assignment so that the producers can assess your abilities, even though they are inclined to offer you a staff job if the pitch goes well. Or you might end up writing one or more freelance episodes for a producer's show before he approaches you about working on staff.

> **Ian Gurvitz:** The agent says, "This writer is brand-new but they've got these hot spec scripts, and I wanted to bring them to you first," that kind of stuff. Which is what they tell everybody to create a feeding frenzy.

You will probably receive one of two job titles when first hired. The lowest staff position is dubbed a *term writer*; this person is hired on a week-to-week basis, though he is usually guaranteed a minimum number of weeks of employment. The next position up is a *story editor*; this position falls into a category of writers who are "also employed in additional capacities,"[47] which means that they receive a more favorable compensation package (as described below). If at all possible, try to obtain the second title—it brings in a lot more money and is a better professional credit to have on your resume.

Whatever a new staff writer's title is, his responsibilities are usually the same from one show to the next. As we discussed in the "Writer's Work Week" section of chapter 12, a staff writer participates in read-throughs, run-throughs, final shoots, pitch meetings from outsiders, and many, many group writing sessions. Plus, he spends time alone or with his partner, dreaming up story lines and cranking out script drafts. His home base is usually a tiny writer's office located in a show's main production offices, on a studio lot. He also spends lots of time in rehearsal halls, the sound stage where his show is produced, and the studio commissary (a guy's gotta eat).

Some shows run so smoothly that they practically have a regular schedule for key production meetings, rehearsals, and even writing sessions. (Many experienced staffs designate one or two nights a week as a regular after-hours rewrite night.) These well-managed shows are usually a pleasure to work on because the producers are efficient and considerate. While you might still be working very long hours, little of that time is wasted and you are not being subjected to one crisis after another.

Then there are the other shows, frequently the newer shows, which have yet to work out the kinks. Working on these shows can be a nightmare of conflicting creative opinions, long hours spent solving problems that should never have occurred, and panicked rewrites at the last possible minute.

Still, a job is a job. Every show that you work for means another credit, money to pay the bills, a chance to make new contacts, and an education about the writing process. And to be honest, no matter how organized a show's producers are, problems will always surface when you are trying to create a half hour of quality television every week.

OFFICE POLITICS

As in any business, a new employee should be particularly sensitive to office politics. Who has the power? How do they use that power? What do they expect of people lower on the food chain? Who is allied with whom? Who dislikes or is jealous of whom? And who might see bright-eyed-and-bushy-tailed you as a threat?

In a perfect world, you would only work on shows where the producers promote a collegial, supportive, sharing environment. In the real world, you might sometimes find yourself in a hostile, every-man-for-himself situation. What should you do? How should you act? Well, you should probably just try to act naturally or you'll just give yourself a headache. Beyond that, you might want to consider the following:

- Do your homework. Get a copy of the draft that will be rewritten next and make notes before going into a roundtable session. That way, you're not just ad-libbing fixes as you go.

- Personal chemistry is very important. Show people that you are fun to have around and they will find ways to keep you around.

- Be open to other people's ideas. It's that whole karma thing—give, and you shall receive tenfold. (Wait, that's a pyramid scheme. Well, same difference.)

- Know that if you embarrass someone in front of his superiors, he is likely to come gunning for you. So try to couch criticism in a nonpersonal way. (See "karma-pyramid scheme" point above.)

- Take time to size up the group before you cut loose. Some established writer-producers are very into the staff hierarchy thing. If a new junior writer comes on too strong, they tend to become annoyed. So unless you feel that it would stifle you intolerably, get to know your co-workers a bit before getting in their faces.

- Think twice before chiming in on someone else's in-joke. Some folks take great offense when an uninvited newcomer butts into a private conversation.

- Be a good sport. Writers kid and harass each other all of the time. Don't take offense, and feel free to respond if a good zinger comes to mind.

- Don't bash others behind their backs, because it will always come back to you. If someone insists on bashing another person to you, be aware that, by listening, you are registering tacit agreement, which can also come back to you.

- Form alliances, preferably with those higher up the ladder. In a staff of fifteen, cliques will always form. Since you're going to be in a clique anyway, why not include a couple of big hitters?

- Don't work at home. Some producers will tell writers who have a draft to write that they can work anywhere that they want. But you need your producers to see your face on a regular basis, to become comfortable with you. Drop out of sight and suddenly you are no longer part of the family.

Gee, next I'll be telling you how to hold a salad fork. I should probably have addressed the whole politics question by offering one simple observation: The best ingredients for success are talent, hard work, and an engaging personality.

ROUNDTABLE WRITING

What does it feel like to work in the room for the first time? Sitting there with ten other writers, beating out stories and punching up scripts? Or even co-writing a first draft from page one? It's probably just what you imagine. Stimulating, yet exhausting. Rewarding, yet frustrating. Fun, frantic, and fattening.

You already know the basics of roundtable writing. A senior producer presides over the group, deciding what goes in and what doesn't. A script secretary or one of the writers records the changes; on some shows, the new words are fed to a big-screen monitor so that everyone can see them as they would appear on paper. Some staffs also put a cork board or dry-erase board up on a wall, to keep track of story beats, serialized story lines, or a season's episodes.

Writing sessions can run late into the night, night after night. Sometimes producers will divide a large writing staff into two groups, one to break new stories and one to rewrite a script. Sometimes producers will send different writers off to write different scenes of a script, and then patch the resulting work together. And sometimes a show will hire a "punch-up person," a superfunny comedy writer who comes in just one or two days each week to help the regular staff punch up that week's episode.

How do you fit in? Some producers believe that junior writers should be seen and not heard; of course, this doesn't do much to help you impress your new bosses. Your best bet is to watch the senior producers for clues. If they want their writers to keep pitching, pitching, pitching, then dive right in. If they seem to frown on poorly formed suggestions, then pick and choose which ideas to toss out. In short, listen, watch, and learn. What do the other writers do, with what results?

ADVICE FROM OUR PRODUCERS

Some other thoughts on landing your first staff job:

Maxine Lapiduss: I want somebody who wants that job. I want somebody who's going to be there and not bitch and moan at eleven o'clock at night if we're having a bad week, rather than someone who's looking at his watch every half hour. I want somebody who's enthusiastic and wants to be there as long as it takes. . . .

At a staff writer level or a story editor level, if you're new and haven't worked in the system, it's almost better to kind of not speak up too much. Because generally, nine times out of ten, the show that gets on the air is a reflection of the executive producers and the producers. It's all funneled through their sensibilities. So if you're new and you're always pitching ideas, sometimes it gets a little invasive because this is the executive producers' chance to put their ideas out there.

Lawrence Konner: Say that a writer comes in [for a job interview and the producer] says, "So, what are you thinking about doing?" If he says, "Well, I want to write drama. I think I can write drama as well as I can write comedy. I think I can write movies and TV. And I have a cable show idea, and there are three radio programs I'm playing around with. . . ."— *that scares the employer.* It might be true, but don't tell them. And don't say that you want to direct, and don't say that you want to star in a show. If you're in to pitch a sitcom, it's "I love sitcoms. I grew up on sitcoms. All I ever wanted to do was sitcoms." If they say, "Well, how come you wrote this drama last year?" your response is, "It's the only work I could get. And dammit, I made it funny. I couldn't help myself." . . .

The ideal candidate, I think, is the person who can have fun throwing Chinese food at three in the morning, when you're all getting a little silly, but who also is prepared, has done his homework, when it comes time to get the work done. . . .

You're in a room full of eight or ten people who like to insult people and often do it very well. So you can expect to hear about everything from your choice of shirts that day to your haircut, but don't take it personally. Try to blend in and show things that demonstrate professionalism. Be on time. Don't take long lunches. Don't make a hundred personal phone calls. You know, all the kinds of things that you would do at any new job apply here. . . .

One of the things that's most difficult to understand is that—because the nature of what we're doing for a living is not corporate—the senior people are sometimes going to flout, to be disrespectful of, the rules. But that doesn't mean that *you* have the right to follow suit. You haven't yet earned the right to show disrespect.

Ian Gurvitz: Every room has its own personality. If it's more autocratic and the executive producer says, "It's this way because I want it this way," then that's that. If you think your idea is better—the only thing you can do is, it's a long week, so you just wait to see who's been proven right. . . .

Not everyone can be big and loud in the room, and you don't want that. Otherwise, nobody gets a word in. If [someone is quiet in the room but a terrific writer], then great. Occasional contribution is fine if the writer's scripts are good. . . .

Some people [tend to always say], "Oh, we need a better joke here," or "No, no, this won't work. That won't work," which pisses everybody off. Because your job is not to just identify the problems, your job is to pitch a better joke or story fix. . . .

Know the show inside and out. Have all of the characters' names in your head. Know what the back-stories are. Know where the show has been for the last year or two so you can talk about it intelligently. . . . One time, I think it was on *Wings*, we were hiring a new writer-producer and he came in and just could talk the show very well, so that we were going, "This guy obviously did his homework." [Which helps, because] there's going to be a very short learning curve [when you join a staff].

Irma Kalish: Don't be afraid to speak up just because you're new. A lot of times, you will be thinking, "Gee, I'll bet we could solve that problem if we did such and such," but you don't say anything and then someone speaks up two minutes later with the same idea and gets all the credit. So don't be afraid; it's okay to be wrong. People throw things out on the table and even if you only have a half-formulated idea, someone might pick up on the other half of it. Norman Lear always impressed me by saying, "Don't be afraid to put your finger on something that's wrong, even if you don't know how to fix it." Other people will say, "Well, if you don't know how to fix it, shut up." But that's not true. It's good to know that something is wrong and then everybody can work on how to fix it.

Sandy Frank: I always think of a TV season as if it's a race with a boulder. You have a head start on the boulder and your job as a producer is to stay ahead. You have to constantly have people out breaking stories, writing new scripts, and tabling scripts. You always have to be two, three, hopefully more scripts ahead. If the boulder catches up with you, you are in big trouble. If you are shooting a show on Tuesday and you don't have a script for the next morning's table reading, you are in trouble. But it happens, it happens a lot. Especially if a show is troubled. And so, when you're under that kind of time pressure and you're starting to lose the race with the boulder, the first scripts might not all be great, you know? You have to either write the show as a group or just write it during the production week, and hope that by Friday or Tuesday or whatever day you shoot that it's working. It's not ideal by any means, but it's the nature of trying to write twenty-two episodes in nine months. . . .

When you're writing in a room, your job is to pitch jokes. And some of your jokes will be funny and some won't. You shouldn't be too inhibited about pitching jokes. That's what you're there for. If people make a face at you or whatever, well, some rooms are more vicious than others. Everyone gets that. Just keep pitching and hopefully things will work out. . . .

When someone says, "I think we should do this," and you or whoever is in charge says, "No. Thanks, but no," or whatever, you try to say it politely the first time. Then, when that person says, "No, no, but I really think we should do this. Here's why, . . ." you think about it and say, "Well, I understand what you're saying, but we're not going to do it that way. We're going to do it this way." "But, but really . . ." All right, by that third time, you just want that person to go away, because you're under a huge amount of pressure—time pressure. You want to finish. You want to go home, maybe see your family every once in a while. And at some point, that person just will be resented for doing that. . . .

I've seen a person pitch to the executive producer; he didn't like the pitch. Then she pitched to the co-executive producer; he didn't like the pitch. Then she pitched to the supervising producer; same thing, he didn't like the pitch. Eventually she's pitching to one of the other story editors, and they're agreeing that it's really funny, and that's not helping anyone.

Matt Williams: I want to see how a new writer is going to contribute to the room. Is this a punch mind? Is this a joke mind? Is this a story mind? Is this somebody who's really good at character? . . .

Usually what happens is, you're focusing on a single problem. It could be a plot problem, or how do we get this character from here to here. . . . Focus on that. Don't worry about the blow of the second act right now. Help the room solve this problem. Later, when you're finally at the end of act two and you need the big blow, shift gears and focus on that. . . . Young writers will try to chase everything in the script at once. Watch the room, see what it's landing on at that moment, what problem. . . . I guarantee you, if a young writer comes into the room and helps me solve two, three, four key problems in a script, I want that person in the room all the time. . . .

Every time we hit a block—and I'm going back to my first year on *Cosby*—I would just keep pushing and keep pushing while other people were checking out. I'd go, "Come on, come on. What if? What if?" And I kept offering them solutions. I didn't give up. I didn't check out, which happens. . . .

I can sit at a table, with ten writers around a table, and the second a writer [mentally] leaves the room or his mind drifts, I feel it. I know it. And a good room runner knows the second someone's checked out and their head isn't in the script. . . . Again, it goes back to, help the head writer solve problems. That's your job.

CONTRACTS AND COMPENSATION

When you are hired as a staff writer, your agent will negotiate your job title, rate of pay, the minimum number of weeks that you will be employed, a guaranteed number of scripts that you will write (for which you might be paid separately), and perhaps a schedule for future promotions. In addition, your contract will incorporate most of the same provisions that are included in a step deal for a freelance script. As with those contracts, a staff writer's deal is a pretty standard agreement and it must conform to the protective rules established by the writers' MBA. (Again, if you have any questions or concerns, consult with your agent or a lawyer.)

As mentioned earlier, a new writer's job title can have a big effect on her compensation. Term writers are hired on a week-to-week basis, usually with a guarantee that they will be employed for a minimum number of weeks, at the least. (Thirteen weeks is common.) The more weeks a producer is willing to guarantee a term writer, the lower the weekly rate that he must pay that writer. (The sliding scale of weekly fees can be found in the WGA's "Schedule of Minimums" pamphlet.) Term writers can be let go at any time but, if they are fired before their guaranteed term of employment has ended, they must still be paid the money that was promised. The fees that a term writer makes for writing episodes of her show are applied against her week-to-week salary, and she must be paid the greater of the two; meaning, if the writer's cumulative script fees represent more money than her staff salary, she must be paid the difference, in addition to her salary.

Writers who are employed as story editors or above are referred to as writers "also employed in additional capacities." These writers "may be employed on a per-episode basis, but the applicable Guild minimum payable to the writer is still the week-to-week or term minimum, based on the number of weeks services are actually to be performed. These payments include compensation for rewrites and polishes, but these payments may not be applied against stories and/ or teleplays or program fees due."[48] In other words, a story editor's rate of pay might be based on a weekly rate or it might consist of a set fee for each episode produced. However, in the latter case, if his cumulative per-episode fees equal less than the cumulative weekly salary fees would normally be for that period of employment, he must be paid the higher (weekly salary) figure. Plus—and this is the best part—story editors get paid separate script fees for each episode that they write, *in addition* to their per-episode compensation. (Rewriting other people's scripts does not count.) And, if the show is produced for ABC, CBS, or NBC, he also gets paid a small *program fee* of about seven hundred dollars for each episode he writes that gets produced.

Exactly how much money are we talking about? Here are a few representative pay rates for term writers and story editors employed on a prime-time network sitcom:

Term writer (if guaranteed up to six weeks):

| From 5/2/99 to 5/1/2000 | $2,971 per week |
| From 5/2/2000 to 5/1/2001 | $3,075 per week |

Story editor (if guaranteed up to nine weeks; does not include script and program fees):

| From 5/2/99 to 5/1/2000 | $5,539 per week |
| From 5/2/2000 to 5/1/2001 | $5,733 per week[49] |

Again, the more weeks of employment that are guaranteed, the lower the pay rate. At the same time, a successful show could mean about forty-five weeks of highly paid employment in a year. (Shows usually get a month or two of hiatus each year.) And agents are frequently able to negotiate higher fees than these, the WGA minimums, for their clients.

If you would like more information regarding compensation for staff writers, get a copy of the WGA,w's current "Schedule of Minimums" by contacting its operations office at (323) 782-4520.

MOVING ON

You've studied the craft of comedy writing, written your specs, found an agent, and landed your first job. What comes next? Let's look at how one turns a job into a career.

Seventeen

Step Six—Climbing the Ladder

MOVING UP

Very few television writers seem to work on one show for any length of time. A typical writer might start out as a term writer on one show and then jump to another show as a story editor. When that show gets canceled after only two episodes, she lands a story editor job on yet another show. A few seasons on that show and the woman is now a co-producer. She gets recruited to serve as a co-executive producer on another show and eventually becomes a show runner. Or a studio lures her into taking a lucrative development deal in the hope that she will create a new hit sitcom for them.

Along the way, the writer's fees are going up, way up, and she gradually gains new responsibilities to go along with her new job titles. She becomes involved in postproduction, casting, promotion, and meetings with executives. She supervises writing sessions and makes decisions regarding budget expenditures. Perhaps she even directs a few episodes.

Of course, the above is just one example of a career path. A writer might ascend the ladder more quickly and find herself running her own show at age twenty-six (e.g., Matt Stone of *South Park*). Or she might stop halfway up the ladder to pursue some other career. Or she might stumble out of work and find that she is unable to get rehired (as a writer).

What should a sitcom writer do to build a healthy career? Good question. Some people bounce happily from one job to another, whether they are talented or not, largely because they happened to work on a hot show early in their career. The spin from that early job gets them other jobs, until their extensive credit list has enough of its own spin to keep them employed.

Some people get occasional boosts up the ladder because they have strong social skills. They develop a network of fans among the industry's heavy hitters and can usually count on landing a new gig through those contacts. (Network and studio executives have recently become more aggressive about forcing their favorite writers on producers when it comes time to assemble a staff.)

But most writers succeed the old-fashioned way—they just work damn hard. They keep turning out good material, which provides ongoing proof of their talent. They bring a positive attitude to the job and they try to develop their own network of professional contacts. When caught between jobs, they sit down and write something, a new sitcom spec for their agent to peddle or perhaps a feature script that they hope to sell.

To advance your career do the following:

- Keep turning out your best work.

- Be a pleasure to have around.

- Take the initiative when it comes to getting work done.

- Keep writing when between jobs.

- Network, network, network! That young term writer or studio executive that you befriended last year might call you about a new gig next year. (And you can return the favor the year after.)

THE CARE AND FEEDING OF AGENTS

The higher up the ladder you climb, the more demands you can make of your agent and the more your agent will want to please you, because you now earn bigger commissions for her.

Ideally, your agent would constantly be looking for better opportunities for you—a new job on a more successful show, ammunition to negotiate a promotion for you, better terms or fees for your current position, or freelance script deals on the side when work is slow. In reality, if you have a steady job on a show, your agent will tend to focus on other clients (which is understandable). So if you feel restless, you sometimes have to nudge her if you want more attention.

As time passes, you are likely to become friends with your agent, which is great, as long as she doesn't take your professional goals for granted. If you have a concern, make it known and both of you can strive toward a solution.

Of course, sometimes an agent will lose interest in a client. Perhaps you have realized that you are being stereotyped as a particular kind of writer and you fear that your career will suffer if you don't move to a different type of show. But your agent pooh-poohs your concern because "at least you have a job," or she expresses concern but then makes no effort to pull your career out of its rut. Or, even worse, perhaps you are out of work and the agent isn't taking aggressive action on your behalf. What can you do?

Call the agent regularly, weekly, to share your job-search updates. Hopefully, she will respond to your aggressive actions by doing her part. To help the joint search, keep cranking out (great) new writing samples so that both of you have fresh material to circulate.

If your calls make it clear that she is not doing her part, ask for a meeting to discuss strategy. If she bothers to prepare and has something to contribute, great. You're on track again. If not, let her know that you are disappointed. Hopefully, she will apologize and start taking action.

Of course, at this juncture, you are running a slight risk. An agent who isn't "working you" is almost certainly considering dropping you as a client. If you pressure her, she might do so.

What would you lose if she did turn you loose? Not much, if she isn't making any efforts on your behalf. But because one of your options is to seek new representation, you might want to tread lightly. It is always easier to land a new agent if you already have one in hand, because the latter lends you a degree of credibility.

> **NOTE:** *If interviewing agents, never disparage your former or current agent. It reflects poorly on you and is likely to get back to that person.*

What if the agent that you need to replace is a friend? That's a tough one. But if that agent isn't able to find work for you, a true friend would understand that you need to find someone who can. As long as you have communicated your concerns and given your agent-friend a chance to make something happen, you have done all that should be expected. And there is nothing to keep you from maintaining the friendship just because you have accepted representation elsewhere. (Many writers even end up re-signing with a former agent later in their careers.)

What if you are happy with your agent but someone from a bigger, hotter agency offers to represent you? If your career is progressing nicely, other agents are likely to seek you out. They might introduce themselves at a taping, or call you out of the blue, or meet you through another client. Next thing you know, you're being invited to lunch or a basketball game, or to the agent's office for a formal hello meeting. The new agent hits you with a lot of flattery and promises of great career moves, all of which is very tempting. Do you switch? Especially when your current agent worked so hard to get you this job, the very thing that made you so marketable? Another tough question. Frankly, I once turned down such an opportunity, out of loyalty, and lived to regret it. Others have made the jump, only to be unceremoniously dumped a year later when their career hit a rough patch. This type of decision involves more than just business considerations; it's also about the relationship that you share with your current agent and your own set of personal values. For once, I won't even try to suggest an answer.

Is it hard to fire an agent? Aren't you bound by your contract? Most agents do not want to keep a client who is unhappy with them. If they discover that you are planning to move elsewhere, they might press you for a second chance, especially if you are a big moneymaker. If you believe that their renewed interest will make the difference, perhaps you should stay with them. But if you or they don't see a future together, they will probably let you terminate the relationship, on one condition: they get to keep all commissions generated by the jobs that they have landed for you to date. This demand is entirely fair. But it might put a crimp in your efforts to secure new representation, since the new agents won't see a dime until you change jobs, which could conceivably take years. Still, the new agents would make the same demand if the situation was reversed.

Sometimes there is a disagreement over who deserves what commissions when a writer changes representation. Rather than taint your relationship with either agency, it is probably best that you step back and ask the agents to resolve the matter. After all, your job is to write comedy, not negotiate commission splits.

TAKING A DEVELOPMENT DEAL

Every sitcom writer dreams of creating and producing his own series. Unfortunately, because of the high stakes involved, only proven writer-producers are given the chance to develop a new show. There are rare exceptions; for instance, a less experienced type might be given a shot if he has unique access to an important star or exclusive rights to a hot literary property.

Doesn't having a great new idea mean anything? This is Hollywood. Everyone has great new ideas. What matters are credentials.

Sometimes a studio or production company will offer a *development deal* to an established writer, and other times a writer's agent might pitch her for such a deal. The writer is usually someone who has worked on a hit show in a mid- to upper-level producing capacity, but she need not be an established show runner. A typical development deal provides the writer with a salary, an office, an assistant, and perhaps a fund for acquiring story rights. The term of the agreement is usually one or two years, with options to extend the deal.

In exchange for receiving this package, the writer is required to give her partners first—or sometimes, exclusive—crack at producing any concepts that she creates. If a series comes out of the deal, the writer will assume some already-negotiated role as one of the main producers.

It sounds like a great deal and often is. But it can also result in a writer going through what is called "development hell." She might dream up a brilliant concept or write an inspired pilot script, only to get a quick "Pass, no thanks" from her partners. If her deal is exclusive, that's it; the writer can't take her baby elsewhere, and must move on to the next project. Sometimes, not only can't the writer get her own projects off the ground but her partners pressure her to consult on other people's projects or to accept a producing job on one of their other shows. Still doesn't sound so horrible? When you have finally reached a position from which you might actually be able to launch your own show, such obstacles can seem intolerable. And more than one writer has derailed a promising career by getting bogged down in go-nowhere development deals.

Still, the chance to create your own series is something to think about.

HOW DO YOU SELL A NEW SERIES?

You don't. Unless you have a development deal, several producer credits, a big star in your pocket, or control of some much-sought-after story rights, please do not even try. Throughout this book, I have attempted to stress the importance of *focusing your energies* and *making the best use of your time*. Sure, if you cough up a clever proposal for a new series, there are plenty of junior executives who will be happy to take the pitch. Why not? Meeting with new writers is part of how they justify their existence.

MEMO TO BOSS: Took pitch today from Sally Sitcomwriter for series titled *Fat Chance in Hell*. Clever concept but not for us *(since we'd never trust a new writer to develop a series)*. Will continue to keep an eye on this promising writer *(and pass on all of her submissions)*.

Have you heard the old adage, "Hollywood is the only place where people die of encouragement"? They were talking about series development.

Focus on work that will maximize your chances of success. Study the craft, write the best scripts that you can, and work your way up the ladder. If you are good enough, and tenacious, someday you'll get your shot at developing your own series.

In Closing

It's a funny thing. Some people look down their noses at comedy, and yet many "experts" are quick to declare that it's the hardest form of fiction to write. (Explain that one.) I can't change people's opinions, but I certainly hope that this book and the thinking behind premise-driven comedy make your work easier, more productive, and more rewarding.

Is becoming a sitcom writer worth all of the effort?

Ian Gurvitz:	It's a great job.
Irma Kalish:	Being with people who are creative and funny . . .
Lawrence Konner:	There's action all of the time.
Matt Williams:	Monday you read it, you start rehearsing, and Friday it's opening night and closing night. And in a matter of weeks, it's on the air.
Lawrence Konner:	It's instant gratification.
Maxine Lapiduss:	Better than driving a cab.
Sandy Frank:	Better than being a coal miner.
Ian Gurvitz:	People bring you food.
Maxine Lapiduss:	The free food's good.
Ian Gurvitz:	And then there's the money.
Maxine Lapiduss:	It pays pretty well.
Lawrence Konner:	It's overpaid.
Ian Gurvitz:	It's a great job to have.
Maxine Lapiduss:	Where else can you sit around with a bunch of people all day and try to make each other laugh?

Whether you choose to pursue a career as a sitcom writer or not, I wish you good fortune. If you would like to share your own thoughts about the craft of comedy writing, please E-mail me at the Newhouse School: evsmith@syr.edu.

Appendix A

Script Format Guidelines

Sitcoms are produced in three formats: live-action videotape, live-action film, and animation. Below are script format guidelines for each type of show.

Please note that these are *generic* guidelines. While they reflect current professional standards, every show is different. If you are writing a spec script for an existing television series, try to obtain copies of scripts produced for that show so that you can precisely duplicate their format. (The more that your script resembles the real thing, the better the chances that it will be well received.) At the very least, if writing for a live-action series, find out whether the show is shot on tape or film so that you can choose the correct generic model.

Also, note that the following models are appropriate for *spec scripts*. They deliberately omit some elements that are usually added only after a script has been put into production. These items include scene numbers, page headers that identify the script draft, cast lists under each scene heading, and separate slugs for sound effects and special effects. While it isn't a crime to include these elements in a spec script, they slow down "the read" and they imply that the script is a production draft (that was probably punched up by the show's staff).

TOPICS COVERED IN THIS APPENDIX

I. The Title Page

II. Writing in Film Format
Page Numbers
Script Headings
Scene Headings
Scene Descriptions
Dialogue Blocks
Transition Cues
Vertical Spacing
Margin Settings
Act Breaks
Tags
Ending a Script

III. Writing in Tape Format
Page Numbers
Script Headings
The First Scene
Scene Headings
Scene Descriptions
Dialogue Blocks
Transition Cues
Vertical Spacing
Margin Settings
Act Breaks, Tags, and Endings

IV. Writing in Animation Format

V. General Guidelines (listed by key words)

I. The Title Page (see Figure 1)

Every spec script starts with a *title page* that identifies the work, its author, and a contact person. Regardless of whether the show is taped, filmed, or animated, the layout of this page is the same. As for typeface, always use the industry standard, **pica-sized Courier font**; this uniformly sized typeface produces ten letters per linear inch.

1. The **series title** is typed 1/3 of the way down the page. It should be centered, written in all caps, and either underlined or printed in bold type.

   NOTE: When "centering" any part of the script, add six extra character spaces to the left margin to compensate for room taken up by the script binding. See "Margin Settings" below.

2. The **title of the episode** appears two lines below the series title, centered, typed in upper- and lowercase letters, and enclosed by quotation marks.

3. The phrase [written by] appears four lines below the episode title, centered, in lowercase.

4. The **writer's name** appears two lines farther down, centered, in upper- and lowercase.

5. **Contact information** (i.e., the address and phone number of the writer or, preferably, the writer's agent) is typed in a single-spaced block in the lower right corner of the page, in upper- and lowercase, typed flush left within the block. You might wish to start the block with the heading [CONTACT:].

6. If the script has been registered with the Copyright Office or the WGA, place the proper **registration notice** in the lower left corner of the page, across from the lowest line in the block of contact information. (See "Protecting Your Work" in chapter 14.)

7. Suggestion: *Do not* label a spec script as a "First," "Second," or other draft. "First draft" implies that the script still needs work, while "second" or later draft designations suggest that the script might have been punched up based on other people's input. Similarly, *do not* write the date that you completed the script on the title page. Doing so will only serve to age your script, since anything over six months old might be perceived as yesterday's news. (Draft numbers and dates are not needed until a script goes into production, when they are used to help producers keep track of rewrites.)

II. Writing in Film Format

The elements of a script written in *film format* are described below. See the sections on "Vertical Spacing" and "Margin Settings" for details on proper positioning.

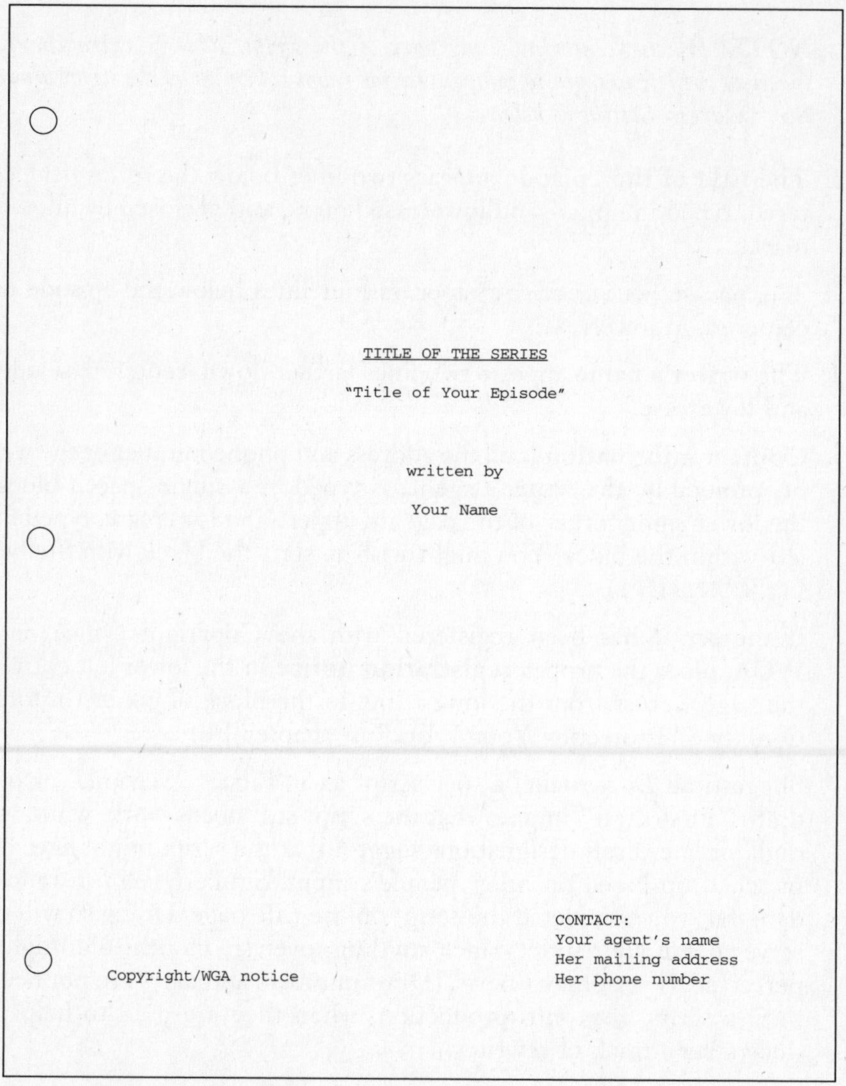

```
                        TITLE OF THE SERIES
                       "Title of Your Episode"


                             written by

                             Your Name
```

```
                                          CONTACT:
                                          Your agent's name
                                          Her mailing address
   Copyright/WGA notice                    Her phone number
```

Figure 1: Title page for a tape, film, or animation script.

PAGE NUMBERS

Starting with the first page of dialogue, type each page number, followed by a period, in the top right corner of the paper, three or four spaces from the top and side edges of the paper.

SCRIPT HEADINGS (SEE FIGURE 2)

Drop five or ten lines below the first page number and type the series title in all caps, centered, underlined or in boldface type. (*Again, when centering any part of the script, add six extra character spaces to the left margin to compensate for room taken up by the script binding.*)

Then, skip a line and type the episode title in upper- and lowercase, centered, in quotes.

Then, skip two lines and type, centered, underlined, in all caps, whichever of the following is used in that television series:

1. [COLD OPEN], if the series starts with a brief teaser before going to the opening title sequence; or,

2. [ACT ONE], if the series shows opening titles before starting the first scene.

Then, skip two lines and type [FADE IN:], flush left, in all caps, to begin your first scene.

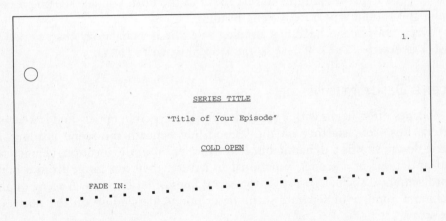

Figure 2: The first page of a film format script.

NOTE: If the first scene is a COLD OPEN or TEASER, then Act One does not begin until after the first commercial break. See "Act Breaks" below.

SCENE HEADINGS (SEE FIGURE 3)

Each scene begins with a scene heading, typed in all caps, flush left, that identifies the location and time of that scene. A scene heading is composed of three parts:

1. The first part is an abbreviation, either [INT.] or [EXT.], that tells us whether we are viewing the **interior** or **exterior** of the scene's location.

2. The second part identifies the scene's **location**, be it [JOEY'S CAR], [THE COURTHOUSE], or [SUE'S BEDROOM].

3. The third part, typed following a dash, identifies the **time** during which the scene occurs. This can be designated as either a day part (e.g., [DAY], [NIGHT], [DAWN], or [DUSK]), or as an indication that time has passed since the last scene (e.g., [30 MINUTES LATER], [MOMENTS LATER], or [LATER]), or as a specific clock time (e.g., [NOON] or [6 P.M.]). If no time has passed since the previous scene ended, that is indicated by typing the word [CONTINUOUS] or by simply leaving the third part of the scene heading blank.

Every time that the story's location or time frame changes, even if your characters are just walking from one room to the next, you are starting a new scene and should type a new scene heading.

Keep your scene headings simple; unless it is mandatory that we know that it is exactly [2:37 P.M.] in the story, just write [DAY].

SCENE DESCRIPTIONS

Scenes often begin with a scene description, typed in upper- and lowercase letters, flush left, starting on the second line beneath the scene heading. A scene description is a dynamic but *brief* description of the location, characters, and/or actions in a scene. Functional in nature, they can range from a one-word sentence, such as [Beat.], to several lines of description. A scene might include a number of separate scene descriptions, depending on the needs of the story.

The first time a new character is identified in a scene description, her name should be typed in all caps. The names of series regulars do not need to be called out in this manner.

Some writers capitalize descriptions of sound effects and/or special effects when they occur within a scene description, while others (this writer included) believe that this only serves to distract the reader.

Scene descriptions are written in the present tense. Some writers use proper grammar when writing them, while others use clipped phrases or a loose conversational style.

DIALOGUE BLOCKS

Dialogue, which is typed in a single-spaced block, consists of three parts (see "Margin Settings" for correct positioning):

1. The first part is the **character's name**, typed in all caps.

2. Then, immediately beneath that, or between segments of speech that follow, come **dialogue cues**. Typed in lowercase and bracketed by parentheses, these brief phrases either indicate how a line should be read or cue a specific movement (e.g., [(claps his hands)]).

3. The third part of the dialogue block is the **dialogue** itself, typed in upper- and lowercase.

If a character's dialogue is interrupted by a scene description, type her name again, followed by the abbreviation [(cont'd)], when she resumes speaking. Then continue her dialogue.

If a character's dialogue is running too long to fit on a page, move the entire speech to the following page. Or, interrupt the speech with a line containing the single word [(MORE)] typed forty-five spaces in from the left side of the page. Then, at the top of the next page, type the character's name and [(cont'd)], and continue the interrupted speech.

NOTE: Go light on dialogue cues—they bog down the read.

TRANSITION CUES

Transition cues describe how the episode will segue from one scene to the next. Typed in all caps, they include the following: [FADE IN:], [CUT TO:], [DISSOLVE TO:], [FADE OUT.], [CUT TO BLACK], [FREEZE FRAME], etc.

The one opening cue, [FADE IN:], is typed flush left, while all other cues are typed sixty spaces in from the left side of the page.

In the past, writers placed a transition cue—usually [CUT TO:]—at the end of every scene. Today, many writers deem ending cues superfluous when writing in film format, unless they are needed to indicate a specific effect (e.g., dissolving to a dream sequence) or to help a script's pacing by "putting a period" at the end of a scene or sequence.

VERTICAL SPACING

In film format, all elements within a scene (including scene headings, scene descriptions, dialogue blocks, and transition cues) are separated from each other by a *single* blank line. However, for ease of reading, many writers insert two blank lines between scenes (i.e., before the next scene heading).

MARGIN SETTINGS (FOR FILM FORMAT)

Top and bottom: There should be one inch of margin space at the top and bottom of the page, regardless of the page number squeezed into the top right corner. Obviously, due to irregular breaks between dialogue blocks, you will often have more than one inch of blank space at the bottom of a page.

Sides: To accommodate the script's binding, the body of a script is shifted six spaces to the right (see "Script Binding" in the "General Guidelines" section). Accordingly, using the standard screenwriting typeface (pica-sized Courier font), set the margins in from the left side of the page as follows:

From space 16 to space 75: Body of the script (including the cue [FADE IN:], scene headings, and scene descriptions)

From space 28 to space 63: Dialogue

From space 34 to space 57: Dialogue cues

From space 40: Character names

From space 60: Transition cues (except for [FADE IN:])

NOTE: *Margin and space settings presented in this document are general guidelines; a few spaces left or right will not mar your script.*

ACT BREAKS

Unless it airs on a "commercial-free" pay-cable network, a half-hour sitcom episode is usually interrupted by two or more commercial breaks. Indicate planned act breaks in your script by doing the following:

1. End the last scene of each act by typing the transition cue [FADE OUT.].

2. Skip two lines, then type [END OF ACT ONE]—or [_ . . . ACT TWO] or [_ . . . ACT THREE], as the case may be—centered, underlined, in all caps.

3. Start the first scene of the next act on a *new page*. Drop five to ten lines below the page number and type [ACT TWO]—or [ACT THREE] or whichever—centered, underlined, in all caps.

4. Then, skip two lines and type the transition cue [FADE IN:].

5. Then, skip one line and begin the first scene of the new act.

NOTE: *If the script's first scene is a COLD OPEN, then the scene that immediately follows the first commercial break will begin ACT ONE. To indicate that the cold open has ended, follow the steps above, substituting* (END OF COLD OPEN) *for* (END OF ACT . . .) *in step two. Then, start Act One on a new page.*

TAGS

Just as some series start with a cold open before showing opening titles, many also close with a *tag*—a brief, amusing scene placed at the end of the episode, after the main story lines have already been resolved. Tags, formatted like the first scene of a new act, are indicated as follows:

1. After indicating that the last act of the episode has ended, start the tag scene on a new page. Type [TAG] five to ten lines below the page number, centered, underlined, in all caps.

2. Then, skip two lines and type the transition cue [FADE IN:].

3. Then, skip one line and begin the tag scene.

ENDING A SCRIPT

End the final scene of the script by doing the following: type the transition cue [FADE OUT.], and then skip two lines and type [END OF EPISODE], centered, underlined, in all caps.

```
INT. JERRY'S APARTMENT — DAY

George helps Jerry rip the package open. They pull out . . .
a real deerskin.

                    JERRY
          Oh my God.

                    GEORGE
          Jesus, is that . . . ?

                    JERRY
          Someone killed Bambi and mailed me
          the corpse.

                    GEORGE
          What sort of horrible, demented
          fiend would do that?

                    JERRY
               (reads the card)
          That would be my mom.

                    GEORGE
          Your mom?

                    JERRY
          Yep. Seems Mom and Dad were
          visiting up north, enjoying the
          great outdoors . . . Thought they'd
          do a little killing.

                    GEORGE
          A little?

George pokes his fingers through several bullet holes.

                    GEORGE (cont'd)
          Arnold Schwarzenegger never shot so
          many bullets.

                                        CUT TO:
```

Figure 3. Dialogue written in film format.[50]

III: Writing in Tape Format

The elements of a script written in *tape format* are described below. See the sections on "Vertical Spacing" and "Margin Settings" for details on proper positioning.

PAGE NUMBERS

Starting with the first page of dialogue, type each page number, followed by a period, in the top right corner of the paper, three or four spaces from the top and side edges of the page.

SCRIPT HEADINGS

Some tape shows include series and episode titles on the first page of dialogue and others don't. If you wish to do so, follow the same guidelines used when writing in film format.

THE FIRST SCENE (SEE FIGURE 4)

Drop five or ten lines below the first page number and type, centered, underlined, in all caps, whichever of the following is used in that series:

1. [COLD OPEN], if the series starts with a brief teaser before going to the opening title sequence; or,

2. [ACT ONE], followed by a blank line and then [SCENE A], if the series is a sitcom that does not start off with a cold open. (In tape format, sequential letters or numbers are usually assigned to all scenes except for cold opens and tags.)

Then, skip three more lines and type [FADE IN:], flush left, underlined, in all caps, to begin the first scene.

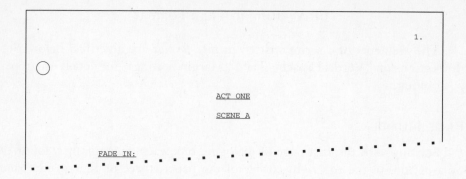

Figure 4: An act heading in a tape format script.

SCENE HEADINGS (SEE FIGURE 5)

As just mentioned, scenes written in tape format are usually assigned letters or numbers (in sequence), and most producers prefer that each new scene start on a new page. To do so, type the scene designation (e.g., [SCENE A]) in all caps, centered, and underlined, five to ten lines below the page number. Then, skip two lines and start the scene.

Each scene begins with a *scene heading*, typed in all caps, underlined, flush left, that identifies the location and time of that scene. A scene heading is composed of three parts:

1. The first part is an abbreviation, either [INT.] or [EXT.], that tells us whether we are viewing the **interior** or **exterior** of the scene's location.

2. The second part identifies the scene's location, be it [JOEY'S CAR], [THE COURTHOUSE], or [SUE'S BEDROOM].

3. The third part, typed following a dash, identifies the **time** during which the scene occurs. This can be designated as either a day part (e.g., [DAY], [NIGHT], [DAWN], or [DUSK]), or as an indication that time has passed since the last scene (e.g., [30 MINUTES LATER], [MOMENTS LATER], or [LATER]), or as a specific clock time (e.g., [NOON] or [6 P.M.]). If no time has passed since the previous scene ended, that is indicated by typing the word [CONTINUOUS] or by simply leaving the third part of the scene heading blank.

Every time that the story's location or time frame changes, even if your characters are just walking from one room to the next, you are starting a new scene and should type a new scene heading (on a new page).

Keep your scene headings simple; unless it is mandatory that we know that it is exactly [2:37 P.M.] in the story, just write [DAY].

SCENE DESCRIPTIONS

Scenes often begin with a scene description, typed in all caps, flush left, starting on the second line beneath the scene heading. A scene description is a dynamic but *brief* description of the location, characters, and/or actions in a scene. Functional in nature, they can range from a one-word sentence, such as [BEAT.], to several lines of description. A scene might include a number of separate scene descriptions, depending on the needs of the story.

The first (and only the first) time that a new character is identified in a scene description, her name should be underlined. The names of series regulars do not need to be called out in this manner.

Every time a character enters or exits a scene, her name and the accompanying verb should be underlined (e.g., [MONICA ENTERS], [KATE EXITS], or [LEWIS RUNS OUT]).

Some writers underline descriptions of sound effects and/or special effects when they occur within a scene description, while others (this writer included) believe that this only serves to distract the reader.

Scene descriptions are written in the present tense. Some writers use proper grammar when writing them, while others use clipped phrases or a loose conversational style.

DIALOGUE BLOCKS

Dialogue, which is typed in a double-spaced block, consists of three parts (see "Margin Settings" below for correct positioning):

1. The first part is the **character's name**, typed in all caps.

2. Beneath that is the **dialogue**, typed in upper- and lowercase.

3. Then, within the dialogue, there are **dialogue cues**. These are brief phrases that either indicate how a line should be read or cue a specific action (e.g., [(CLAPS HIS HANDS)]). Dialogue cues are typed in all caps, bracketed by parentheses, and positioned as if they were just another sentence in the character's speech.

If a character's dialogue is interrupted by a scene description, type her name again, followed by the abbreviation [(CONT'D)], when she resumes speaking. Then continue her dialogue.

If a character's dialogue is running too long to fit on a page, move the entire speech to the following page. Or interrupt the speech with a line containing the single word [(MORE)] typed forty-five spaces in from the left side of the page. Then, at the top of the next page, type the character's name and [(CONT'D)], and continue the interrupted speech.

NOTE: Go light on dialogue cues—they bog down the read.

TRANSITION CUES

Transition cues describe how the episode will segue from one scene to the next. Typed in all caps, they include the following: [FADE IN:], [CUT TO:], [DISSOLVE TO:], [FADE OUT.], [CUT TO BLACK], [FREEZE FRAME], etc.

The one opening cue, [FADE IN:], is typed flush left and underlined, while all other cues are typed sixty spaces in from the left side of the page and not underlined.

Unlike film format, every scene in tape format ends with a transition cue, usually [CUT TO:] or [DISSOLVE TO:]. And as mentioned, many producers prefer that each new scene start on a new page.

VERTICAL SPACING

In tape format, all elements within a scene (including scene headings, scene descriptions, dialogue blocks, and transition cues) are separated from each other by a *single* blank line. However, lines within the dialogue blocks themselves (including character names and lines of dialogue) are *double-spaced.*

MARGIN SETTINGS (FOR TAPE FORMAT)

Top and bottom: There should be one inch of margin space at the top and bottom of the page, regardless of the page number squeezed into the top right corner. Obviously, due to irregular breaks between dialogue blocks, you will often have more than one inch of blank space at the bottom of the page.

Sides: To accommodate the script's binding, the body of a script is shifted six spaces to the right (see "Script binding" in the "General Guidelines" section of this appendix). Accordingly, using the standard screenwriting typeface (pica-sized Courier font), set the margins in from the left side of the page as follows:

From space 16 to space 70: Body of the script (including the cue [FADE IN:], scene headings, and scene descriptions)

From space 26 to space 60: Dialogue (including dialogue cues)

From space 40: Character names

From space 60: Transition cues (except for [FADE IN:])

NOTE: *Margin and space settings presented in this document are general guidelines; a few spaces left or right will not mar your script.*

ACT BREAKS, TAGS, AND ENDINGS

Follow the guidelines presented in the film format section.

IV. Writing in Animation Format (see Figure 6)

The script formats used for animated sitcoms vary widely from show to show. For instance, scripts for *The Simpsons* use double spacing for dialogue blocks while scripts for *South Park* use single spacing, and scripts for *King of the Hill* use traditional transition cues while those for *South Park* skip most cues. Given such inconsistencies, it is difficult to describe a generic format for animated scripts. At the same time, since so many variations exist in the field, who's to say that a format that you choose to follow is incorrect?

If you are unable to obtain a copy of a produced script from a series to use as a template, I suggest that you do the following: Format your script as if you were writing for a *live-action film* show, but make these changes:

HEADINGS AND TRANSITION CUES

All script headings and transition cues should be in boldface type.

SCENE DESCRIPTIONS

Scene descriptions should stop seventy spaces in from the left side of the paper, leaving an inch and a half of right-hand margin. Since animated shows are not bound by the limitations of live-action production, it is acceptable to include some camera directions in an animation script.

DIALOGUE BLOCKS

Dialogue blocks should be double-spaced.

SCENE C

INT. JERRY'S APARTMENT — DAY

George helps Jerry rip the package open. They pull out
. . . a real deerskin.

                    JERRY

        Oh my God.

                    GEORGE

        Jesus, is that . . . ?

                    JERRY

        Someone killed Bambi and mailed me

        the corpse.

                    GEORGE

        What sort of horrible, demented

        fiend would do that?

                    JERRY

        (READS THE CARD) That would be my

        mom.

                    GEORGE

        Your mom?

                                        CUT TO:

Figure 5. Dialogue written in tape format.

INT. JERRY'S APARTMENT — DAY

George helps Jerry rip the package open. They pull out
. . . a real deerskin.

                    JERRY

        Oh my God.

                    GEORGE

        Jesus, is that . . . ?

                    JERRY

        Someone killed Bambi and mailed me

        the corpse.

                    GEORGE

        What sort of horrible, demented

        fiend would do that?

                    JERRY

        (READS THE CARD) That would be my

        mom.

                    GEORGE

        Your mom?

                    JERRY

        Yep. Seems Mom and Dad were visiting

        up north, enjoying the great

        outdoors . . . Thought they'd do a

        little killing.

                                CUT TO:

Figure 6. Dialogue written in animation format.

DIALOGUE CUES

Dialogue cues should be typed in all caps and bracketed by parentheses, and positioned as if they were just another sentence in the character's speech.

SCRIPT LENGTH

Script length should be forty to fifty pages.

V. General Guidelines (listed by key words)

The following apply to all three script formats:

CAMERA ANGLES

Do not include camera angles in your script. Or, if you must include some, try to limit your directions to suggestions regarding dramatic focus (such as [ANGLE ON TOYOTA]), rather than specific camera commands (such as [CAMERA ZOOMS IN FOR ECU (extreme closeup) OF THE TOYOTA]). Script-format-wise, camera angles appear in one of two ways: typed in all caps on a separate line, flush left, like a scene heading, or typed in all caps within the body of a scene description.

INTERCUTTING BETWEEN LOCATIONS

If you need to cut back and forth between characters at different locations (say, during a phone call), establish the second location via a scene description and then type [INTERCUT BETWEEN name AND name] as if it were a scene heading. Then, just type the dialogue blocks as if both/all characters are at the same location.

INTERRUPTIONS BY ANOTHER CHARACTER

If one character is interrupting another, indicate this by cutting off the first character's speech with a dash. Then, begin the second character's dialogue block. There is no need to type [(interrupting)] as a dialogue cue when the second character begins speaking.

LENGTH OF SCRIPT

On average, one page of a script written in *film format* equals about a minute of screen time. Accordingly, a sitcom script written in film format usually runs about thirty pages in length. A script written in *tape format*, which features double-spaced dialogue, usually runs forty-five to fifty pages in length. And a script written in *animation format* usually runs forty to fifty pages in length. Of course, every show is different, so read scripts produced for the show to determine the correct length for your spec.

> *NOTE: Longer is not better when it comes to script length; only your mother wants to see that three-hundred-page* Frasier *script that you wrote.*

MONTAGE

A montage is a quick succession of related scenes, often sans dialogue, that offers a compressed view of some development—a dream sequence, a blossoming relationship, a training sequence, etc. To start a montage, simply [DISSOLVE TO:] a scene heading that reads [MONTAGE], or some variation thereof, such as [TRAINING MONTAGE]. Then list three, five, or more scenes, describing each in just a sentence or two, in separate paragraphs, typed as regular scene descriptions. To end the montage, simply [DISSOLVE TO:] the next regular scene heading.

PAPER

Use a standard-quality white bond—no fancy, flimsy, erasable, or perforated paper.

PAUSES

To indicate a pause in action or between lines of dialogue, type [beat], [a beat], or [pause] as a line of scene description or a dialogue cue, capitalized, or not, per the appropriate script format. Or to indicate pauses *within* a line of dialogue, or that a sentence fades off before its last words are spoken, use an ellipsis (typed [. . .]).

SCRIPT BINDING

The script should be three-hole-punched on the left side, with brass brads placed in the *top and bottom holes only*. (Fancy binders suggest that the writer is an amateur, as does a third, superfluous brad.) If you wish to add a script cover, place two sheets of simple, blank card stock on the front and back of the script; pick a solid, plain color and avoid any patterns or designs.

SOUND/SPECIAL-EFFECTS CUES

When a script is being prepped for production, cues for sound effects and special effects (SFX) are all typed as separate, underlined slugs. However, in a spec script, it is best to simply write these effects into scene descriptions to avoid distracting the reader.

TYPEFACE

Use the industry-standard typeface, pica-sized Courier font; it produces ten characters per horizontal inch.

NOTE: *Presentation counts; if you get too creative with type faces, type size, spacing, etc., or if your spelling and grammar are sloppy, that script that you slaved over will end up on the recycling pile.*

VOICE-OVER NARRATION

One can indicate voice-over narration by typing [(V.O.)] after a narrator/character's name, on the same line. If we hear the voice of a character in a scene but cannot see her (e.g., she's yelling from another room), type [(O.C.)] after her name, on the same line, to indicate that she is off camera.

WHITE SPACE

Do not cram your script pages full of ink. Producers and executives, who usually have dozens of other scripts to read, love white space because it makes the read go faster, the script feel lighter. Feel free to break longish scene descriptions into paragraphs and leave big bottom margins when dialogue will not fit on a page.

Appendix B

Additional Resources

Below is a list of resources for sitcom writers. For ease of reference, some information that has already been presented in the text is repeated in this appendix.

RECOMMENDED BOOKS

While many books have been written about television, sitcoms, and the craft of screenwriting, I believe that a writer should devote most of his reading time to fiction. That said, I recommend that every sitcom writer add the following craft-oriented books, all of which are available through local bookstores, to his library:

Campbell, Joseph. *The Hero with a Thousand Faces*. Princeton: Princeton University Press, 1973.

Egri, Lajos. *The Art of Dramatic Writing*. New York: Touchstone/Simon & Schuster, 1960.

Helitzer, Melvin. *Comedy Writing Secrets*. Cincinnati: Writer's Digest, 1987.

Josefsberg, Milt. *Comedy Writing For Television & Hollywood*. New York: Harper & Row, 1987.

Jowett, Benjamin & Thomas Twining, trans. *Aristotle's Politics & Poetics*. New York: Viking Press, 1974.

Saks, Sol. *The Craft of Comedy Writing*. Cincinnati: Writer's Digest, 1985.

Seger, Linda. *Making a Good Script Great*, 2d ed. Hollywood: Samuel French, 1994.

Wolff, Jurgen. *Successful Sitcom Writing*. New York: St. Martin's Press, 1988.

SITCOM SCRIPTS

In addition to the resources described in chapter 7, you can order some scripts over the phone, for about fifteen dollars per episode, by contacting the following companies:

Larry Edmunds Books
6658 Hollywood Blvd.
Hollywood, CA 90028
(323) 463-3273

Script City
8033 Sunset Blvd.
Los Angeles, CA 90046
(323) 871-0707

RECOMMENDED PERIODICALS

The following periodicals explore topics ranging from recent industry developments to the craft of screenwriting:

Written By (the official journal of the Writers Guild of America, west)
7000 W. Third Street
Los Angeles, CA 90048
Toll-free subscription line: 888-WRITNBY
writtenby@wga.org
Published monthly; single issues for $5 (minimum order of $10), annual subscriptions for $40, free subscription for WGA,w members; features interviews with screenwriters, essays about the craft, industry news, and a regularly updated TV production contact list.

Creative Screenwriting
6404 Hollywood Blvd., Suite 415
Los Angeles, CA 90028

(213) 957-1405
SCRNWRT@aol.com
Annual subscriptions cost $30; features critical and historical essays about screenwriting.

The daily edition of either *Variety* or *The Hollywood Reporter* if you live *in* Los Angeles, or the weekly edition of either if you live *outside* of Los Angeles. Similar in style and content, these publications provide news about the business of Hollywood; coverage includes announcements of production deals, the hiring of personnel, network scheduling news, and weekly ratings charts. Subscriptions for *Variety* (either format) can be ordered by calling (800) 323-4345, and those for *The Hollywood Reporter* (either format) can ordered by calling (323) 525-2000.

WRITERS GUILD OFFICES

Though most sitcom writers end up joining the WGA, *west*, here are individual department numbers for both branches of the Writers Guild.

WGA, west
7000 W. Third St.
Los Angeles, CA 90048
General information: (323) 951-4000
www.wga.org

(area code 323):

Agency	782-4502
Contracts	782-4501
Credits	782-4528
Library	782-4544
Membership	782-4532
Publications	782-4542
Script registration	782-4540
Signatories	782-4514
Written By	782-4522

WGA, east
555 W. 57th St.
New York, NY 10019
General information: (212) 767-7800
www.wgaeast.org

(area code 212):

Agency	767-7821
Contracts	767-7803
Credits	767-7804
Membership	767-7802
Publications	767-7800
Script registration	767-7801
Signatories	767-7821

U.S. COPYRIGHT OFFICE

To request a free informational pamphlet or a copyright application form ("Form PA"), contact:

Copyright Office
Library of Congress
101 Independence Ave., S.E.
Washington, DC 20559-6000
(202) 707-3000

INTERNSHIPS

Below are several internship programs designed to develop promising screenwriters. Admittance is competitive, some programs pay a stipend, and all programs involve a workshop experience with industry professionals. Contact each organization for a description of its program and application process.

Academy of Television Arts & Sciences
Internship Program
5220 Lankershim Blvd.
N. Hollywood, CA 91601
www.emmys.org
(818) 754-2830

Walt Disney Studios Fellowship Program
500 S. Buena Vista St.
Burbank, CA 91521-0880
(818) 560-6894

Warner Brothers Comedy Writers Workshop
4000 Warner Blvd.
Burbank, CA 91522
(818) 954-7906

SEMINARS AND WORKSHOPS

Contact the following organizations to request a current catalogue. My comedy-writing seminars are usually presented through the American Film Institute.

American Film Institute
2021 N. Western Ave.
Los Angeles, CA 90027
www.afionline.org
(323) 856-7690

International Film & Television Workshops
P.O. Box 200
2 Central St.
Rockport, ME 04856
www.meworkshops.com
(207) 236-8581

UCLA Extension Program
Dept. of Entertainment Studies
10995 Le Conte Ave., Room 437
Los Angeles, CA 90024
www.unex.ucla.edu
(310) 825-9064

INDUSTRY DIRECTORIES

A number of industry directories are published and updated on a regular basis. Below are several reasonably priced options:

Hollywood Creative Directory and *Hollywood Agents & Managers Directory*
3000 W. Olympic Blvd., Suite 2525
Santa Monica, CA 90404
(800) 815-0503 (outside California) or (310) 315-4815

www.hcdonline.com
Published three times a year; single issues (of either directory) available for $49.50, yearly subscription for $99; in addition to general contact information for companies, provides names of individual staff members. Web site has free job board that lists non-writing positions.

Pacific Coast Studio Directory
P.O. Box V
Pine Mountain, CA 93222-0022
(805) 242-2722
www.studio-directory.com
Published three times a year; single issues available for $13, yearly subscription for $30; some free listings available at publisher's Web site.

Ross Reports
P.O. Box 5018
Brentwood, TN 37024-5018
(800) 817-3273
Published monthly; single issues available for $7, yearly subscription for $50.

Endnotes

[1] Charles Slocum, "More Than Ever," *Written By* (September 1997), 34.

[2] Sigmund Freud, *Jokes and Their Relation to the Unconscious: The Standard Edition*, ed. James Strachey (New York: W.W. Norton, 1989), 171–93.

[3] Dana Sutton, *The Catharsis of Comedy* (Lanham, Maryland: Rowman & Littlefield, 1994), 19–31.

[4] Herbert Spencer, "The Physiology of Laughter," *Macmillan's Magazine* (March 1860), 395.

[5] Robert Storey, "Comedy, Its Theorists, and the Evolutionary Perspective," *Criticism* 38 (summer 1996), 424–37.

[6] Freud, *Jokes*, 9.

[7] David Wild, *Friends: The Official Companion* (New York: Main Street Books, 1995), 98.

[8] Freud, *Jokes*, 107–39.

[9] Theodor Lipps, *Komik und Humor* (Hamburg and Leipzig, 1898), 90, quoted in Freud, *Jokes*, 11.

[10] Freud, *Jokes*, 248–53.

[11] Steven Levitan, *Just Shoot Me*: "Pilot Episode," revised first draft (Brillstein/Grey, April 18, 1996), 39–40. Television script.

[12] Sol Saks, *The Craft of Comedy Writing* (Cincinnati: Writer's Digest, 1985), 34.

[13] Steve Chivers & Curt Shepard, *The Parent 'Hood*: "Beauty Call," shooting script (Warren-Rinsler/Townsend Entertainment, August 7, 1997), 19–20. Television script.

[14] Adam Chase & Ira Ungerleider, *Friends*: "The One with Fake Monica," final

draft (Bright/Kauffman/Crane Productions, March 3, 1995), 4–5. Television script.

[15]Ibid., 8–9.

[16]David Cohen, *Simpsons*: "Lisa the Vegetarian," production draft (Gracie Films, March 1995), 24–25. Television script.

[17]Bill Masters, *Seinfeld*: "The Alternate Side," table draft (Castle Rock, November 1, 1991), 15–16. Television script.

[18]Les Firestein, *The Drew Carey Show*: "The Sex Drug," table draft (Warner Bros., February 12, 1998), 1. Television script.

[19]Ibid., 6–7.

[20]Chase & Ungerleider, *Friends*: "Fake Monica," 6.

[21]Evan Smith, *Seinfeld*: "Someone Killed Bambi" (May 1992), 40–41. Television spec script.

[22]Ibid., 47.

[23]John Swartzwelder, *The Simpsons*: "Bart the General," table draft (Gracie Films, June 1989), 15–17. Television script.

[24]Ibid., 20–21.

[25]Ibid., 25.

[26]Melvin Helitzer, *Comedy Writing Secrets* (Cincinnati: Writer's Digest, 1987), 57.

[27]Firestein, *Drew Carey*: "Sex Drug," 20.

[28]Philip Vaughn, *King of the Hill*: "Pulp Arlen," draft status unknown (March 23, 1998), 3. Television script.

[29]Freud, *Jokes*, 157.

[30]Saks, *Craft*, 31–32.

[31]Larry Gelbart, "One Question . . . ," *Written By* (May 1998).

[32]Jurgen Wolff, *Successful Sitcom Writing* (New York: St. Martin's Press, 1988) 64.

[33]Linda Seger, *Making a Good Script Great*, 2d ed. (Hollywood: Samuel French, 1994), 62.

[34]Benjamin Jowett & Thomas Twining, trans., *Aristotle's Politics & Poetics* (New York: Viking Press, 1974), 230–57.

[35]Lajos Egri, *The Art of Dramatic Writing* (New York: Touchstone, 1960), 33–59.

[36]Robert Storey, "Comedy, Its Theorists, and the Evolutionary Perspective," *Criticism* 38 (summer 1996), 424–37.

[37]William Goldman, "Rocking The Boat," *Premiere* (April 1998), 85.

[38]Seger, *Making a Good Script*, 74.

[39]Smith, *Seinfeld*: "Bambi," 1.

[40]Writers Guild of America, west, "1996 WGA,w Membership Manual" (Los Angeles: WGA Publications, 1996), 4:1.

41U.S. Copyright Office, "Copyright Basics: Circular 1" (Washington, DC: U.S. Government Printing office, 1996), 3.

42Ibid., 5.

43Writers Guild of America, west, "General Information," 3d ed. (Los Angeles: WGA Publications, 1998), 9–12; phone conversations with representatives of the Script Registration departments at WGA,w and WGA,e.

44Writers Guild of America, west, "The Writers Guild Series: Creative Rights" (May 1992), 15.

45Writers Guild, west, "General Information," 5–8; phone conversations with representatives of the membership departments at WGA,w and WGA,e.

46Writers Guild of America, west, "1998 Schedule of Minimums" (Los Angeles: WGA Publications, May 2, 1998), 6, 10.

47"Writer/Agent Alert: Do I Have to Do the Math?" *Written By* (April 1997), 65; phone conversations with representatives of the contracts department at WGA,w.

48"Writer/Agent Alert," *Written By*, 65.

49Writers Guild, west, "1998 Schedule of Minimums," 16.

50Smith, *Seinfeld*: "Bambi," 15–16.

Index

Academy of Television Arts and
    Sciences, 79, 206
Act breaks
    dramatic acts vs. commercial
        breaks, 99–100
    in all script formats, 252
    starting Act One after a cold
        open, 250
    See also Story structure
Ageism, 176
Agent(s), 8, 181–198
    approach via telephone, 187
    commissions, 182
    developing a hit list, 183–186
    if you fail to land an, 194–195
    interviewing, 196
    replacing your, 239–240
    signing with an, 197
    vs. entertainment lawyers, 183
    vs. managers, 183
    working with your, 202, 238–240
Aggression (a characteristic of
        comedy), 16
Alliteration, 66

American Film Institute, viii, 2, 78,
    269
Animation format, 259, 261–262
    sample script page, 261
    script length, 145, 263
Aristotle, 93
Art of Dramatic Writing, The (Egri),
    101

Beat
    defined as a pause, 147
    defined as a plot point, 91–92
Beat sheet, creating a, 91–92
Bigger is better, 68
Brevity, the importance of, 17
Broadcast format, 81, 99–100, 113
Budget limitations, 108, 158
Buttons, 143

Camera directions, 120, 146, 262
Career paths, 8–10
Casting's impact on comedy, 40–41
Catharsis of Comedy, The (Sutton), 12
Censorship and comedy, 69
Character arcs, 96

Character flaws, exploiting, 97
Character mix, 26, 32–36, 102
   stirring up the, 43–44
Character types, 103–106
Characteristics of comedy, 14–18
Characters, creating funny, 33, 101–106
Choreographing action sequences, 146
Closing credits, 100
Cold opens (or teasers), 81, 114
   in an outline, 117
   in broadcast format, 100, 113
   in script format, 249, 253–255
Cold-calling producers, 204–205
Comedic nuances, 149–150
Comedic voice, developing your, 70
Comedy
   block, 45
   output, 20
   theory, 12–18
"Comedy, Its Theorists, and the
   Evolutionary Perspective"
   (Storey), 13, 103
Comedy Writing (Josefsberg), 32
Comedy Writing Secrets (Helitzer), 18, 63
Comedy's impact on story, 98
Commercial breaks, 100
Compensation
   for freelance assignments, 225
   for staff writers, 234–235
Conflict, the value of, 97
Consistency, 20
Contact file, 179, 194
Contracts
   for freelance assignments, 223–224
   for staff writers, 234–235
Copyright, 208–211
   contact information, 211, 268
   definition, 208
   notice on title page, 117, 209, 247

   vs. WGA script registration, 209
   works made for hire, 211, 224
Courier font. *See* Typeface
Craft of Comedy Writing, The (Saks), 18, 48, 68
Creative control, 172–173

Day jobs, 177–179
Deal-driven production
   commitments, 171
Developing an episode premise, 83–89
   generating ideas, 84–85
   high concept ideas, 88
   producers' advice, 83
   turning ideas into springboards, 86–88
   See also Springboards
Development deals, 240
Dialogue blocks
   in animation format, 259
   in film format, 251–252
   in tape format, 257–258
   interrupting at bottom of page, 252
Dialogue cues
   excess cues slow the read, 151
   in animation format, 262
   in film format, 251–252
   in tape format, 257–258
Dialogue, writing, 147–151
Drew Carey Show, The, script
   excerpts, 53, 55, 63

Egri, Lajos, 101
Ensemble shows, 95
Entertainment lawyers (vs. agents), 183
Exposition, 151–153
   characters expressing emotions
   and beliefs, 152

describing characters and settings, 120
the exposition test, 142

Film format, 247–254
  sample script page, 254
  script length, 145
First draft, writing a, 140–165
  first scenes are critical, 141
  just do it, 140
Fish-out-of-water, 34
Fixing it in post, 23
Following up on a submission, 193
Foreign accents, 67
Foreshadowing, 114, 152
Frank, Sandy, vii, 84, 123, 156, 159, 163, 222, 233, 243
Freelance assignment(s)
  hiring windows, 201
  landing, 8, 79, 199–205, 228
  living outside of L.A., 179, 192
  pitching for, 111, 216–223
  receiving notes, 157–164
  time frame, 157, 165
  vs. staff jobs, 227
  See also Contracts; Compensation
Freud, Sigmund, 12–14, 17, 36, 67
Friends script excerpts, 16, 50, 56
Funny actions, 64–66
Funny sounds, 66–67

Gay characters in sitcoms, 35, 41
Genres (defining a style of comedy), 37–41
Gurvitz, Ian, vii, 84, 123, 163, 206, 220, 228, 232, 243

Helitzer, Melvin, 18, 63
High concept ideas, 88
Hiring windows, 171, 201–202
Hollywood Reporter, 77, 178, 185, 267

Home Improvement story outline, 123–139
Hooking the reader quickly, 114

Incongruity, comedic, 14, 18
  between a character and his environment, 102
  building jokes, 47–48, 63
  in a predicament, 26–27
  in physical humor, 65
Industry directories, 178, 185, 269
Intercutting between locations, 262
Interruptions by another character, 262

Jokes and Their Relation to the Unconscious (Freud), 12
Josefsberg, Milt, 32
Just Shoot Me script excerpt, 47

Kalish, Irma, vii, 123, 154, 164, 220, 232, 243
King of the Hill script excerpt, 66
Konner, Lawrence, vii, 84, 155, 164, 182, 194, 206–207, 221, 231, 243

Labels, about all of these, 69
Lapiduss, Maxine, vii, 122, 141, 154, 163, 221, 231, 243
Leave-behinds, 217–218
Legal release, signing a, 191
Less is more, 17, 68
License fees, 169
Literal punch lines, 63
Locations and sets, 108
Los Angeles, moving to. *See* Moving to L.A.

Making a Good Script Great (Seger), 91, 141
Managers (vs. agents), 183

Mannerisms, 64
MBA. *See* Minimum Basic Agreement
McKee, Robert, 152
Minimum Basic Agreement (writers' MBA), 224, 234
Montage sequence, 143, 263
Moving to L.A., 10, 179
   testing the waters before, 192–193

Network development process, 169–172
Newhouse School, viii, 244
Ninety-day clause, 197
   See also Agent(s)

Odd couples, 34
Office politics. *See* Staff jobs
Opening credits, 100
Opponents (or antagonists), 107
Outline, creating an, 111–139
   a selling tool, 111–113
   describing characters and scenes, 119
   including dialogue, 119
   incorporating broadcast format, 113
   layout on paper, 113, 115–118
   producers' advice, 122–123
Over-scale (or above-scale) fees, 182, 223, 225

Page numbers (in a script), 249
Painting the picture, 120, 145
Paper used in scripts (industry standard), 263
Parent 'Hood, The, script excerpt, 48
Passive representation, 195, 204
Pause, indicating a, 146, 263
Phone spiel, preparing a, 188
Physical comedy. *See* Funny actions
"Physiology of Laughter, The" (Spencer), 13

Pitching stories, 215–223
   possible outcomes, 222
   preparing, 216–222
   producers' advice, 219–222
Poetics (Aristotle), 93
Power-of-attorney (granted to agent), 198
Predicaments, comedic, 27–32
   compounding, 43–45
Premise-driven comedy, 23–71
   in dialogue and actions, 46–71
   in sequences and scenes, 42–45
   in the story, 25–41, 84
Pretense, 36
Producer and writer titles, 172
Production crew titles, 173
Production process (impact on stories), 108–109
Production schedule, typical, 173–174
Punch lines, 54–63
   don't go past the joke, 55
   last things last, 55
   literal, 63
   problem might be in the setup, 63
   running gags, 57–62
   topping a joke, 55–56

Query letters, 186–190

Reaction, indicating a, 147
Regulations regarding program ownership, 169
Rejection, dealing with, 207
Repetition, avoiding, 93, 108
Researching a series, 78–79
Residuals, 160, 182, 212, 225
Rewriting a script, 157–165
   producers' advice, 163
Rewriting an outline, 121–123
   producers' advice, 122–123
Rewriting process, The traditional, 21–23

Rider W, 197
Role reversal, 33
Room, the, 122, 156–158, 164, 174, 230, 232–234
Roundtable writing, 21, 229–234
   See also Staff jobs
Runners, 62
Running gags, 57–62
   part of a series premise, 62
   vs. story runners, 62

Saks, Sol, 18, 48, 68
Scene descriptions, 115, 145–147
   in a montage sequence, 263
   in animation format, 259
   in film format, 250–252
   in tape format, 257–259
   offensive language in, 151
   sound and effects cues in, 264
   write in present tense, 119, 145, 251
Scene headings, 250, 257
   in an outline, 118
   in animation format, 259
   in film format, 250–252
   in tape format, 256, 258
Scenes, writing, 141–147
   ending with a button, 143
   entrances and exits, 143
   first scenes are critical, 141
   harvesting comedy in story premise, 144
   pacing, 143
   scene descriptions, 145
   scene length, 142
   scene structure, 115
   start late, finish early, 142
"Schedule of Minimums" (writers' fees), 225, 234
Script binding, 263
Script format, 81, 144
   See also Animation format; Tape format; Film format; Appendix A: Script Format Guidelines
Script headings
   in animation format, 259
   in film format, 249
   in tape format, 255
Script length, 262–263
Scripts, finding produced, 79, 266
Seamless humor, 19–21, 97
Seger, Linda, 91, 141
Seinfeld script excerpts, 52, 57, 254
Self-addressed, stamped envelope, 191
   See also Submitting scripts
Selling a new series, 241
Seminars and workshops, 269
Series bible, 79
Series development schedule, traditional, 169–170, 201
Setups, 46–54
   bolstered by shared experiences, 52–54
   bolstered by story, 54
   different shapes and forms, 48–49
   no hints, 51
   should be reasonable, 47
   spreading out, 50–51
Sexual tension, 35
Show runners, 172
Signatories to the WGA, 182, 184, 186, 197, 213–214, 223
Signature lines, 151
Simpsons, The, script excerpts, 51, 59
Slapstick, 65
Smith, Evan (E-mail address), 244
Some Like It Hot, 26–27
Sound and effects cues, 109, 245, 250, 257, 264
Spacing and margins
   in animation format, 259
   in film format, 252
   in tape format, 258

Spec scripts, 7–11, 21
  and copyright, 211
  are outlines necessary, 91, 112–
    113
  before moving to L.A., 192
  getting work via, 8–11
  physical comedy in, 87
  producers' advice, 153–156
  rewriting, 162–163
  sets and locations, 108–109
  studying the series, 78–82
  submitting, 200–205
  submitting old scripts, 203
  time frame of story, 98
  which series to pick, 76–77
  why write specs, 75–76
Special effects. *See* Sound and effects
    cues
Speech patterns, 55, 147–150
Springboards, creating, 86–89
  an example, 87
  pitching, 111, 216–222
Staff jobs
  landing, 8–9, 78, 171–173, 199–
    202, 215, 227–236, 238
  office politics, 229–234
  producers' advice, 231–234
  rewriting a script, 157–165
  typical work week, 172–175, 228
  vs. freelance assignments, 21–22,
    227
  writing a first draft, 112, 230–234
  See also Contracts (for staff
    writers); Roundtable writing;
    Hiring windows
Stage business, 64
Standing sets, 108
Step deals, 223
Storey, Robert, 13, 103
Story breakdowns, 79
Story editors, 172–175, 228, 235, 237
  terms of employment, 235
Story structure, 91–96
  linear vs. thread, 92–95

serialized story lines, 95
  stories without endings, 95
  threads vs. subplots vs. ensemble
    stories, 94
  vs. broadcast format, 99–100
Story, the importance of, 90–91
Studying a series, 80–82
Stunts, 109
Style of comedy, 37–39
  being consistent, 39
  genres, 37
  questions that define, 38
Submitting scripts, 77, 190–191, 203
Subplots, 91, 94
Successful Sitcom Writing (Wolff), 76
Surprise (a characteristic of comedy),
    15, 47, 51, 55, 159
Sutton, Dana, 12
Sweeps months, 109
Swing sets, 108

Table readings, 174
Tags, 100, 114
  in animation format, 259
  in film format, 253
  in tape format, 259
Takes and doubletakes, 65
Tape format, 255–260
  sample script page, 260
  script length, 145
Tension, comedic, 13–14, 23, 27–28,
    44, 64–65
  caused by predicaments, 27–28
  compounding, 43–45
  in a joke setup, 47–48, 52
  in a story premise, 24
  the importance of, 18
Tension, dramatic, 13, 23, 54, 91,
    93, 98, 142
Term writers, 228
  job rank, 172
  moving up, 237
  terms of employment, 234–235

Three-act structure, 93–94
See also Story structure
Tickler file, creating a, 194, 203
Time frame of a story, 98
Title page (of a script), 209–210, 246–248
designating draft version or completion date, 247
registration notice, 209
sample title page, 248
Topping a joke, 55–57
Trade publications, 178, 185
Transition cues
in animation format, 259
in film format, 251
in tape format, 258
Triples, 49
Truby, John, 43, 93
Truth (in comedy), 15–16, 85, 99
Typeface
in a script (the industry standard), 246, 252, 258, 264
in an outline, 116, 121

Valéry, Paul, 22
Variety, 77, 178, 185, 267
Visiting characters, 39, 81, 101, 106–107
describing in an outline, 115

receiving too much attention, 86, 106, 108
Visuals, funny, 65, 114
Voice-over narration, 264

WGA script registration, 209–210
contact information, 211
notice on title page, 117, 210, 247
vs. copyright registration, 209–211
White space, 120, 264
Williams, Matt, vii, 19, 83, 98, 106, 122, 124, 153, 164, 215, 220, 234, 243
Wolff, Jurgen, 76
Wordplay, 150
Writer's block, 207
Writers Guild of America
agency list, 185
contact information, 267
joining the, 212–214
library, 79
script registration service. *See* WGA script registration
west vs. east, 185
Writing dialogue, 147–156
See also Comedic nuances; Speech patterns
Writing in teams, 206
Written By, 212, 266–267
television market list, 204

NOTES

NOTES

NOTES

NOTES

NOTES

NOTES

NOTES